Meiji Graves in Happy Valley

Royal Asiatic Society Hong Kong Studies Series

Royal Asiatic Society Hong Kong Studies Series is designed to make widely available important contributions on the local history, culture and society of Hong Kong and the surrounding region. Generous support from the Sir Lindsay and Lady May Ride Memorial Fund makes it possible to publish high-quality works that will be of lasting appeal and value to all, both scholars and informed general readers, who share a deeper interest in and enthusiasm for the area.

Recent titles in the series:

Outlaws of the Sea: Maritime Piracy in Modern China by Robert J. Antony (2024) (Hong Kong University Press)

Man in a Hurry: Murray MacLehose and Colonial Autonomy in Hong Kong by Ray Yep (2024) (Hong Kong University Press)

Hong Kong Public and Squatter Housing: Geopolitics and Informality, 1963–1985 by Alan Smart and Fung Chi Keung Charles (2023) (Hong Kong University Press)

Grounded at Kai Tak: Chinese Aircraft Impounded in Hong Kong, 1949–1952 by Malcolm Merry (2022) (Hong Kong University Press)

Hong Kongers in the British Armed Forces, 1860–1997 by Kwong Chi Man (2022) (Oxford University Press)

More than 1001 Days and Nights of Hong Kong Internment: A Personal Narrative by Chaloner Grenville Alabaster; edited by David St Maur Sheil, Kwong Chi Man, and Tony Banham (2022) (Hong Kong University Press)

My Dearest Martha: The Life and Letters of Eliza Hillier, edited by Andrew Hillier (2021) (City University of Hong Kong Press)

War and Revolution in South China: The Story of a Transnational Biracial Family, 1936–1951 by Edward J. M. Rhoads (2021) (Hong Kong University Press)

A Death in Hong Kong: The MacLennan Case of 1980 and the Suppression of a Scandal (2nd Edition) by Nigel Collett (2020) (City University of Hong Kong Press)

A Pattern of Life: Essays on Rural Hong Kong by James Hayes, edited by Hugh D. R. Baker (2020) (City University of Hong Kong Press)

A Stormy Petrel: The Life and Times of John Pope Hennessy by P. Kevin MacKeown (2020) (City University of Hong Kong Press)

Settlement, Life, and Politics—Understanding the Traditional New Territories by Patrick H. Hase (2020) (City University of Hong Kong Press)

Meiji Graves in Happy Valley

Stories of Early Japanese Residents in Hong Kong

Yoshiko Nakano and Georgina Challen

Hong Kong University Press
The University of Hong Kong
Pok Fu Lam Road
Hong Kong
https://hkupress.hku.hk

© 2025 Hong Kong University Press

ISBN 978-988-8876-85-3 (*Paperback*)

All rights reserved. No portion of this publication may be reproduced or transmitted in any form or by any means, electronic or mechanical, including photocopying, recording, or any information storage or retrieval system, without prior permission in writing from the publisher.

British Library Cataloguing-in-Publication Data
A catalogue record for this book is available from the British Library.

Digitally printed

For Saki

Contents

List of Illustrations	viii
List of Tables	xi
Preface	xii
Acknowledgements	xiv
Note on Romanisation	xvi
Chapter 1. A Community of Two Halves	1
Chapter 2. The *Karayuki-san*	22
Chapter 3. Boarding House and Restaurant Operators	40
Chapter 4. A Japanese Ship in Victoria Harbour	60
Chapter 5. A Developing International Business Elite	78
Chapter 6. Tradespeople and Professionals	98
Chapter 7. Conclusion	117
Brief Timeline	127
Annex: List of Japanese-Related Graves	129
Notes	136
Bibliography	172
Index	187

Illustrations

Cover image: Japanese Women at the Happy Valley Racecourse, circa 1910

Front Matter

Map of Japan showing present-day prefecture boundaries   xvii

Map of Hong Kong in 1888   xviii

House flags of the Mitsubishi Mail Steamship Company and Mitsui Bussan
  Kaisha in the *Chronicle & Directory* 1885   xix

English-language inscription on Kiya Saki's grave   xx

Japanese graves in the upper reaches of the Hong Kong Cemetery   xxi

Chapters

Figure 1.1: Andō Tarō in Paris in 1873   5

Figure 1.2: The Hong Kong Central waterfront in the late 1860s   8

Figure 1.3: Location of Japanese boarding houses, brothels, and concubines in
  Central in 1886   12

Figure 1.4: Section from the diary of French author and politician Victor Hugo   14

Figure 1.5: Postcard of Happy Valley, circa 1905   15

Figure 1.6: Hong Kong Governor Sir John Pope Hennessy during his visit to
  Japan in 1879   16

Figure 1.7: Obelisk of Japanese student Kondō Kizō   17

Figure 1.8: Grave of Yukawa Onsaku   19

Figure 1.9: Map showing the division of the Hong Kong Cemetery in 1909   21

Figure 2.1: Obelisk of Kiya Saki   23

Figure 2.2: Postcard of Wellington Street in the 1880s   32

Figure 2.3: Base of Kiya Saki's obelisk with sixty-two women's names   34

Figure 2.4: Yamamoto Hisa's afterlife name, the 'big sister of tourism'   37

Figure 2.5: Japanese nannies in Hong Kong, circa 1910–1913   38

Illustrations

Figure 3.1: Chinese restaurant Heng Fa Lou — 43

Figure 3.2: A Japanese pearl diver and crew in the waters off Thursday Island — 44

Figure 3.3: Advertisement for the Tokyo Hotel with Uetsuki Yoneko — 48

Figure 3.4: A beach outing organised by a Japanese youth society, circa 1911 — 51

Figure 3.5: Matsheds at the Happy Valley Racecourse, circa 1910 — 51

Figure 3.6: Count Ōtani Kōzui and members of Hong Kong's Japanese community — 55

Figure 3.7: Happy Valley Racecourse fire of February 26, 1918 — 56

Figure 3.8: Grave of boarding house operator Matsubara Jisaburō — 57

Figure 3.9: Memorial to Ten Thousand Souls — 58

Figure 4.1: Caricature of Governor John Pope Hennessy in the *Japan Punch* — 63

Figure 4.2: Advertisement for the Mitsubishi Mail Steamship Company's Shanghai service — 65

Figure 4.3: Mitsubishi passenger fares from Hong Kong to Japan in January 1880 — 65

Figure 4.4: Mitsubishi executives, circa 1877 — 67

Figure 4.5: A page from Honda Masajirō's first report on Hong Kong — 69

Figure 4.6: Monument erected in memory of Honda Masajirō — 72

Figure 4.7: Sketch of the Hong Kong waterfront in Inokuchi Ushiji's travelogue — 76

Figure 5.1: An 1878 woodblock featuring Japan's four most prominent industrialists — 80

Figure 5.2: Photo of twenty-two-year-old Ataka Yakichi taken in 1895 — 81

Figure 5.3: Grave of Kusakabe & Co. employees Hirose Matsujirō and Horii Yasaburō — 83

Figure 5.4: Fukuhara Kayo's grave in the Hong Kong Cemetery — 87

Figure 5.5: Group of Japanese executives with their families and associates — 88

Figure 5.6: Advertisement for Mitsui Bussan Kaisha in the *Chronicle & Directory* 1908 — 89

Figure 5.7: The Yokohama Specie Bank's entry in the *Chronicle & Directory* for 1900 — 92

Figure 5.8: Menu for the 'Mikado Ball' held on November 3, 1905 — 94

Figure 5.9: Decorative menu for a March 1906 dinner at the Hongkong Club — 96

Figure 6.1: Details of Moore's hairdressing services in 1882 — 100

Figure 6.2: A late nineteenth-century tattoo design template from Nagasaki — 101

Figure 6.3: Noma Denjirō tattoo shop sign in Queen's Road photographed circa 1907–1909 — 103

Figure 6.4: Senior Belilios Scholar Yamasaki Munenao in 1906 — 105

Figure 6.5: Beaconsfield Arcade in Central — 107

Figure 6.6: A page from the second edition of *Honkon Nippō* — 109

Figure 6.7: Yokohama Specie Bank manager Hozumi Tarō 110

Figure 6.8: An advertisement for Umeya's photographic services in 1903 111

Figure 6.9: A sketch of the dissection room in the Kennedy Town plague hospital 113

Figure 6.10: The hospital hulk *Hygeia* in 1905 114

Figure 6.11: Thistle and butterfly engravings on the marble gravestone of Haruno Ino 115

Figure 7.1: Section of a 1900 map showing the Happy Valley cemeteries 123

Figure 7.2: Miura Seiichi's funeral at the Japanese crematorium in early 1920 124

Figure 7.3: Front of O-Sai-San (Tanaka Seiko)'s headstone 126

Figure 7.4: O-Sai-San's headstone lies shattered on the ground in 2022 126

While every effort has been made to contact copyright holders for their permission to reprint material, the authors would be grateful to hear from any copyright holder who is not acknowledged here and will undertake to rectify any errors or omissions in future editions.

Tables

Table 1.1: First ten Meiji-era Japanese graves in the Hong Kong Cemetery	2
Table 1.2: Number of Japanese residents in Hong Kong, 1880–1911	9
Table 1.3: Occupations of Japanese residents in 1886	10
Table 1.4: Top ten occupations of Japanese residents in 1916	13
Table 2.1: First line of names on Kiya Saki's grave	34
Table 3.1: List of Japanese liquor licence applicants in October 1919	59
Table 4.1: Lobnitz & Co. financial records	62
Table 4.2: Number and nationality of vessels entering Hong Kong ports, 1872–1912	76

Preface

On November 13, 1879, the *China Mail* carried a full report of a luncheon – or tiffin – held to mark the launch of Japan's first commercial service between Yokohama and Hong Kong by the Mitsubishi Mail Steamship Company. Over sixty guests, including the governor of Hong Kong, John Pope Hennessy, were ferried out to the *Niigata Maru*, which was anchored in the harbour and where they were greeted by Honda Masajirō (本田政次郎), Mitsubishi's Hong Kong office general manager. Following a toast to 'The Queen', Pope Hennessy, who was recently returned from a three-month visit to Japan, offered a toast to 'His Majesty the Mikado of Japan', adding that he believed that this was the first time the health of the Mikado had been proposed in Hong Kong. Honda made the only Japanese-language contribution to the speeches with 'Gentlemen, *macotoni arigato*' (I am really obliged to you).

Sadly, Honda would pass away from consumption less than a year after the tiffin. A monument erected to his memory survives in the Hong Kong Cemetery in Happy Valley, somewhat hidden behind larger English and German headstones and crosses. Eighteen graves to the left, in the same row, stands the obelisk of a Japanese sex worker, Kiya Saki (木谷佐喜), who died in 1884. Its base bears the names of the sixty-two women who paid for it.

These are just two of the approximately 470 Japanese graves in the Hong Kong Cemetery. Over 80 per cent of these graves belong to individuals who, like Honda and Saki, died during the Meiji era (1868–1912), a remarkable period of modernisation and opening up of Japan that saw thousands of its people travel to other parts of the world to study, work, and settle. Who were these people and what were they doing in Hong Kong? How did they live? Furthermore, why were unbaptised Japanese buried in what was called at one time the 'Protestant Cemetery'?

Little has been published in English about the city's Japanese community prior to the two world wars, more specifically during the late nineteenth and early twentieth centuries. While much has been written and shared through memoirs and other first-hand accounts about the horrors of the occupation of Hong Kong by Japanese forces and Japan's post–Second World War efforts to re-establish itself in the city, far less is known about these earlier residents. The official biographies of prominent Japanese businesspeople often deal very briefly with their operations in Hong Kong during the Meiji era and focus on Shanghai instead. Yet, by 1912, over a thousand Japanese resided in Hong Kong and advertisements for Japanese companies and services featured prominently in the English-language press. However, their contributions

Preface

to Hong Kong's diversity have been largely overshadowed by the traumatic historical events that followed and, therefore, left unexplored.

In 2020, the Hongkong Japanese Club, whose involvement with the Japanese section of the cemetery dates back to 1982, initiated a project to document a small number of these Meiji graves, including Saki's. As we began investigating the subject and searching for information, we realised that these were human stories that deserved to be told. Combing through the English-language newspapers of the time, we chanced upon an item in the *China Mail* that described the discovery in the harbour of the body of a Japanese woman who had committed suicide, Saki.

This heartbreaking find led us to expand the scope of our research beyond the club's project. We began to make connections between the names on the graves and a broader range of primary materials in English and Japanese, which increased digitisation has made more accessible. In addition to newspapers, government correspondence, official reports, and death registers, we drew from travellers' accounts and memoirs, many of which are only available in Japanese. Using our Japanese and English cultural perspectives and the names on the graves as a starting point, we pulled these fragments together to form an impression of the Meiji-era Japanese community in Hong Kong. We looked at how its members related to each other and to the wider society, as well as their roles in transnational networks that extended beyond the colony.

Most of all, we wanted to make these stories accessible in a way that they have not been before and throw some light on the more remote areas of the Hong Kong Cemetery that few people, even long-term residents like us, visit. By revealing the personal journeys of these mostly forgotten Japanese, we hope to add a further dimension to discussions of Hong Kong and its relationship with Japan during the Meiji era and increase recognition of their place in the development of this wonderfully diverse city.

Acknowledgements

When the Hongkong Japanese Club first approached us with this project in 2020, we never imagined the journey of discovery that awaited us. Our exploration of the Meiji graves in the Hong Kong Cemetery has been a fascinating and joyous shared experience – one that has enriched our understanding of the city both of us have called home for most of our adult lives.

This book would not exist without the support of the Hongkong Japanese Club. We are particularly indebted to the club's deputy manager, Tomoko Sugimura, with whom we collaborated closely on the original initiative to document eight of the graves, Yoshiko as project manager and Georgina as English writer. Our thanks also to the 2021 Hongkong Japanese Club Cemetery Preservation Committee – Takeo Iwami (Chair), Tsuyoshi Ebihara, Kosaku Kawai, Takafumi Kido, Shunichiro Mizukami, Jun Toda, and Masakazu Yagyu. Special mention must go to the late Takeo Iwami, who was the first to recognise, in 1982, the importance of preserving these markers of a bygone time. We are grateful for the assistance and enthusiasm of other members of Hong Kong's Japanese community: the Consul-General of Japan, Kenichi Okada; the former President of the Hongkong Japanese Club, Yoshikazu Shimauchi; the former co-chair of the Century 21 Club, Kenichiro Washikita; and photographer Miyuki Kume, who braved the heat and mosquitoes to document the graves. Kosaku Kawai's generous introduction made it possible for us to access the Mitsubishi Archives in Tokyo, which shed invaluable light on Hong Kong's nineteenth-century maritime links with Japan.

We have sought to build on previous work on the Hong Kong Cemetery and the city's early Japanese community by writers and researchers such as Chan Cham Yi, Lee Pui-Tak, and Patricia Lim. Chan Cham Yi taught in the Department of Japanese Studies at the University of Hong Kong until 2012 and his office was just two doors down from Yoshiko's. His compilation of accounts of Japanese travellers and residents in the city proved to be a precious resource that we returned to again and again.

We are grateful to the staff of the various archives and offices we consulted in our search for clues as to the identity and lives of Hong Kong's Meiji-era Japanese, with particular thanks to Yumiko Ito at the Mitsubishi Archives; Yoshiro Saito at the Nagasaki Museum of History and Culture; Vito Chiu, Wilson Lee, and Alex Ng at the Hong Kong Public Records Office; Philip L. Wickeri and Michelle Lin at the Hong Kong Sheng Kung Hui Archives; Joseph Yu of the Queen's College History Museum; Shannon Koo at the Hong Kong Museum of Medical Sciences; and Andy Yeung and Kwan Yin Yee in the University of Hong Kong Libraries. We appreciate the assistance

Acknowledgements

we received with our enquiries from the Bibliothèque centrale de l'École polytechnique (France); Hong Kong Births and Deaths General Register Office; Hong Kong Cemeteries and Crematoria Office in Happy Valley; Imperial College London; National Records of Scotland and University of Glasgow Archives & Special Collections; and the Queensland State Archives.

We have sought to include a wide variety of illustrations and thank the following for access and permissions to reprint materials: Bibliothèque nationale de France; Bodleian Libraries; C. K. Lee; Ko Tim Keung; Susann Lombeck (Louise Helen Petersen Collection, with thanks to David Bellis for introducing us); Hirochika Matsuoka; The Mitsubishi Archives; the Museum of Fine Arts Budapest–Hopp Ferenc Museum; National Archives of the UK, Kew; Special Collections, SOAS Library; the University of Hong Kong Libraries; and Wellcome Collection. Two photographs taken at the Happy Valley Racecourse were reproduced by permission of the Government of the HKSAR from the collection of the Hong Kong Museum of History. Benjamin Iaquinto and Lewis Tse in the HKU Department of Geography and Masaki Yagisawa in the Department of International Design Management at the Tokyo University of Science provided very welcome last-minute help with maps of Japan and Hong Kong.

John Carroll gave us generous feedback on our initial proposal and Elizabeth Sinn on one of our earliest chapters. We also thank the two anonymous reviewers of our manuscript for their positive and helpful comments, the members of Hong Kong University Press's Editorial Board, and the Press's publisher, Michael Duckworth, acquisitions editor, Kenneth Yung, and the editing and production team for their guidance and support throughout this process. Our sincere gratitude to the Royal Asiatic Society Hong Kong for contributing to the volume's publication costs.

We have both benefitted from incredibly supportive colleagues at our two places of work – the University of Hong Kong and Tokyo University of Science – while writing this book. We are particularly grateful to Janet Borland, Junichi Iijima, and Charles Schencking, as well as Daniel Elam, Lin Yiping, Gina Marchetti, Alvin K. Wong, Winnie Yee, and everyone in the HKU Department of Comparative Literature.

Last but not least, a huge thank you to our friends Emily, Kazu, Kelvin, Kangsoon, Naoko, Sachiko, Saori, Tomoko T., Tonja, and Took, and to our families, especially Yoshiko's sister Akiko and brother Yoshimasa, and Georgina's brother Tim and husband Jo Yan, who have spent hours listening to us talk about graves and cemeteries with patience and good humour.

We end with a special thought for our own departed loved ones, Takashi, Yoko, John, Jane, and Sophie. We feel their loss every day. Peace. Perfect Peace.

Note on Romanisation

Japanese names appear in the customary order with the family name first, followed by the given name.

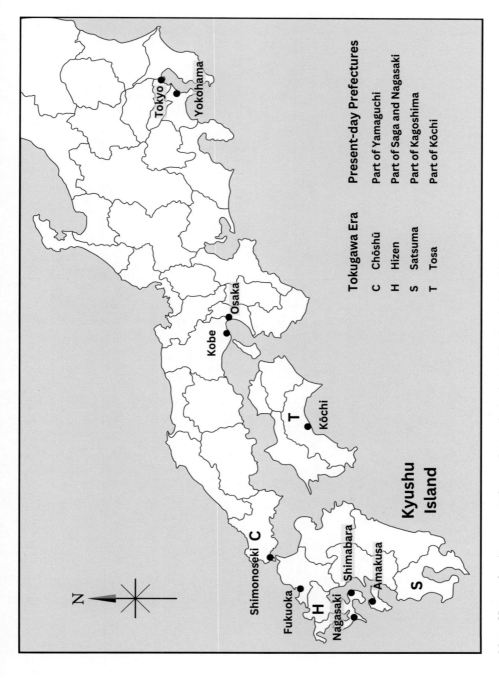

Map of Japan showing present-day prefecture boundaries. (Design by Masaki Yagisawa.)

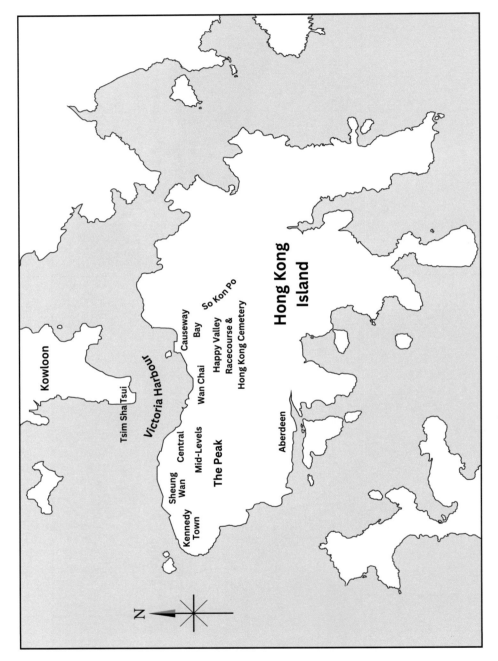

Map of Hong Kong in 1888. (Design by Masaki Yagisawa.)

House flags of the Mitsubishi Mail Steamship Company and Mitsui Bussan Kaisha (fourth row from the bottom). (Source: *Chronicle & Directory* 1885.)

English-language inscription on Kiya Saki's grave. Her memorial also features a two-metre-tall obelisk with inscriptions in Japanese. (Photo credit: Miyuki Kume.)

The graves of Japanese company executives, sailors, and a boarding house owner stand among the banyan trees in the upper reaches of the Hong Kong Cemetery. (Photo credit: Miyuki Kume.)

1

A Community of Two Halves

In Hong Kong, I work for the publisher of a paper that reports news from many far-flung places. And I occasionally take care of drifters from Japan, who have found their way to the city. I have a wife and children there. Hong Kong treats me well and my life is comfortable, so I have no plans to leave and return to Japan.[1]

[Former shipwrecked sailor Rikimatsu during a British expedition stopover in Hakodate in 1855]

One of Hong Kong's first documented Japanese residents following the island's cession to Britain in 1842 was a shipwrecked sailor. In 1835, the fourteen-year-old Rikimatsu (力松) was delivering sweet potatoes to Amakusa (天草) in Kyushu when his vessel encountered bad weather and sank. He and three companions drifted at sea for thirty-five days before finally coming ashore in the Philippines.[2] Despite surviving this ordeal, Rikimatsu could not return to Japan.

In 1635, the Tokugawa government – or *bakufu* (徳川幕府) – enforced a ban on overseas travel without official authorisation that was to remain in place until its rescinding in May 1866. Anyone caught trying to leave Japan without the *bakufu*'s permission faced the death penalty.[3] This included unfortunate Japanese sailors shipwrecked outside the country's waters who then attempted the voyage home at their peril.

Rikimatsu eventually found his way to Macau, where he became a protégé of the influential German Lutheran missionary and sinologue Karl Gutzlaff (1803–1851). He converted to Christianity, adopting the name Adonia Rickomartz. Following a failed attempt by the American ship *Morrison* to return him and six other Japanese to Japan in 1837, Rikimatsu settled in Hong Kong.[4] He served as an interpreter for the British and worked as a compositor preparing text for print for the English-language newspaper *Friend of China*. In 1849, he married an American woman, Henrietta Ambrook, in an Anglican ceremony with Gutzlaff in attendance. Together they had five children, though only two daughters, Louisa Jane and Henrietta Elizabeth or 'Bessie', and a son, Edward Adonia, appear to have survived into adulthood.[5] Bessie later trained as a missionary and had hoped to travel to Japan but died before she could fulfil her wish of seeing her father's homeland.

Rikimatsu passed away on September 23, 1860, and was buried in the Hong Kong Cemetery. Following its opening in 1845, the Hong Kong Cemetery was under the charge of the Anglican chaplain, who maintained a list of burials. Though the emplacement of his grave is lost, Rikimatsu is the first known Japanese man listed in this register and the only one interred during the Tokugawa – or Edo – period (1603–1868).[6]

It would be another eighteen years before the next Japanese burial in the cemetery. In August 1878, YUKAWA Onsaku (湯川温作)'s grave joined Rikimatsu's in Happy Valley. Yukawa's is the first of the Meiji era (1868–1912), which immediately succeeded the Tokugawa shogunate. Indeed, over 80 per cent of the approximately 470 recorded Japanese graves in the cemetery – from a total of at least 7,000 – belong to individuals who died during this era.[7]

These early graves belonged to Japanese residents and visitors from different walks of life. They are often the only remaining record of their presence in the city and offer a lens through which to gain a greater understanding of the make-up of a community of two halves that occupied an ambiguous space in Hong Kong's colonial society and was too fragmented to demand its own, dedicated burial ground. The nine Japanese graves after Yukawa's were for a barber, two infants, two employees of the Mitsubishi Mail Steamship Company, three seamen, and a student who, like Yukawa, was on his way home from Europe.[8]

The final column in the Anglican registers listed who conducted the funeral ceremony, if there was one. For the majority of Japanese burials, this entry simply read 'no ceremony', that is, no Christian ceremony. Since none of the Japanese religious sects

Table 1.1: First ten Meiji-era Japanese graves in the Hong Kong Cemetery

Burial Date	Name	Profession	Age	Cause
August 6, 1878	YUKAWA Onsaku (湯川温作)	Overseas student	22	Consumption
October 27, 1878	HIRASAWA Rokujirō (平澤録二郎) aka Jorio Kitchey, Christian convert	Barber	33	Unknown
May 23, 1879	SHIMIZU Masanosuke (清水政之助)	Navy sailor	22	Diarrhoea
July 24, 1879	Infant son of HATSU (ハツ)	–	–	Debility
March 18, 1880	Stillborn child of Mr & Mrs TERADA Ichirō (寺田一郎), Japanese Consulate	–	–	–
November 2, 1880	HONDA Masajirō (本田政次郎)[1]	Mitsubishi general manager	35	Consumption
February 21, 1881	YAMAGUCHI (山口某)	Seaman	21	Diarrhoea
June 8, 1881	MURAKAMI Hideshi (邨上秀士)	Mitsubishi clerk	23	Fever
September 11, 1881	'KAUSTIONI, Oto'	Seaman	32	Diarrhoea
December 29, 1881	KONDŌ Kizo (近藤貴蔵)	Overseas student	27	Tuberculosis

Sources: Burial Registers 1853–1930, Hong Kong Sheng Kung Hui Archives, PRO HKMS44–1. Additional details from the Hong Kong Births and Deaths General Register Office and 奥田 [Okuda] (1937), 202–7.

1. For more on Honda's grave, see Chapter 4.

had a presence in the city at that time, they had no one to officiate at the interment. This record of early burials is indicative of the overall make-up of the Meiji-era graves in the Hong Kong Cemetery. Other than individuals passing through, such as students and sailors, most belong to Japanese residents in lower-class occupations in the colony, such as small retailer or prostitute.

These names and dates offer unique opportunities for further investigation. The infant son of Hatsu, for example, was born aboard the Messageries Maritimes steamship *Anadyr* that was taking UENO Kagenori (上野景範; 1845–1888) home after his five-year stint in London as Japanese Minister to Britain. Hatsu was a maid travelling in his entourage and must have lost her child either just before arriving in Hong Kong or during the ship's stopover in the city.[9] The other infant on the list was the stillborn child of Hong Kong consular official Terada Ichirō and his wife. Of the ten entries recorded above, only six monuments, including Yukawa's, are still identifiable.[10]

As mentioned previously, Yukawa Onsaku's was the first Meiji-era Japanese grave in the Hong Kong Cemetery. The twenty-two-year-old military cadet was returning to Japan after six years spent studying at various educational institutions in France. He left Yokohama for Marseille in 1872 as part of a wave of students sent overseas to acquire direct experience of novel technologies and practices from Europe and the United States. After two hundred years of managed contacts with the outside world during the Tokugawa period, Yukawa and hundreds like him were to provide the new Meiji government with the necessary tools and expertise to modernise Japan's infrastructure and institutions.

Re-engaging with the Outside World

The Tokugawa ban that meant Rikimatsu risked death should he return to Japan did not preclude foreign contact altogether. However, what interaction did take place was strictly regulated and private travel without official approval was almost impossible. The Dutch were permitted to remain, though they were later confined to the small artificial island of Dejima in the Nagasaki harbour (長崎出島). The *bakufu* also maintained its trading relationships with China and Korea throughout the Tokugawa period.[11]

By the mid-nineteenth century, the behaviour of Western powers in the East Asian region had grown increasingly predatory. China's defeat at the hands of the British in the First Opium War (1839–1842) and regular forays by foreign ships into Japanese waters highlighted Japan's vulnerability and technological deficiencies.[12] On July 8, 1853, Commodore Matthew Perry of the US Navy sailed into the harbour of present-day Tokyo with a squadron of warships and a letter from the US president that demanded the opening of Japan's ports to trade. This incursion led to the Convention of Kanagawa in 1854 and a further agreement in 1858. These documents, together with the commercial treaties signed with Britain, France, Holland, and Russia around the same time, formally established Hakodate, Niigata, Yokohama, Kobe, and Nagasaki (函館, 新潟, 横浜, 神戸, 長崎) as treaty ports, and Tokyo and Osaka as open cities.[13]

The treaty-port and open-city system, to some extent modelled on the First Opium War settlement with China, created enclaves in which the Japanese government had to surrender both its tariff autonomy and legal jurisdiction over foreign residents living in the cities covered by the treaties. These systems were a form of 'informal imperialism' that gave Europeans and Americans access to Japan's resources on their own, advantageous terms.[14] Despite this humiliating loss of sovereignty, the *bakufu* did succeed in its demand that the opium trade, so crucial to Hong Kong's early prosperity, be outlawed in Japan.[15]

With the opening up of the country's ports and the unprecedented arrival of foreign traders and diplomats, the *bakufu* realised that overseas travel could no longer be avoided. The ban was officially rescinded in 1866.[16] Japanese individuals were now free to venture abroad for study or trade, seamen to work on foreign ships, and merchants to associate with foreigners at the treaty ports without government interference.[17]

The unequal treaties further weakened the Tokugawa regime's already ailing grasp on power. The negative economic impact of the treaty-port arrangement caused domestic unrest, and powerful *daimyō* [大名; provincial lords], particularly those of Satsuma, Chōshū, Tosa, and Hizen (薩摩, 長州, 土佐, 肥前), called for reforms. In December 1867, following years of turmoil, the armies of Satsuma and Chōshū marched on Kyoto. In January 1868, the newly anointed Emperor Meiji, who had ascended the throne in February 1867, proclaimed the end of the Tokugawa shogunate. A government of nobles and *daimyō* under the emperor replaced the *bakufu* and signalled the beginning of the era known as the Meiji Restoration.[18]

Learning from Western Technology and Expertise

Meiji officials, several of whom had clandestinely travelled overseas during the 1860s, understood that the study and selective incorporation of foreign practices and technology into virtually every aspect of Japanese society were vital to resisting the encroachment of Western interests and preserving the country's resources. To this end, they accelerated a number of outward-looking initiatives that the Tokugawa regime had, somewhat reluctantly, undertaken in the final decade of its rule: the hiring of foreign experts to act as advisors and provide instruction in Japan, the deployment of fact-finding missions abroad, and the sending of Japanese students to train at overseas institutions of learning, mainly in Europe and the US.[19]

The Iwakura Embassy of 1871–1873 was the most famous of all Meiji-era foreign delegations. The Embassy, headed by Prince IWAKURA Tomomi (岩倉具視; 1825–1883), left Japan bound for San Francisco on December 23, 1871, and did not return until September 13, 1873. At the time of its departure, the eminent group counted forty-six official members, fifteen other participants, and forty-two students, including five young women. Accompanying Prince Iwakura were several other significant players in the Meiji regime, among them ITŌ Hirobumi (伊藤博文; 1841–1909), who would become Japan's first prime minister under a newly introduced cabinet system in 1885.[20] ANDŌ Tarō (安藤太郎; 1846–1924) was one of the mission's junior secretaries.[21] Originally from Yotsuya (四谷) in Tokyo, Andō had fought for the forces loyal to the last *shōgun* but switched sides following the latter's defeat.[22] He later served as Japan's most senior consular representative in Hong Kong from 1874 to 1882.

The expedition spent close to seven months in the US before leaving for Britain, where it was received by Queen Victoria. Delegates then embarked on an extensive tour of various European countries, meeting dignitaries and visiting military installations, shipyards, prisons, factories, sewage plants, banks, schools, and cultural landmarks.

The mission had a diplomatic agenda as well: the renegotiation of the unequal treaties that the *bakufu* had signed with foreign powers. Though unsuccessful in this regard, it had a lasting impact on Japan's development and the overhaul of its institutions.[23] Articles in Hong Kong's English-language press debated the Embassy's accomplishments, including an editorial in the *China Mail*, which recognised the value of the endeavour in raising Japan's profile on the world stage.

> Granted that the envoys and their suite have returned no wiser than they went after spending a mint of money, they have achieved something which no other device could possibly have achieved in visiting Europe. They have removed Japan from the list of *terra incognita* to the average Briton or Continental. The have personally demonstrated that their country boasts men of fair intelligence . . . and have shown that they understand diplomatic usages, can appreciate western appliances, and desire to encourage foreign enterprise amongst their countrymen. These, be it noted, are things which all the books in the world, and all that could be done in their own country could never have achieved.[24]

The Iwakura Embassy stopped for two nights in Hong Kong on its way back to Japan from Europe. Members of the delegation arrived aboard the Messageries Maritimes ship *Ava* on August 27, 1873, just four months after the opening of the city's Japanese Consulate.[25]

Figure 1.1: Andō Tarō during the Iwakura Embassy's visit to Paris in 1873. Andō later served as Japanese Consul in Hong Kong. (Source: National Diet Library Digital Collections.)

A Japanese Consulate for Hong Kong

Britain first occupied Hong Kong Island in 1839, as part of its efforts to establish a base from which to promote its trade with China. Portugal had Macau, Spain Manila, and Holland Jakarta [Batavia], but the closest British-controlled territory to the Chinese mainland of any significance was in India. The latter was also the source of Britain's main export to China: opium. The Qing government ceded Hong Kong Island to the Crown during the First Opium War. The Convention of Peking [Beijing] signed at the end of the Second Opium War (1856–1860) extended British territorial rights to include the Kowloon Peninsula.[26]

The bustling colony's population tripled to over 20,000 people within just five years – the majority Chinese arrivals from neighbouring Guangdong – and imposing, European-style office buildings made their appearance along the harbourfront. Yet Britain's remote outpost was better known for its high crime rates, deadly diseases, and pirate-infested waters. The situation improved in the 1850s, with Hong Kong attracting a more affluent class of Chinese migrants seeking refuge from the ravages of the Taiping Rebellion (太平天国の乱; 1850–1864) and the city profiting from the transit of Chinese labourers to the US. Increasing numbers of European and American companies, along with Jewish, Armenian, and Indian, including Parsee, merchant houses, opened offices in Hong Kong to capitalise on its status as a free port and the growth in the transshipment trade with China, particularly in opium. The opening of the Suez Canal in 1869, which greatly reduced sailing times to European destinations, further boosted Hong Kong's position as a commercial and migratory hub connecting China, India, Southeast Asia, the US, Europe, and even Australia.[27]

Japan's lifting of the two-hundred-year travel ban and change to the more outward-looking Meiji regime made it possible for previously unseen numbers of Japanese to go abroad for work and study in the early 1870s. The voyage to Europe aboard the steamships of commercial shipping companies such as the British Peninsular and Oriental Steam Navigation Company (P&O) and its French competitor Messageries Maritimes always involved a stopover or change of vessel in Hong Kong.[28]

The Meiji government selected Hong Kong as one of five cities in which to establish a diplomatic presence in 1872, along with Shanghai, New York, Fuzhou, and Venice.[29] Japanese Ministry of Foreign Affairs official Ueno Kagenori, who would later serve as resident minister in London from 1874 to 1879, announced the decision in a letter to the British Minister to Japan, Harry Parkes (1828–1885). Ueno explained that in view of the rise in the number of his compatriots travelling to Hong Kong, the ministry had appointed HAYASHI Michisaburō (林道三郎) as Japan's vice-consul in the colony. The letter caused something of an upset, with Parkes complaining that Hayashi had not followed proper procedures with regard to the notification of his appointment. Parkes blamed the latter's insufficient grasp of English for the confusion, commenting that it was 'very likely that Mr. Hayashi's knowledge of English may not have been sufficient to appreciate what was said to him exactly'. This was despite the Japanese government selecting Hayashi for this important post precisely because of his English- and Chinese-language abilities.[30] English-language competency would, indeed, prove a challenge for many of the Japanese living and working in the colony.

Japan finally opened its consulate in Hong Kong on April 20, 1873, with the thirty-year-old Hayashi at its head.[31] His duties included intelligence gathering, reporting to

Tokyo on Hong Kong's growing Japanese community, and handling issues connected to the transit passengers arriving and departing 'nearly every week'.[32] Despite his knowledge of the language, Hayashi had little overseas experience and clearly found managing the Hong Kong mission a challenge. With the funding provided by the Foreign Ministry insufficient to cover the consulate's high staffing and rental costs, Hayashi was soon in debt. He committed suicide on September 22, 1873, while on home leave in Tokyo.[33]

First Encounter with a Modern Colonial City

Japanese travellers going overseas in the early 1870s had limited knowledge of the world outside Japan. They could only rely on translated books, newly published guides on Western-style clothing and manners, and encounters with foreigners in the open ports for an idea of what to expect once they left home.[34] Hong Kong was their first experience of a comparatively modern city. Some recorded their impressions of the colony in the diaries that they kept of their travels. Much like today, visitors were awed by views of the city at night, comparing the multitude of gaslights to fireflies.[35] Sailing into the harbour on his way to France in September 1872, the writer NARUSHIMA Ryūhoku (成島柳北; 1837–1884) was moved to pen a verse:

> In the tall buildings along the waterfront, ten thousand lights;
> The passenger and trade vessels call and answer one other.
> Here in the southern seas, the ninth month is still fiery hot;
> Everyone races to buy a few pieces of ice from a silver bowl.[36]

Furthermore, these narratives convey a sense of the ambiguous feelings that the British colony inspired. In addition to its adoption of modern technology, such as the telegraph, and European-style architecture, Hong Kong provided an opportunity to view the workings of British imperialism up close. The discriminatory treatment of the city's Chinese inhabitants shocked Japanese visitors. However, rather than empathising with the former's plight, they blamed them for it. This disdain for a country previously admired for its scholarship emerged in the 1860s as increasing numbers of Japanese officials and students transited through the treaty port of Shanghai and Hong Kong.[37] In their diaries, they condemned the inability of the Qing government to resist or at least manage foreign encroachment and ban the trade in opium, as Japan had. They sought to distance themselves from the Chinese by commenting on the extent of their addiction to the drug and their unsanitary living conditions. Journal entries on the high rates of robbery and the unhygienic environment in the predominantly Chinese quarters of the city portrayed Hong Kong's Chinese population as dirty and dishonest.[38] They contrasted a China in decline with the visible successes of British colonial power.

While Britain's advanced technology, commercial ambitions, and military might were to be admired, they were also to be feared. If a vastly outnumbered foreign power could submit the local population to its rule, what was there to prevent it from doing the same in Japan? The race was on to match Britain's achievements and join it as one of 'the two great Island Empires'.[39]

Figure 1.2: The Hong Kong Central waterfront in the late 1860s. (Photograph by John Thomson. Source: Wellcome Collection.)

Occupations of Hong Kong's Meiji-Era Japanese Residents

Not all Japanese passed through Hong Kong merely on their way to somewhere else. Though just a handful at first, the number of Japanese living in the city would exceed a thousand by 1912. Despite achieving this milestone, the Japanese in Hong Kong remained a community of two halves throughout the Meiji era: one centred around the sex industry and the other focused on advancing Japan's technology and commerce to a level where it could compete with the Euro-American powers dominating global trade, with tradespeople and professionals falling somewhere in between.

Prior to 1897, Hong Kong's official census reports divided the population into three main categories: Europeans and Americans, Chinese, and a third grouping for anyone who did not fit into the other two, which included the Japanese.[40] This lack of distinction makes it difficult to estimate the number of Japanese residing in Hong Kong during the 1870s with any precision, though there were certainly less than a hundred. Japanese and later colonial government sources provide a clearer indication of the make-up and spatial configuration of the city's Japanese community from the 1880s onwards and highlight issues that would cause friction and division within it for several decades to come.

Table 1.2: Number of Japanese residents in Hong Kong, 1880–1911

Year	Japanese Residents					Total Civilian Population as per HK Government Census
	Female	%	Male	%	Total	
1880	60	70%	26	30%	86	
1881						153,544
1886	96	66%	50	34%	146	
1889	142	58%	101	42%	243	
1891						215,194
1901	224	53%	197	47%	421	281,794
1906	379	44%	478	56%	857	315,843
1911	483	44%	616	56%	1,099	450,098

Sources: Hong Kong Government Censuses for 1881, 1891, 1901, 1906, and 1911, totals exclude the navy and military establishments, and the mercantile marine; 奥田 [Okuda] (1937), 111, 189–200, 270, 313–16; and 外務省通商局 編 [International Trade Bureau, MOFA, ed.] (1917), 348.

The Japanese Consulate counted eighty-six short-term or long-term Japanese residents in the city on April 7, 1880, with 30 per cent men and 70 per cent women. The majority of men were sailors or involved in the trade and retail of seafood and sundry items. Though no names or occupations were provided for women, the gender imbalance pointed to the fact that most were *karayuki-san* – or prostitutes.[41]

KIMURA Shūzō (木村修三) was one of about a hundred Japanese residing in Hong Kong in the early 1880s.[42] He recalled that there was a lot of petty crime, which an inadequate police force failed to tackle, and that the authorities required him to show a night pass if he wanted to move from Central to Wan Chai after dark. From as early as 1842, the colonial government had sought to restrict the night-time movements of the colony's Chinese population 'to provide for the better security' of its residents. In 1870, it was unlawful for any Chinese 'to be at large in the city of Victoria, between the hour of 9 in the evening and sunrise without a pass'. Clearly, this legislation was applied selectively to Japanese residents as well, despite the relevant ordinance making no mention of other ethnicities.[43]

The consulate recorded occupations for women in its count for 1886, with fifty out of ninety-six female residents described as managing or working in 'cafés' and *kashizashiki* (貸座敷; rental rooms), a euphemism for prostitution, and thirteen as concubines of Western men.[44] Their average age of twenty-four, single status, and geographical provenance were further indications of their occupation.[45] Indeed, over two-thirds of the women hailed from Nagasaki prefecture, which was the point of origin for a significant proportion of trafficked prostitutes during the early years of the Meiji era.[46]

Table 1.3: Occupations of Japanese residents in 1886

Men – 26		Women – 77	
Mitsui Bussan Kaisha employee	4	*Kashizashiki* worker	44
Kashizashiki/'Café' manager	4	Concubine of Westerner	13
Chinaware dealer	3	Servant	11
Photographer	3	*Kashizashiki*/'Café' manager	6
Hairdresser/Barber	3	Hairdresser	1
Boarding house operator	2	Boarding house operator	1
Kimono dealer	2	*Shamisen* player	1
Servant	2		
Tailor	1		
Shop assistant	1		
Employee of US shipping company	1		

Source: 奥田 [Okuda] (1937), 190–200. There were also nine boarders, fifteen family members, and nineteen with no occupation given.

The average age of the male residents came to 28.65.[47] The professions for thirty-five of the men revealed a more diverse range of occupations. They included kimono and chinaware dealers, as well as tailors, hairdressers, and boarding house and restaurant operators. The concentration of workers in these occupations echoed that of nineteenth-century Chinese migrants to Japan, who, besides trading, featured prominently in the clothing, hairdressing, and restaurant industries, otherwise known as the 'three-blades' (三刀): chef's knife, tailor's scissors, and barber's razor.[48]

MINAMI Teisuke (南貞助; 1847–1915), who was consul at the time of the 1886 census, was keen to promote Japanese trade and find new markets for Japanese-manufactured products in the colony.[49] At least this was the claim made by the consulate's English-speaking secretary, John William Jones (1859–1942). Jones arrived in Hong Kong in 1884 to join the colonial administration as a teacher at Hong Kong's Government Central School. In 1886, he took up a temporary private position with the consulate, which he kept until Minami's departure two years later. In a letter to the secretary of state to the colonies detailing his appointment, Jones writes that 'with Mr. Minami as Consul (a gentleman of great sagacity & perseverance) no stone was left unturned to increase the commerce of Japan. Before he left the Colony therefore he had the extreme satisfaction of seeing much readier markets than when he arrived in Hong Kong for such products as:– matches, porcelain, peppermint oil, copper, inferior soaps, rough gauze cotton cloths, to say nothing of the much increased British trade, of which he greatly favoured.'[50]

The number of company representatives certainly increased during Minami's tenure. The 1886 survey listed four male staff members of the merchant firm Mitsui Bussan Kaisha (三井物産會社), including the newly arrived, twenty-six-year-old acting manager FUKUHARA Eitarō (福原榮太郎).[51]

Closely connected to occupation, class affiliations played a divisive role in the make-up of the early Japanese community in Hong Kong. After coming to power in 1868, the Meiji government had officially abolished the four divisions of society – *samurai*, farmers, artisans, and merchants (士農工商) – to facilitate social mobility.[52] Despite this, class distinctions persisted, with members from a *samurai* background often occupying the most important positions in commercial and governmental enterprises. Of the 146 residents, just five men, including the four Mitsui employees, were from the *samurai* class, while over 80 per cent were categorised as 'commoners'.[53]

Separations between those connected with the sex industry and the city's burgeoning Japanese elite, which included senior consular staff and company managers, played out spatially as well. In Japan, the terms 'downtown' (下町; Shitamachi) and 'uptown' (山の手; Yamamote) were commonly used during the Edo period to discriminate between those from lower social strata who lived close to the water and those from the *samurai* class dwelling on higher ground. In Hong Kong, the 'downtown' brothels and stores of several small tradespeople were concentrated in the nether reaches of Central – roughly the area now traversed by the first three sections of the Central to Mid-Levels Escalator. The 'uptown' Mitsui executives, meanwhile, resided further up the hill, at Remedios Terrace on Arbuthnot Road, very close to the Japanese Consulate on Caine Road.[54]

Japan's victory in the first Sino-Japanese War of 1894–1895, and the significant indemnity paid by China, signalled the country's emergence as an economic and military rival to European powers in Asia.[55] By the turn of the century, Japanese residents in Hong Kong numbered 421, with female residents accounting for 53 per cent of the total.[56] Improved hygiene and increased access to the services they enjoyed at home made it more attractive for executives to bring their families to the city, and the number of company representatives skyrocketed, from fewer than ten in 1886 to eighty-five in 1901. A growing number of established Japanese commercial entities, such as banks and shipping firms, began setting up offices in Hong Kong, causing the social make-up of the Japanese community to diversify.

The Russo-Japanese War of 1904–1905 marked a turning point in the gender ratio, with men outnumbering women in the years following the end of the conflict. By 1910, the Japanese resident population in Hong Kong had passed the one thousand mark. A Ministry of Foreign Affairs report for 1916 recorded a total of 1,460 Japanese residing in the city, 43 per cent female and 57 per cent male, and listed their occupations. In addition to consular employees and students, the census distinguished fifty-four different areas of employment.[57]

A significant percentage of women continued to work in the sex industry. The census counted nineteen brothel owners, thirty-seven concubines of foreign men, and 156 prostitutes, all women, for a total of 212. This equated to close to 15 per cent of the total Japanese population in Hong Kong. The proportion of residents connected to the sex industry increased further if it included boarding house operators involved in the traffic of *karayuki-san* and other trades, such as hairdressing, tailoring, and kimono selling, that relied to a significant extent on prostitutes and their brothels for business.

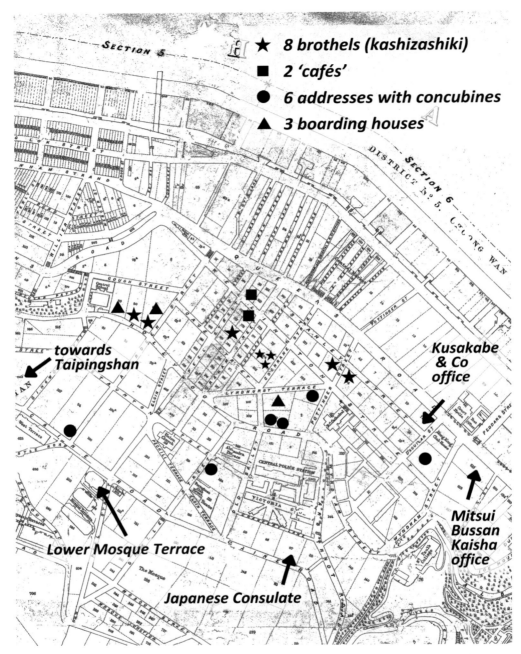

Figure 1.3: Location of Japanese boarding houses, brothels, and addresses with concubines in Central in 1886. (Source for addresses: 奥田 [Okuda], 1937, 190–200.)

A Community of Two Halves

Table 1.4: Top ten occupations of Japanese residents in 1916

Men		Women	
Company worker	171	Prostitute	156
Shipping office worker	44	Company worker	66
Kimono and sundry goods shopkeeper	38	Concubine of Western man	37
Tailor	37	Food and beverage worker	33
Hairstylist	34	Shipping office worker	27
Shoemaker and shoe seller	33	Geisha	24
Carpenter	33	Tailor	21
Peddler	33	Brothel operator	19
Ryokan and boarding house worker	31	Kimono and sundry goods shopkeeper	16
Art and curio dealer	30	Broker	15

Source: 外務省通商局 編 [International Trade Bureau, MOFA, ed.] (1917). The counts for each occupation included dependents, such as children, spouses, and servants, if applicable.

Hong Kong was by no means home to the largest Japanese diasporic community during the Meiji era. In the nineteenth century, colonial powers and expanding economies in the Americas began looking to Asia for the provision of a cheap and submissive workforce to toil in agriculture, mining, and construction projects. China was one source of labourers, both free and indentured; Japan was another.[58] The first batch of Japanese contract workers departed for Hawaii in 1868 and a further 30,000 arrived between 1885 and 1895 to work on Hawaiian plantations. Other major destinations for predominantly male migrant workers in the last decade of the Meiji era included Brazil, Canada, Peru, the US, and the Australian pearl diving centres of Thursday Island and Broome.[59]

Unlike in these locations, where a large diasporic community grew up around labourers employed in a specific industry such as agriculture or pearl diving, Hong Kong's early Japanese residents followed a different pattern. Japanese women initially outnumbered men, but they were quickly joined by established commercial concerns that recognised the colony's strategic importance as a centre for trade and maritime expansion. The opening of the Japanese Consulate in 1873 was a clear indication of the Meiji government's intent to enhance its diplomatic and business presence in the city. The make-up of the Japanese community in Singapore followed a similar pattern to that of Hong Kong, though Japan did not have a permanent consular presence there until twenty years later.[60]

Nevertheless, Japanese residents in Hong Kong occupied an ambiguous space throughout the Meiji era. Neither European nor Chinese, British officials sometimes struggled with how to categorise them within the colony's highly stratified and discriminatory society. With no aristocracy or traditional upper class to speak of, high-ranking British civil servants and wealthy merchants sat at the top of the social ladder and nearly all Chinese at the bottom. The Hongkong Club, which opened its doors on May 26, 1846, and whose membership was one of the city's principal indicators of high status, excluded even the most prominent members of the Chinese community.[61] In the case of the Japanese, senior consular officials and company representatives appeared regularly on the guest lists of prestigious European social occasions, whereas the colonial government grouped Japanese in lower-class occupations with the Chinese.

Meiji Graves in the Hong Kong Cemetery

The ambiguous position of Hong Kong's Japanese residents in the 1870s extended to the handling of their dead. Hampered by class distinctions and the absence of a defined middle class, the early Japanese community failed to achieve the critical mass needed to secure its own burial ground. It required the intervention of the Japanese Consulate for the colonial government to permit the interment of an unbaptised Japanese in the Hong Kong Cemetery. On August 6, 1878, Yukawa Onsaku became the first Meiji-era Japanese buried there.

Born in 1856 in the Chōshū domain (now part of Yamaguchi prefecture 山口県), Yukawa was a student at the Osaka Military Academy (大阪兵學寮; *Ōsaka heigakuryō*) when he won a scholarship to travel to France for military training in 1872.[62] His arrival in the country on December 16 coincided with that of the Iwakura Embassy.[63] Yukawa attended several French educational institutions before officially registering at the prestigious École Polytechnique in Paris on April 30, 1877. His surviving academic record reveals that he took classes in mathematical analysis, geometry, chemistry, mechanics, physics, and stereotomy. The latter is the art or technique of cutting solids, particularly stonecutting.[64]

'Japonisme' was very much in vogue following the Paris Exhibition of 1867, to which both the Tokugawa government and the Satsuma domain had sent exhibits, and there is evidence that Yukawa moved in the French capital's artistic circles towards the end of his six-year stay.[65]

An entry in the diary of politician and author Victor Hugo, who had an interest in *ukiyo-e* woodblock prints, seems to indicate that he met Yukawa. The passage, dated January 30, 1876, reads, 'A Japanese man, You Ka Va, welcomed me in. [Art critic Philippe] Burty brought him to see me a month ago, and he lives in the hotel.' Hugo was seeking relief from the crowds following his election to the upper house of the French parliament. He found refuge at the Hôtel d'Égypte, 46 Rue Gay-Lussac, and encountered Yukawa, who was staying there.[66]

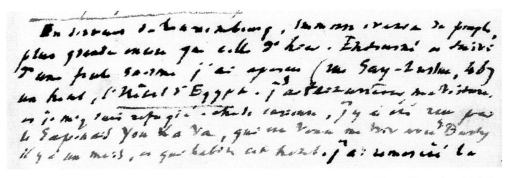

Figure 1.4: An excerpt from the diary of French author and politician Victor Hugo in which he mentions meeting 'You Ka Va' (second line from the bottom) at the Hôtel d'Égypte in Paris in January 1876. (Source: Bibliothèque nationale de France. Fonds Victor Hugo. III – CARNETS. 1er janvier–31 décembre 1876.)

A Community of Two Halves

Figure 1.5: Postcard of Happy Valley, circa 1905. (Source: Hong Kong Memory Project/Ko Tim Keung.)

Yukawa became ill and was unable to complete his first year at the École Polytechnique, deciding instead to head home. He and two companions, HIRO Toraichi (廣虎一; b. 1850) and KOSAKA Chihiro (小坂千尋; 1850–1891), left Marseille for Yokohama aboard the *Djemnah* on June 30, 1878.[67] The Messageries Maritimes ship made a scheduled stopover in Hong Kong on August 4. Yukawa's condition had worsened during the voyage and his two friends attempted to secure passage on an earlier ship so as to get him home as soon as possible.[68] However, Yukawa succumbed to consumption the day after their arrival.[69] The question then arose of how to ensure he was laid to rest in a suitable location.

The Protestant Graveyard, renamed Colonial Cemetery and now Hong Kong Cemetery, opened in 1845 in the area known as the 'Wong Nei Chung Valley'.[70] The location, across the road from the racecourse, proved popular as a final resting place. Between 1848 and 1870, land was designated for dedicated Catholic, Parsee, Jewish, and Muslim cemeteries. The name 'Happy Valley' likely arose from this agglomeration of burial grounds rather than any connection to the enjoyment of horseracing; the name was often used in Britain as a euphemism for cemeteries in the nineteenth century.[71]

In contrast to Happy Valley's other religious burial grounds, the Hong Kong Cemetery was government-funded and not exclusively reserved for Anglican civilians and military personnel. It functioned to some extent as a public cemetery, accepting deceased members of other Protestant faiths, as well as European destitutes. The burial registers list seven Asians – six Chinese and one 'Malay' – buried in the Hong Kong Cemetery in the 1850s.[72] The former shipwrecked seaman Rikimatsu was the first Japanese man interred there, in 1860. Yukawa, in 1878, was the second.

Some Japanese residing in or passing through the colony must have died in the eighteen years following Rikimatsu's decease. Yet there is no record of any new Japanese burials in the Hong Kong Cemetery prior to 1878. As those who perished during that time were most likely non-Christians and employed in lower-class occupations, friends or relatives might have arranged for interments in one of the Chinese burial grounds. The latter were poorly regulated and temporary in nature, with the government only starting to designate land specifically for Chinese burials in 1871.[73] Yukawa's higher status as an army cadet made it necessary for the Consulate to secure a more appropriate arrangement.

Andō Tarō arrived in Hong Kong in 1874 to head up the Japanese Consulate for the next eight years.[74] As a junior member of the Iwakura Embassy, he had travelled extensively in the US and Europe and had considerable exposure to Western ideas and practices. His time in Hong Kong coincided with that of the colony's eighth governor, John Pope Hennessy (1834–1891).

Unlike his predecessors, Pope Hennessy actively looked to give Chinese members of the population more of a say in the colony's affairs. In February 1878, he demonstrated his respect for the Chinese community's most influential institution, the Tung Wah Hospital (東華醫院), by paying an official visit to its facilities on the occasion of the Chinese New Year. His efforts to overhaul certain discriminatory practices caused many members of the British expatriate community to regard him with hostility.[75]

As Japan's official representative in Hong Kong, Andō was a guest at many of the city's important social functions and he and Pope Hennessy were well acquainted. In the summer of 1879, Andō coordinated and accompanied the governor, his wife, Catherine 'Kitty' Elizabeth Low (1850–1923), and their son, Bertie, on a three-month private visit to Japan. The daughter of senior colonial administrator Hugh Low, Kitty was a quarter Malay through her mother and sixteen years younger than her husband. Pope Hennessy had met and married her during his posting to Labuan in present-day Malaysia, where he was governor from 1867 to 1871.[76] They travelled together throughout the country, from Hakodate in the north to Osaka further south and, of course, to Tokyo. Andō ensured that the governor was received by the Meiji Emperor and Japan's most eminent politicians and businesspeople.[77]

Figure 1.6: Hong Kong Governor Sir John Pope Hennessy during his visit to Japan in 1879 (back row, third from right). The photograph also includes Japan's Finance Minister Ōkuma Shigenobu (third from left). Andō Tarō, Japan's Consul in Hong Kong (second from left), has his hand resting on the chair of his wife, Fumiko (front left). Hennessy's wife, Kitty, sits in the centre of the first row with their son Bertie. (Source: 江森編 [Emori ed.], 1909, iv.)

Figure 1.7: The obelisk of Japanese student Kondō Kizō stands amid Christian crosses and headstones in the Hong Kong Cemetery. Kondō spent a year in London at the Royal School of Mines before contracting tuberculosis. Like Yukawa, he was on his way home when he passed away on December 27, 1881, aged twenty-seven. (Photo credit: Miyuki Kume.)

In view of his more racially egalitarian outlook, Pope Hennessy would certainly have supported any request to allow the burial of unbaptised Japanese in a government cemetery almost exclusively reserved for European and American Protestants.[78] Yukawa's affiliation with the Japanese army must have counted in favour of his inclusion, but the more than 470 recorded graves that joined his in the ensuing decades belonged overwhelmingly to Japanese civilians from the lower social strata.

Japanese gravestones like Yukawa's were scattered around the remoter terraces of the cemetery, at some distance from the more accessible and better maintained areas near the chapel, which were reserved for Westerners of the Protestant faith.[79] The Japanese community in Singapore acquired its own, exclusive burial ground in 1891, when the members of an organisation predominantly associated with the sex industry secured a plot of land in the north-eastern part of the city.[80] In Hong Kong, it did not even have a dedicated section within which to bury its dead. Indeed, the consulate's arrangement to have Yukawa buried in the Hong Kong Cemetery set a course that then made asking for an exclusive plot for this purpose more difficult.

This intermingling of Japanese graves with those of Protestant residents explains the hybrid nature of the monuments erected in their memory. Yukawa's incorporates a tall, four-sided, non-tapered obelisk with inscriptions in Chinese characters (漢字; *kanji*). The design choice, which was not widespread in Japan, complied with an army edict issued in 1874 that dictated the shape and dimensions of monuments erected for deceased Japanese soldiers overseas. The army advocated wooden markers, but stone pillars were acceptable, if not too costly.[81] However, many of the cemetery's Japanese gravestones for civilians used this format too. It was similar to the Egyptian motifs in vogue at the time and possibly an attempt to fit in with the styles adopted for other grave markers in the cemetery. Having a gravestone made in Japan and shipped to Hong Kong was not an option. There were also grave fees to be paid. In 1883, these amounted to 16 dollars – 15 dollars for the ground fee and 1 for the digging – the equivalent of a steerage class fare from Hong Kong to Kobe.[82] Therefore, families and friends relied on local monumental masons, who did not offer more traditional Japanese formats.

Another unusual feature was the juxtaposition of inscriptions in Japanese and English. Yukawa's is the only grave to display an epigraph in French, a nod to the six years he spent in France.

> TOMBEAU DE ONSAKU YUKAWA
> OFFICIER JAPONAIS
> MORT A HONGKONG
> LE 5 AOÛT, 1878,
> À L'ÂGE DE 22 ANS
> EN RENTRANT DE LA FRANCE
> À SA PATRIE.[83]

Student Kondō Kizō's grave marker also takes the form of an obelisk and features an inscription in English. The Chinese characters etched on the monuments detail information about the deceased, such as their name and birthplace, as well as the person – or persons – who erected the grave. Later Meiji monuments sometimes included an afterlife name. Buddhist priests charged a premium for this mark of prestige that signified an entrance into a 'state of buddhahood' and it was out of reach for most.[84] The majority of the Japanese gravestones are made of granite, with far fewer carved from marble.[85]

With the growth of the colony's other expatriate communities, grave space became an issue. Japanese burials in the Hong Kong Cemetery occurred at a rate of about ten a year in the final decades of the nineteenth century, but this number had doubled by the beginning of the twentieth century.[86] European, especially British, Christians complained about the rituals associated with Japanese funerals, such as the burning of incense, ultimately compelling the government to take a stand and find a compromise that could accommodate all parties. Though members of the Japanese community had come to think of the sections in the upper left-hand corner of the Hong Kong Cemetery, where the largest number of Japanese graves were located, as 'the Japanese Cemetery', they were in danger of losing it as their place of burial.

A 'Japanese Cemetery'

When the Japanese finally secured a designated space for their burials in the cemetery, it was by default. In October 1908, the Hong Kong Sanitary Board passed a bye-law prohibiting the 'burning of joss sticks and firing of crackers' in the 'Colonial Cemetery'.[87] The board members in favour of the ban claimed to be unaware of its impact on the Japanese community, whose graves now took up a remote but significant portion of the cemetery. Furthermore, an editorial in the *China Mail* pointed out the

Figure 1.8: The grave of Yukawa Onsaku stands in a more remote area of the Hong Kong Cemetery. His funeral and burial cost 259 dollars. The Japanese Army and Foreign Ministry argued for two years over which department should cover this amount. (Photo credit: Miyuki Kume.)

board's misconceptions with regard to Buddhist and Shintō funeral practices, which, unlike certain Chinese rituals, do not use firecrackers: 'The speakers at the Sanitary Board meeting . . . were evidently unaware that the ritual of the Shin-shu sect, which is served by the Hongwan-ji priests, and to which most of the Japanese residents nominally belong, does not require the firing of crackers, and only a very limited amount of incense burning . . . while in the case of Shintoists the ceremonies and paraphernalia are even more meagre from a spectacular point of view.'[88]

The prohibition was a not-so-subtle attempt by some board members to exclude non-Christian – and, by extension, non-European or American – burials from an increasingly overcrowded cemetery; other faiths had dedicated cemeteries, and the Protestants should have one too. A subsequent review of the bye-law generated heated discussions within the board as to how to resolve the situation. Chinese members were particularly vocal in maintaining that the Hong Kong Cemetery, as a non-consecrated space, should be open to all, irrespective of nationality and religion, though perhaps not necessarily class.[89] Indeed, they felt aggrieved by the lack of a proper burial ground for the city's 'better class' of Chinese and saw this as an opportunity to promote their own demands for a permanent Chinese cemetery.[90] Citing a proclamation of 1841 that 'secures to all inhabitants the exercise of their religious rights and ceremonies', Japanese Vice-Consul FUNATSU Tatsuichirō (船津辰一郎; 1873–1947) wrote to various colonial officials to defend the use of incense in the Colonial Cemetery, 'the only place for Japanese to bury their dead'.[91] Ultimately, it was agreed that the government would provide land for a new cemetery for all Buddhists and other non-Christian faiths in So Kon Po, near Causeway Bay.

As the establishment of this new burial ground might take some time, an interim measure was needed. The Hong Kong Cemetery was effectively carved into two sections, a significantly larger, consecrated Christian ground and a separate zone for non-Christians, where incense could be burned.[92] The Legislative Council passed the relevant ordinance in November 1909 and the governor, Frederick Lugard, attended a religious dedication ceremony led by the Anglican Bishop of Victoria on March 29, 1910.[93] With Japanese accounting for the majority of non-Christians buried in the cemetery, the separation effectively created a de facto 'Japanese Cemetery'.

The Meiji-era graves in the Hong Kong Cemetery, and the stories of those who are buried in them, provide a lens through which to understand the make-up of Hong Kong's Japanese community in the late nineteenth and early twentieth centuries – a community of two halves. They provide insight into not only how its members perceived one another, but also where they ranked within Hong Kong's highly stratified and discriminatory society. Chapters 2 and 3 discuss those regarded by their fellow Japanese as working in the lowliest of occupations, the *karayuki-san*, or prostitutes, and the boarding house owners involved in their traffic. Chapters 4 and 5 consider those occupying the upper echelons of local Japanese society, the senior shipping and trading company representatives. Lastly, Chapter 6 looks at the small tradespeople and professionals, such as doctors, who navigated the space in between these two extremes of social class and status.

The graves and their occupants reveal the internal tensions and external pressures that explain why Hong Kong's Meiji-era Japanese residents failed to unite on communal issues, such as a dedicated burial ground. They also allow us to rediscover people and their social networks that might otherwise be overlooked and offer a personal connection to the past of this vibrant and multicultural city.

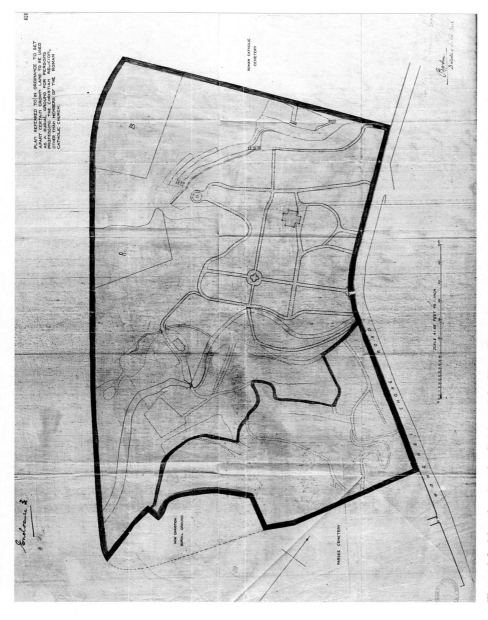

Figure 1.9: Map showing the division of the Hong Kong Cemetery into Christian and non-Christian burial grounds in 1909. The non-Christian section is the small, unshaded area in the upper left-hand corner of the map. (Source: TNA: CO 129/358, 428.)

2
The *Karayuki-san*

> Yesterday, about one o'clock, the dead body of a Japanese woman, aged about 22 years, was picked out of the water, about 80 yards to the East of Tsim Tsa Tsui Wharf by Acting Police Sergeant Mann, whose attention was called to the body by a Chinese boatman who observed it a few minutes before. The body was full dressed except that it had no shoes on. In each sleeve of a loosely fitting jacket was tied a pretty heavy stone. A pair of Japanese woman's shoes was found on the Praya Wall at Kowloon about 15 yards East of the Wharf.[1]

So began a report in the June 10, 1884, edition of the *China Mail*, one of Hong Kong's main English-language newspapers. The article stated that upon further enquiries, the police had determined that the deceased was named Osaki and was an 'inmate of an immoral house' at 27 Graham Street in Central. When questioned, the female brothel keeper advised that Osaki had received a letter from her family a few weeks prior informing her that her father was ill and asking her to return to Japan. Unable to afford the voyage home, she received a second letter a little later with the news that her father had died. At seven o'clock on June 8, 1884, a Sunday, Osaki left the house, never to return. The coroner opened an inquest at the Government Civil Hospital, but with no further details available, the jury returned a verdict of 'found drowned'.[2]

Osaki was KIYA Saki (木谷佐喜), a thirty-year-old woman from Nagasaki, whose grave stands prominently adorned by a two-metre-tall obelisk in the Hong Kong Cemetery.[3] The base of the obelisk bears the names of sixty-two women in the *katakana* syllabary rather than the usual *kanji* (Chinese characters) used for grave inscriptions. The headstone refers to Saki as a 'commoner (平民)', an indication that she was not from the *samurai* class.[4] Saki's is the oldest known grave of a woman in the Japanese section of the cemetery, and the character for 'woman (女)' was, somewhat unusually, included on the obelisk. An inscription in English at the foot of the monument indicates that it was erected by her friends.

The imposing size of the obelisk when compared with other Japanese graves in the Hong Kong Cemetery, the inclusion of the terms 'woman' and 'commoner', and the inscription of the sixty-two names on its base made a strong statement. It proclaimed that, although Saki may have come from what were considered the lowest rungs of both Hong Kong and Japanese society, her disappearance was just as deserving of acknowledgement as that of her compatriots of higher status and should be accorded

Figure 2.1: Kiya Saki was the first Japanese woman buried in the Hong Kong Cemetery. Her two-metre-tall obelisk (centre) dwarfs the much shorter one of Japanese seaman Yokote Umejirō, which stands directly behind hers. (Photo credit: Miyuki Kume.)

the same visible reminder. The coroner's inquest made evident the circumstances of Saki's death, and their tragic nature must have resonated among members of the small *karayuki-san* community, though they were unlikely to have had the same effect on more 'respectable' Japanese residents in Hong Kong, such as consular officials and company representatives.

Hardship at Home: Shimabara and Amakusa

Women made up a large percentage of the Japanese population in Hong Kong in the late nineteenth century. Many of them, like Saki, were prostitutes, predominantly from the southern island of Kyushu, who came to be known as *karayuki-san*. As mentioned in the previous chapter, Japanese consular records for 1886 put the number of Japanese in Hong Kong at 146, with ninety-six female and fifty male residents. Some of the women were listed as family members of Japanese men posted to the territory or as domestic helpers; there was also a *shamisen* (三味線) player and a hairdresser. Two-thirds of the women were described as working in *kashizashiki* (rental rooms), a euphemism for prostitution, and 'cafés', or as concubines of Western men.[5]

This imbalance in the numbers of Japanese men and women in Hong Kong was highlighted in an article published on the day prior to the announcement of Saki's death. In reference to a translated piece from the *Hōchi Shimbun* (報知新聞) on the 'Profligacy of Japanese Women', the columnist writes that the 'subject is a painful one, and it is sad to find that almost the only emigrants from Japan are immoral women'.[6] These demographics were reflected in other popular destinations for *karayuki-san*, such as Singapore.[7]

Early Japanese sex workers in Hong Kong were mostly poorly educated young girls from the rural parts of Kyushu, more specifically from the Shimabara Peninsula (島原半島), near the port of Nagasaki, and the Amakusa Islands (天草諸島). The Amakusa Islands lie to the south of the Shimabara Peninsula and the two are separated by a narrow strip of the Ariake Sea (有明海). In addition to the area's paucity of natural resources, inhabitants faced further hardship due to their embrace of Christianity during the Tokugawa shogunate (1603–1868). Their unsuccessful revolt against high taxation known as the Shimabara-Amakusa Rebellion in 1637–1638 forced their Catholic beliefs underground and caused them to be subject to unfavourable policies and discrimination that added to their already desperate circumstances.[8]

The economic innovations of the new Meiji government did not benefit all segments of society equally. In fact, for some, these developments led to a significant worsening of their circumstances. Fiscal policies initiated by Meiji leaders between 1881 and 1884 that included selling off state-run industries, cuts in government spending, tax increases, and shrinking the money supply sent agricultural commodity prices crashing and forced small-scale farmers into debt. Japan's rapid industrialisation led by the textile and mining industries called for a substantial workforce, and young women from impoverished farming families found employment in mills and factories. Large numbers were also enticed, deceived, or sold into the thriving sex industry, or what historian Andrew Gordon calls the 'expanding brothels of the new Japan'.[9]

An 1892 census of the now renamed Minami Takaki district (南高来郡) of Nagasaki prefecture, which included the town and village of Shimabara, provides insight into the difficult circumstances faced by many families and their need to reduce the number of mouths to feed by having some of their members, especially young women, migrate to find work in Japanese cities or overseas. Only wealthy families could afford rice-only diets, a sign of prosperity. The poorest had to make do with dried or fresh sweet potato, millet, and barley.[10]

Published in 1893, the census listed the numbers of abandoned children and destitutes in the district's thirty towns and villages. In a total population of 161,346, the census recorded 174 abandoned children and 146 destitutes.[11] The practice of abandoning or even killing infants, which came to be known as *mabiki* (間引き) or 'thinning', was a form of family planning adopted by the poorest villagers to avoid starvation and by wealthier farmers to reduce the number of potential heirs.[12] In her 1976 book *Karayuki-san*, MORISAKI Kazue (森崎和江) argues that infanticide may have been less widely practised in Shimabara and Amakusa because of the relatively larger number of Christian converts. This would help explain why the mindset of the villagers turned towards labour migration rather than *mabiki* as a means of reducing the number of family members to feed.[13] At least nineteen of the graves in the Hong Kong Cemetery belong to men or women from the Minami Takaki district.

The Meiji government's lifting of the ban on Christian worship and the surveillance that it had engendered, and further opening of the port of Nagasaki, particularly for the export of coal, encouraged many in Shimabara and Amakusa to leave and find work overseas. The term *karayuki-san* (唐行きさん), literally 'person travelling overseas', initially applied to both male and female migrant workers; only later was it used to exclusively reference female sex workers.[14] The colonial government's push to develop Hong Kong into a major trading port meant that the city was home to a growing number of predominantly male, transient workers, both Chinese and foreign. The *Hong Kong Blue Book* for 1884 records a total of 115,369 men to just 45,033 women.[15] This population of soldiers, sailors, merchants, manual labourers, construction workers, and domestic servants created a demand for female sex workers, mostly from China, but also from other nations, including Japan.[16]

It is not known when the first *karayuki-san* made their way to Hong Kong. However, they were probably among the earliest Japanese residents in the city, possibly even during the final decades of the Tokugawa era.[17] The previously discussed survey conducted by the Japanese Consulate in 1880 to determine the number of its nationals in Hong Kong established that there were twenty-six men and sixty women, over 40 per cent of whom were undocumented, that is, likely to be *karayuki-san*.[18] The leader of the Japanese Liberal Party, ITAGAKI Taisuke (板垣退助), on a visit to Hong Kong in November 1882, lamented that a significant percentage of the Japanese population in the colony at that time consisted of prostitutes. 'Most [Japanese] women here sell their bodies for a living. Alas, will this not be taken as evidence that the East is failing to prosper and worthy of contempt.'[19]

Coal, Steamships, and the Nagasaki Connection

Key to this increase in the traffic of women to Hong Kong were the greatly enhanced maritime transportation links between the British colony and Japan. The agreements that the *bakufu* had signed with several Western powers between 1854 and 1858 had led to the opening of the first treaty ports of Hakodate, Niigata, Yokohama, Kobe, and Nagasaki and an expansion in overseas networks. Nagasaki already had a long history as Japan's only 'official port of reception' during the Tokugawa shogunate. As historian Catherine L. Phipps writes in *Empires on the Waterfront*, 'this southern harbour had been formally charged with overseeing foreign exchange with the Chinese and the Dutch since the early seventeenth century, providing Japanese officials there with valuable experience managing defense and foreign trade'.[20]

The reconfiguration of Nagasaki as a treaty port formally opened it up to commerce with new trading partners, and the Tariff Convention of 1866 brought further opportunities for trade. The growth in global shipping created a high demand for coal to power the sizeable fleets of steamships that served these routes, and coal was something Japan, and Kyushu especially, had large supplies of in the nineteenth century. Two mining concerns are of particular interest to the development of a Japanese community in Hong Kong since they involve the first major Japanese companies to open offices in the city.

The Takashima mine (高島炭鉱), situated on an isolated island about fifteen kilometres from the port of Nagasaki, was the first mine in Japan to be mechanised, through the involvement of Thomas Blake Glover. The Nagasaki-based Scottish merchant cooperated with the Saga domain (佐賀藩; part of Hizen [肥前] province at the time) to develop the mine during the final years of the Tokugawa shogunate. The founder of Mitsubishi, IWASAKI Yatarō (岩崎彌太郎), eventually acquired the Takashima mining enterprise in 1881. The Miike coal mines (三池炭鉱), once Japan's largest, were also located near Nagasaki. Originally operated by the Miike *daimyō* – or governor – during the Tokugawa era, they were nationalised by the new Meiji government in 1873 and ultimately sold to Mitsui Bussan in 1888.[21]

What started as a resupply business for visiting Western steamers would turn into a major industry by the 1880s, with Kyushu supplying coal to ports and depots across Asia, including Hong Kong.[22] The majority of steamships used to ferry coal from Japan to other Asian ports in the late nineteenth century were European charters, at a significant cost to coal exporters. In 1879, for example, payments made by the operators of the Kyushu coal mines to foreign ships amounted to 570,000 yen.[23] The Meiji government actively encouraged the development of the Japanese shipping industry. The Mitsubishi Mail Steamship Company (郵便汽船三菱會社) launched Japan's first regular service overseas with a weekly operation between Yokohama and Shanghai in January 1875 and started a Hong Kong line four years later. Despite these efforts, however, Western shipping companies dominated the waters.[24]

Foreign coal ships would become the preferred, clandestine mode of trafficking *karayuki-san* like Saki from Nagasaki to Hong Kong in the 1880s and 1890s. The steady supply of ships and murky legal environment engendered by the extraterritoriality extended to foreign nationals in the treaty ports facilitated the smuggling of some male, but predominantly female, illegal migrants aboard the steamers. In addition to Nagasaki, the special trading port of Kuchinotsu (口之津), located on the tip of the Shimabara Peninsula and less than fifty kilometres by sea from the Miike mines, was another favoured point of embarkation for the traffickers.[25]

During the heyday of the Miike and Takashima coal mines, it was common for foreign ships, including those chartered by major British trading companies such as Jardine Matheson & Co. and Butterfield & Swire, to call into Nagasaki and Kuchinotsu to pick up coal bound for Hong Kong or Singapore if no other commodity was available for their return journey.[26] The close connection between these foreign ships and the traffic of *karayuki-san* is immortalised in the 'Lullaby of Shimabara', a mournful ballad that recounts the tale of a young Japanese woman compelled to leave her home and travel across the seas.

Though many versions of the lullaby exist, almost all contain the verse 'Oh where have our girls gone by the *ao-entotsu no Battanful*?', a reference to 'the blue funnelled ships of Butterfield'. Commonly known as the 'Blue Funnel Line', the Ocean Steam Ship Company employed Butterfield & Swire as its agent in the Far East and, by 1888, its ships called regularly at Nagasaki.[27]

Clandestine Journeys: Fear and Tragedy

Most estimates put the number of *karayuki-san* who made their way from Japan to Hong Kong and destinations around the world during the Meiji and early Taishō eras in the tens of thousands.[28] The journey was an arduous one and fraught with danger. Instances of officials intercepting ships carrying *karayuki-san* appeared regularly in local newspapers and in Japanese consular reports. On March 21, 1888, for example, seventeen Japanese prostitutes were found hidden aboard the German steamer *Tetartos* when it docked in Hong Kong. The ship, chartered by the Takashima colliery, had left Nagasaki some ten days prior bound for the city and the women had stolen aboard under the cover of night. Their interception was attributed to a tip-off, and the Japanese consul in Hong Kong had them repatriated to Nagasaki the same day.[29]

Discovery was still preferable to death, a fate that befell many *karayuki-san* and, occasionally, their procurers. Hiding aboard often meant stowing away inside the coal storage compartment. Dangers included being crushed to death when the coal shifted in rough seas and being burnt alive or asphyxiated should any of the coal catch fire.[30] One of the most infamous incidents is the tragedy that took place aboard the *Fushiki Maru* (伏木丸) in March 1890.

The steamer had arrived in Hong Kong on March 26 from Nagasaki with a cargo of coal. For some time prior to its arrival, crew members had detected a sickening stench emanating from the engine room, which they initially attributed to dead rats. Upon further investigation, they encountered the decomposing corpses of seven women and one man, along with four survivors in a small compartment between the engine room and the hold normally reserved for the examination of the freshwater tanks. The dead had succumbed to the intense heat and fumes that had pervaded the three-foot-wide space between the port and starboard bulkheads during the six-day journey. The marine police had the bodies of the eight deceased covered with lime and sprinkled with carbolic acid before giving orders for their burial.[31]

The disaster was widely covered in the Hong Kong and Japanese press, including details of the coroner's inquiry that was attended by the acting consul of Japan. The captain, P. J. C. Franck, and all four survivors testified. The first to take the stand was a thirty-seven-year-old widow, WATANABE Kiku (渡邊きく).[32] She claimed that the deceased man, NISHIKIDE Kumakichi (錦出熊吉), was from Ōura (大浦) in Nagasaki and that he had approached her on several occasions to go to Hong Kong and work as a domestic helper. She had stolen onboard two days prior to the ship's departure and had tried to escape but her screams went unheard. Seventeen-year-old SHIOSAWA Setsu (鹽澤せつ) stated that the man, who used to visit her parents' house to sell oil, had told her that she would be able to get a better situation in Hong Kong and send money home.[33] Both eighteen-year-old MATSUOKA Hama (松岡はま) and twenty-year-old KANEKO Suma (金子すま) claimed Nishikide had asked them to disguise themselves as coal coolies before smuggling them aboard the ship.[34] There is no intimation that Setsu, Hama, and Suma knew they would be working as *karayuki-san* in Hong Kong, despite this being their likely fate.

A health officer determined that suffocation was the cause of death for all eight victims. However, the statements made by the four surviving women shortly after their rescue suggest that the man's death may actually have resulted from assault: 'From what the poor creatures say it would appear that in the frenzy which their terrible condition induced, they attacked the man who brought them there; and the appearance of his body when brought out was suggestive of violent treatment.'[35]

A Japanese visitor to Hong Kong, HONDA Seiroku (本多静六), commented with poignancy on the events, which occurred just a few days prior to his arrival in Hong Kong on April 1, 1890. In his account, he discussed meeting the acting consul of Japan, who provided him with the details of the case and described his collection of the bodies two days earlier. Honda writes, 'Eight died and four barely survived. Though one might say they brought this upon themselves, it is still heart-breaking to think that this happened to our fellow Japanese.'[36]

The four survivors eventually returned to Nagasaki on the *Asagao Maru* (朝顔丸), which departed Hong Kong on April 24, 1890. A later report alleged that Japanese authorities had placed Kiku under investigation for her role in the human trafficking network.[37]

Two articles appearing around the time of the tragedy provided further evidence of the numbers prepared to risk discovery or worse for the chance of better economic opportunities overseas. One stated that in the first three months of 1890, Nagasaki police arrested thirty-two men and ninety-three women trying to leave the country without a passport. 'It is surmised that their intention was to get on board the German S.S. *Deuteros*, which vessel was leaving for Hongkong on that date, under charter to the Mitsui Bussan Kaisha.'[38] Another mentioned that disaster was narrowly averted aboard the steamship *Kashgar* bound for Manila from Kobe on March 21. The captain of the ship inadvertently came upon a dozen stowaways and saved them from a certain death.[39]

These attempts to intercept the traffic of *karayuki-san* to Hong Kong were predominantly led by a Japanese government increasingly conscious of its image and reputation overseas. It accused the *karayuki-san* of bringing the country into disrepute at a time when it was anxious to project an image of modernity equal to that of the US and European nations such as France and Britain.[40] In 1884, Japan's former consul to Hong Kong, ANDŌ Tarō (安藤太郎), newly stationed in Shanghai and a devout Christian, was horrified at the number of Japanese prostitutes in the city and lobbied the government asking that it take strenuous action to regulate this 'ugly' business.[41] In July 1885, the Japanese Foreign Ministry instructed the governors of six prefectures with open ports, including Nagasaki and Kobe, to question any unaccompanied young woman as to her purpose for wanting to travel overseas. In the absence of a convincing answer, she should be refused a passport and barred from proceeding with her journey.[42] These and other similarly ineffective endeavours to stem the traffic simply resulted in more women being smuggled aboard ships clandestinely or finding other ways to evade detection.

There is some debate about the extent to which *karayuki-san* left Japan of their own accord and with full knowledge of the nature of their work in Hong Kong. A rural and patriarchal society that placed less value on female offspring along with an already well-established brothel system within the country combined to make sex work a legitimate and higher-paying alternative to other forms of manual labour for these women.[43] There was probably a range of experiences, with some women knowingly boarding ships to Hong Kong with the expectation that they would work as prostitutes. However, a considerable number of *karayuki-san*, especially in the 1880s and 1890s, were most likely tricked into believing that they would be employed as servants or shop assistants, abducted, or sold by their families to brokers with no choice but to comply.

Reporting on the attempted kidnapping of four Japanese girls from their homes in Shimabara, a *China Mail* journalist concludes that from time to time the Hong Kong community is 'shocked either by stories coming direct from Japan or by incidents occurring in our own harbour which forcibly illustrate the illegal lengths which some persons go to secure Japanese girls for houses of ill-fame here and elsewhere. To the casual citizen the life led by these unfortunate women is scarcely of any concern, they imagining that the girls are merely following it from choice. In many instances such

The *Karayuki-san*   29

is not the case, and another story from Japan demonstrates conclusively that a large proportion of the women are kidnapped.'[44]

Policing Race, Class, and Sexuality in Hong Kong

Japan's efforts to stem the numbers of *karayuki-san* in Hong Kong received nominal support from the city's colonial officials. Indeed, Hong Kong's nineteenth-century colonial government was predominantly concerned with regulating Chinese prostitutes as a further means of policing the territory's majority Chinese population, and with limiting the spread of venereal disease among the lower classes of the non-Chinese community, including sailors, ordinary soldiers, and working-class Europeans.[45] As historian and anthropologist Ann Laura Stoler concludes in her book *Carnal Knowledge and Imperial Power*, sexual control was a 'fundamental class and racial marker implicated in a wider set of relations of power'. Stoler further elaborates on these intersections of gender, race, and class by claiming that 'it was through the policing of sex that subordinate European military and civil servants were kept in line and that racial boundaries were maintained'.[46]

The colonial government's regulation of prostitution along racial lines was apparent in all legislation enacted to address the issue in the second half of the nineteenth century. The 1857 *Ordinance for Checking the Spread of Venereal Diseases* required brothels to be registered and initially all prostitutes, but later only those catering to non-Chinese customers, to be subjected to a weekly examination by a Western doctor. The ordinance further allowed for the removal of any prostitute found to be infected with a venereal disease to a dedicated hospital.[47] Hong Kong's Lock Hospital opened in 1858, one of many such hospitals established by the British across their colonial outposts; the name comes from the practice of detaining or 'locking up the prostitutes who were found to be suffering from a venereal disease'.[48]

The 1857 ordinance was superseded by the *Contagious Diseases Ordinances, 1867*, which expanded on the provisions of its predecessor.[49] It also gave the police greater powers to enter a premise suspected of operating as an unlicensed – or sly – brothel without a warrant and arrest its occupants, leaving the system wide open to abuse and corruption.[50] A commission was appointed in November 1877 to investigate these abuses, and it submitted its report on the effectiveness of government efforts to curb the spread of venereal diseases and unlicensed prostitution in December 1878 (hereafter 1878 Report).

In practice, brothels were very much classified along racial lines into those catering to Chinese customers and those catering to non-Chinese customers. The distinction was implied by the aforementioned ordinances' requirement that only those prostitutes visited by non-Chinese customers need submit to a weekly examination. It was made even clearer in the 1878 Report, which stated that this 'illegal division' between 'brothels licensed for Chinese only' and 'brothels licensed for foreigners only' was an inevitable outcome of the 'social gulf' that separated 'all classes of Chinese in Hongkong from the corresponding classes of foreign residents'.[51]

Debates around the regulation of prostitution in late nineteenth-century Hong Kong were very much connected to investigations of the *mui-tsai* (妹仔) system, a practice that involved the selling of young women to wealthy Chinese families as bondservants. There were concerns that some of the trafficked girls were kidnapped and sold on as prostitutes. In an attempt to allay these fears and avoid the outlawing of the *mui-tsai* system by the colonial government, Chinese elites petitioned for the establishment of an anti-kidnapping society, and the Po Leung Kuk (保良局; Society for the Protection of Women and Children) was officially approved in 1880.[52]

Not Chinese, Not European

Much like the Japanese community as a whole, Japanese prostitutes occupied an ambiguous space in Hong Kong's segregated brothel system, being neither Chinese nor European yet having to operate within these strictly enforced parameters. While they did not appear at all in the main body of the 1878 Report, they did feature briefly in the Appendix, as an afterthought. Members of the commission met with a variety of colonial officials and the keepers of licensed brothels for Europeans and for Chinese in order to compile the Report. In their interview with the Registrar General, he states that 'the European women do not give me much trouble. There are about 17 of them, and 6 or 8 Japanese besides. All these submit themselves to voluntary medical examination.'[53]

In 1877, the estimated number of Chinese prostitutes working in Hong Kong was well over 1,500.[54] While acknowledging the presence of Japanese prostitutes in the city, their vastly smaller number (though six to eight is probably an underestimation) when compared with Chinese prostitutes helps explain why the Hong Kong government was reluctant to expend resources on their removal.

This perception that Japanese prostitutes were more compliant and 'represented as superior to other nonwhite women' was echoed in correspondence between the colonial surgeon, Dr Philip Ayres, and the colonial secretary.[55] In a letter dated April 26, 1893, Ayres argued for maintaining the regular examination of prostitutes for venereal disease. He writes that '[Japanese women] are more anxious to be looked after than even the Chinese women. Often they come to the Hospital after I have gone and request to be admitted and the Matron to look after them until I can see them the following day.'[56] Furthermore, the fact that Japanese prostitutes had to undergo examination by a Western doctor confirms that they had foreign customers.

The 1878 Report's extensive interviews with government officials and Chinese brothel keepers shed some light on the living circumstances of prostitutes in late nineteenth-century Hong Kong. While obviously applying to the situation of predominantly Chinese prostitutes, one can imagine that the city's *karayuki-san* faced similar conditions. Chief Inspector of Brothels William Foulkes Whitehead provides an idea of their earnings according to the type of customer:

> In East Street, West Street, Tai-ping Shan and in Wàn-tsai [Wan Chai] I think the women are of the lowest class. In the central districts they are the best, in Tai-ping Shan the next, and in Wàn-tsai the lowest class. In the central districts they would not allow Blue Jackets to enter. In these districts they charge $1 to $2 for a night. In Tai-ping Shan, men-of-war's men, merchant sailors, soldiers, Lascars and Malays go. They charge there 30 cents to 50 cents, but $1 for the night. That depends on whether it is a European or Malay. In Wàn-tsai they are cheaper still, from 10 to 15 cents. They would take 10 cents. Some merchant seamen, but chiefly soldiers, go there.[57]

Higher-class brothels offered dinner and entertainment, with some of the 'girls' able to sing or play an instrument.[58] The keeper of a 'first class' brothel at 4 Hollywood Road advised that the earnings for a prostitute in her establishment amounted to between 16 and 17 dollars a month on average.[59] This compared with the monthly salary of 8 dollars earned by a Chinese nurse in the Government Civil Hospital, for example.[60] The keeper added that her brothel had twenty-six girls.[61] Japanese brothels like Saki's operated on a much smaller scale; each brothel generally had between five and eight *karayuki-san* attached to it, both working and living on the premises.

A Japanese Brothel at 27 Graham Street

In 1885, Hong Kong had eight licensed Japanese brothels – or *kashizashiki* (rental rooms) – with fifty-two prostitutes. These numbers were the result of an informal agreement between the Japanese and colonial governments to restrict the issuance of prostitution licences.[62] However, there is little indication that the administration ever enforced this measure and there were undoubtedly several unlicensed Japanese establishments operating in the city as well. Japanese prostitutes provided sexual services to mainly working-class residents of various nationalities and visiting sailors and merchants.[63] In his 1935 oral interview, long-term Japanese resident KIMURA Shūzō (木村修三) recalled two brothels and one 'café' that also sold sexual services active in the early 1880s. The *karayuki-san* only took Western or Indian men as customers and did not accept Japanese sailors. If they did take higher-class Japanese customers, it was only secretly.[64]

Most licensed Japanese brothels in the 1880s were located in Central, in the areas around Stanley Street, Hollywood Road, Graham Street, and Cochrane Street, eventually expanding to other districts such as Wan Chai in the final years of the nineteenth century. By 1901, all but two of the thirteen *kashizashiki* were in Wan Chai. Eleven Japanese establishments occupied numbers 1 to 27 in Ship Street. Originally intended as a high-class residential neighbourhood for Europeans in the earliest days of the colony, the character of the area began to change and it was soon attracting the city's less affluent inhabitants. By the 1870s, Wan Chai was synonymous with the lowest class of brothels catering to common soldiers and sailors.[65]

Though recorded in 1918, thirty-four years after Saki's time, the poet KAWAHIGASHI Hekigotō's (河東碧梧桐; 1873–1937) impressions of a Japanese brothel in Wan Chai provide a rare glimpse into the decor that distinguished Japanese from Chinese and European establishments. A famed haiku poet, Kawahigashi travelled around southern China between April and July 1918 and brought a poetic sensibility to the travelogue he published in 1919. He noted the sound of *geta* (下駄; wooden slippers) clip-clopping down the wooden corridors or the sight of them laying scattered around the entrance to a room. Inside each partitioned room was a Western bed and dresser and two tatami mats. He was particularly fascinated by the eclectic but somehow pleasing mix of Western, Chinese, and Japanese styles. Visitors found sake cups on American-made tin trays, Majolica ashtrays, and Chinese rather than Japanese chopsticks. There were calligraphy scrolls and *zabuton* (座布団) cushions, but when you lifted your head and looked up, the Japanese feel was spoiled by an absent ceiling and exposed roof joists.

Figure 2.2: A postcard looking up Wellington Street from its intersection with Wyndham Street in the 1880s. This is just a few streets away from Graham Street and the area where most Japanese brothels were operating at the time. (Source: Hong Kong Memory Project/Ko Tim Keung.)

Kawahigashi also devoted space in his account to describing the attire and lifestyle of the *karayuki-san* in Wan Chai. *Karayuki-san* on the brothel's ground floor dressed in loudly coloured *yūzen* (友禅), which were typically worn as an undergarment inside the kimono, comparable to lingerie, rather than as an outer garment. Women inside the partitioned rooms, however, sported starched *yukata*, a cotton kimono. 'In the morning they might toast their bread on a gas heater. At night they order sashimi and clear soup which are eaten at *ozen* (お膳) – or low short-legged tables. They sing a song of foreign sailors and are competent with the *shamisen*.'[66] This mix of Japanese, Chinese, and Western elements would certainly have been characteristic of Saki's life at 27 Graham Street in 1884, as would the precarious architecture and unsanitary nature of the dwellings in which they lived. Houses had little or no drainage and hardly any natural light.[67]

The brothel at 27 Graham Street in Central was the scene of a tragedy involving another *karayuki-san* buried in the Hong Kong Cemetery, twenty-three-year-old TOMINAGA Matsu (富永松) from Nagasaki, just four years after Saki's death.[68] On

The *Karayuki-san*   33

April 13, 1888, a 3 a.m. fire in the cook-house of 29 Graham Street led to the collapse of the two adjoining houses at 27 and 31 Graham Street and the death of one of seven women inside 27 Graham Street at the time. An inquest was held the same afternoon, at which one of the firemen testified as follows:

> On getting onto the street I saw that the two houses had fallen in. The front wall of each house fell on the street and the other walls had collapsed. The whole of each house had come down. They were two storied houses. No 27 was a Japanese brothel and 31 was a carpenter's shop below and a Chinese brothel on the upper floor. . . . After I got on the street I heard cries from the ruins of the houses. Some of the firemen made a hole in the front wall of house No. 27. There was a part of the wall about six feet high at the corner of the house standing. It was in this portion of the wall they made a breach and got out about six women through it. They were all Japanese.[69]

The inquest also heard the testimonies of two Japanese: a young woman who confirmed that she and the victim resided at 27 Graham Street, and a man, named as 'Ushino' in the article, but actually MIYANO Yoshijirō (宮野芳治良/芳次郎), the 'café' manager, who paid for the deceased's grave in the Hong Kong Cemetery. After hearing all the evidence, the jury returned a verdict of 'accidental death', with asphyxia as the cause.

The age and poor construction of the houses was given as one of the reasons for their collapse. The Government Inspector of Buildings Herbert Francis Hayllar, reporting on his investigation of the scene, advised that the 'houses are very old. They were very badly constructed. The walls were two rows of bricks with headers every five feet or so and no mortar in the joints.'[70]

'An Unusual Family': The *Karayuki-san* Community

Both Saki's and Matsu's deaths are recorded in the burial register maintained by the Hong Kong Cemetery's Anglican chaplain. A hand-written note next to Saki's entry identified her as a 'stranger' rather than a 'resident' and indicated that her interment did not include a Christian service.[71] These annotations serve as markers of Saki's race and low status within Hong Kong's colonial society. However, the prominence of her grave, and the manner in which the women who paid for it came together in just over a month to erect it, demonstrate the solidarity within the *karayuki-san* community.

The sixty-two names of Saki's friends are all listed in the *katakana* syllabary. Each name is made up of two characters, the person's first rather than surname, which indicates that they were all women. The names are arranged in four lines, two of eleven and two of twenty. The first line would likely have featured the most prominent of Saki's friends. Many of the women whose names appear on Saki's grave bear similarities to those included in the 1886 census, with a few recorded as being from Nagasaki and domiciled at 27 Graham Street.[72]

Assuming that this cross-referencing with the 1886 record is correct, female *kashizashiki* managers and the wives of brothel owners occupied the central positions in the list of names on Saki's grave. This was a mark of their higher-ranking status within the Japanese brothel community and the groups of small traders and boarding house owners that benefitted from these operations. MIYANO Matsu (宮野マツ), the wife of Miyano Yoshijirō, the 'café' manager who paid for Tominaga Matsu's grave, is

Figure 2.3: The base of Kiya Saki's obelisk bears the names of sixty-two women in the *katakana* syllabary rather than the usual *kanji* (Chinese characters) used for grave inscriptions. (Photo credit: Miyuki Kume.)

Table 2.1: First line of names on Kiya Saki's grave

Name on Grave	Potential Full Name	Address	Occupation/Status	Provenance	Age
エイ	Kawasaki Ei	27 Cochrane Street	*Kashizashiki* worker	Kanagawa	36
キク	Tatebayashi Kiku	71 Hollywood Road	Wife of a porcelain shop owner	Nagasaki	30
ヌイ	Maeda Nui	29 Cochrane Street	*Kashizashiki* worker	Nagasaki	30
コト	Maeda Koto	38 Stanley Street	*Kashizashiki* worker	Nagasaki	17
エイ	Itō Ei	27 Cochrane Street	Wife of *kashizashiki* manager	Hyōgo	36
キヌ	Itō Kinu	27 Cochrane Street	Daughter of *kashizashiki* manager	Hyōgo	13
マツ	Itō Matsu	75 Hollywood Road	*Kashizashiki* manager	Nagasaki	31
テル	Hoshino Teru	19 Hollywood Road	Concubine of a foreigner	Kanagawa	26
サツ	Honmura Satsu	38 Stanley Street	*Kashizashiki* worker	Nagasaki	18
カネ	Miike Kane	38 Stanley Street	*Kashizashiki* worker	Nagasaki	21
ケイ	Fujiwara Kei	122 Wellington Street	'Café' manager	Nagasaki	35

Full names, ages, addresses, and occupations are extrapolated from the 1886 census. Source: 奥田 [Okuda], (1937), 190–200.

acknowledged on either the first or second line. She, her husband, and her daughter resided at 6 Peel Street with four employees.

Saki is not the only *karayuki-san* whose grave was paid for by 'friends'. However, the long list of names inscribed on it is a unique feature. This may be because hers was the first for a Japanese woman in the Hong Kong Cemetery and the tragic nature of her death struck a particular chord within the small community of Japanese women whose livelihoods depended on the brothel industry. These engravings hint at a system of mutual support among the *karayuki-san* in the absence of a more formal mechanism of assistance.

Kawahigashi commented at length on this sense of solidarity in his discussion of the Wan Chai brothel. He was impressed by the *karayuki-san*'s forthright approach to their situation, never attempting to conceal their ultimate goal, which was to make money. He describes them as a self-governed small group. 'They form an unusual family and live without petty arguments or competition. They operate under unspoken rules.' He concludes by stating that though there are those who feel the *karayuki-san* bring shame to Japan, if you witness how they live, there are things to be learned from them.[73]

Kawahigashi's more positive views spoke to the contempt with which most Japanese male travellers visiting the city regarded the *karayuki-san*. Novelist and editor ŌHASHI Otowa (大橋乙羽; 1869–1901), for example, writes of his encounter with a group of Japanese prostitutes at a Hong Kong photography shop with utter disdain.

> Suddenly three women in the ugly business came walking up the stairs to the second floor [studio]. One was fat, one was thin, and one had a syphilis chancre between her eyes; their dull hair was put up in buns that resembled cow pats [i.e. in a Western-style coiffure]; they wore dark blue kimonos with geometric patterns and a white cotton cloth served as an *obi*; one had a huge bottom; one wore dark blue, casual *tabi* (socks) and *zori* (sandals) with linen bottoms. They were oohing and aahing over photographs taken with their [presumably foreign] lover. It was shocking and disgusting.[74]

Stay or Return Home: Beyond Life as a *Karayuki-san*

When a *karayuki-san* was sold to a brothel, she was expected to take on the price paid for her by the brothel keeper as a 'debt', which had to be paid off. Most of her earnings, therefore, went towards covering this 'debt', as well as any other daily expenses she incurred, such as food, lodging, and kimonos. This left many *karayuki-san* bound to their brothels for years, and once they had made remittances to their families in Japan, there was little left for their own future security.

Nevertheless, large numbers of *karayuki-san* were able to return to their villages and towns. On his pre-1918 visit to Shimabara, the poet Kawahigashi writes about the distinctive houses built there by returning *karayuki-san*. Their tiled, grey roofs and whitewashed walls made them stand out from the more commonly seen cob-walled and thatched farmhouses. Looking more like the storerooms attached to the houses of the wealthy – or 'treasure houses' – Kawahigashi dismissed them as ostentatious and short-lived displays of wealth, with many *karayuki-san* spending all their hard-earned money within one or two years.[75]

Other than returning home, futures for the *karayuki-san* who remained in Hong Kong included concubinage, becoming the 'kept woman' of a foreigner, or doing well enough to set up their own brothel or small business venture. Some of the Japanese graves belong to women who initially came to the city as *karayuki-san* but then transitioned to one of these situations.

In his interview for the 1878 Report, the acting captain superintendent of police states that a 'great many of the Europeans live in concubinage'.[76] Indeed, concubinage – or the cohabitation of European men with non-European women – was considered preferable to visiting prostitutes, despite the issues surrounding the children that these unions produced. As Ann Laura Stoler notes, 'unlike prostitution, which could and often did increase the number of syphilitic and therefore non-productive European men, concubinage was considered to stabilize political order and colonial health'.[77]

By 'non-European women' the senior policeman largely meant 'Chinese women'. Yet by the 1880s 'Japanese girls' were 'crowding them out of favour'.[78] In his oral history interview, Kimura Shūzō claimed that one of the Meiji era's most famous concubines, MICHINAGA Ei (道永栄; 1860–1927), was living in Hong Kong as the consort of a Russian admiral in the early 1880s.[79] As mentioned previously, thirteen Japanese women with an average age of twenty-eight recorded their occupation as 'concubine of a Westerner' in 1886.[80]

In Nagasaki, setting up house with a Japanese woman was a common occurrence in the second half of the nineteenth century, and the practice quickly came to be referred to as a 'Japanese marriage'.[81] These informal relationships were famously – or infamously – immortalised by the French lieutenant Julien Marie Viaud, better known by his pen name Pierre Loti, in his semi-biographical work *Madame Chrysanthème*, published in 1887. Loti arrived in Nagasaki in July 1885 and spent about a month in the city, during which time he contrived, through the intermediary of a pimp, a liaison with a teenage Japanese girl as part of his research for the book. However, the unequal arrangement that informed Loti's work, and subsequently formed part of the source material for Puccini's 1904 opera *Madame Butterfly*, was, by that time, no longer the only option.

The Japanese government began recognising international unions in 1873.[82] As social historian Brian Burke-Gaffney writes, 'illicit relationships between Japanese women and foreign men were still common in the 1880s, but bona fide international marriages had increased significantly since receiving government approval in March 1873, and families with one foreign and one Japanese parent were anything but rare in Nagasaki and the other treaty ports'.[83] Even without the official sanction of marriage, not all common-law arrangements resulted in the callous abandonment of a Japanese cohabitant.

In Hong Kong, the American-born Lawrence Mallory, who owned a timber yard in Wan Chai and died in September 1904, left his household furniture and other possessions, along with the sum of 3,000 dollars, to his Japanese housekeeper and likely lover HAYASHIZAKI Kiku (林崎キク), and a further 1,500 dollars to her 'niece' HAYASHIZAKI Komatsu (林崎小松).[84] Kiku was a *karayuki-san* before she went to live with Mallory and Komatsu was probably her daughter.[85]

YAMAMOTO Hisa (山本ヒサ), who died on December 7, 1902, at the age of forty-seven hailed from Hyōgo. She was a *shamisen* player and teacher in 1886, and lodging with the concubines of two foreign men at 19 Hollywood Road. Hisa went on to become a major procurer and brothel manager, working with her Kobe-based mother, YAMAMOTO Uta (山本ウタ), to traffic young women to Hong Kong for the purposes of prostitution.[86] In 1900, the Japanese Consul in Hong Kong suspected Hisa of fraudulently obtaining a passport for twenty-year-old MIYAMOTO Chiyo (宮本チヨ) to travel from Kobe under the pretext that Lawrence Mallory had offered her employment as a domestic helper, when she was in reality destined for Hisa's brothel.[87]

By 1901, Hisa was running a *kashizashiki* with twelve *karayuki-san* at 7 Gage Street. That same year, she and four others, including Mallory's housekeeper Hayashizaki Kiku, paid to erect the gravestone of fellow *kashizashiki* manager KANDA Nobuko (神田信子).[88] Nobuko had died seven years before, in October 1894, and presumably had been buried in a numbered grave. It took Hisa's increased influence within the Japanese brothel world to afford her a proper memorial.

Hisa's own white marble headstone bears the unusual nine-character afterlife name of 寶珠院賽霧観光大姉, which can be translated as 'big sister of tourism who is like a beautiful and precious sphere that lifts the mist'. This name indicates that Hisa occupied a high position within the lower half of the Japanese community, and the use of the word tourism is likely connected to her role as a procurer, facilitating the flow of young women from Kobe to Hong Kong.[89]

Figure 2.4: Yamamoto Hisa's afterlife name, the 'big sister of tourism'. (Photo credit: Miyuki Kume.)

UMETSU Sami (梅津サミ) died of apoplexy on April 10, 1910, aged forty-two. Her grave is not in the Japanese style and bears the following inscription in English: 'In loving memory of "nurse" Sami Umetsu'. Japanese nurses were working in Hong Kong during the 1910s.[90] However, the inverted commas around the term imply that Sami was not a nurse in the medical sense. More plausible is that she came from Minami Takaki to Hong Kong as a *karayuki-san* but then took on the position of nanny with a foreign family. Her sister, Koku (梅津コク), who died in 1907 aged forty-seven, is buried nearby, in a grave paid for by Sami.

Figure 2.5: Japanese nannies in Hong Kong, circa 1910–1913 (Source: MS 381233/097, Henry Rue Photograph Album, Special Collections, SOAS Library.)

The bilingual nature of many of the Japanese headstones, as in the cases of Saki and Sami, is unusual and evidence of the multinational environment in which they lived and worked, at the intersections of Japanese, Chinese, and Western imperialist cultures. While some *karayuki-san* eventually returned to their hometowns, enjoyed relatively more comfortable lives as concubines, or became brothel keepers or procurers themselves, a significant number ended up sick and destitute and, like Saki, died without ever seeing Japan again.

Parallel Japanese Communities in Hong Kong

As mentioned earlier in this chapter, Japanese consular officials in Hong Kong actively sought the colonial government's assistance to put a halt to the traffic of *karayuki-san*

The *Karayuki-san* 39

and their 'life of shame abroad'.[91] This denial of their existence as anything but shameful meant that the lived experiences of the *karayuki-san* as individuals in their own right, with their own voices, were largely overlooked until the 1970s. The publication of two books in particular, Tomoko Yamazaki's (山崎朋子) *Sandakan Hachiban Shōkan* [*Sandakan Brothel No. 8*] in 1972 and Kazue Morisaki's *Karayuki-san* in 1976, was instrumental in reversing this trend.[92] Both authors offer accounts of the *karayuki-san* from a sympathetic woman's perspective and re-evaluate their significance to Meiji-era Japan. Academic works, notably on the *karayuki-san* in Singapore, Australia, and more recently the North American West, have added to a growing literature that seeks to restore these women's voices to histories of this period.[93]

In his discussion of the *karayuki-san* in the Netherlands Indies (now Indonesia) from the late nineteenth century to the 1930s, economic historian Hiroshi Shimizu considers several ways in which they may have contributed to Japan's economy and its relations with colonial powers, including helping to make up for the 'wide sex disparity' through the 'offering of their services', acting as an informal bridge between their own and other foreign and local communities, and the remittance of 'large amounts of foreign exchange', Mexican silver dollars in the case of Hong Kong.[94]

Shimizu emphasises the role that the *karayuki-san* played in the development of an early Japanese community and network of support, before the establishment of a more official Japanese presence. *Karayuki-san* certainly paved the way for the growth of other Japanese economic activities in Hong Kong, and a whole local industry of small retailers grew up around them and relied on their and their brothels' custom to prosper.

However, while it is clear from the 'friends' who came together so quickly to pay for Saki's grave that such a community existed, it did not extend beyond the brothel and boarding house owners and other small traders who benefitted from their traffic and work. Rather, it functioned in parallel to a more 'respectable' segment of the Japanese community, keen to distance itself from an industry that placed its members on a par with the lower rungs of Chinese society. Japan opened its consulate in Hong Kong in April 1873, and several larger Japanese trading companies had started to establish themselves in the city by the 1870s, intent on promoting a modernising version of Japan.

Historian Carol Gluck traces the beginnings of a concerted effort by the Meiji government to cultivate a sense of national identity and belonging to the promulgation of the Japanese Constitution in 1889. This text confirmed the emperor as a symbol of unity. Together with the 1890 Imperial Rescript on Education, the constitution formed the basis of attempts to define a 'civil morality' centred around shared notions of family, as well as reimagined customs and values of the past. This unity was required both to counter external threats during the Sino-Japanese and Russo-Japanese wars and to address the internal social upheavals resulting from the government's rush to modernise.[95] This idea of a national purpose and of creating a country that could rival Western colonial powers was in sharp contrast to the *karayuki-san*'s attachment to a district or village and their focus on their own day-to-day survival and that of their families. The controversies surrounding the *karayuki-san* and the trafficking network built around them were, in fact, obstacles to the establishment of a unified Japanese community and added to the ambiguity with which the Japanese were regarded in Hong Kong in the late nineteenth century.

3
Boarding House and Restaurant Operators

> Dinner was at the Consulate. I had marinated fish, rice and pickles. The meal was sufficient to take away the vile taste of the Western food I had endured during my ten days aboard [the French ship *Menzaleh*].[1]
>
> [Mori Ōgai's diary entry for September 1, 1884]

Japanese army doctor MORI Ōgai (森鴎外; 1862–1922) wrote this entry in the diary he kept of his voyage from Yokohama to Cologne in 1884.[2] Mori spent four days in Hong Kong, arriving on August 31 aboard the French Messageries Maritimes ship *Menzaleh*. He was sailing to Germany to further his medical studies, one of a group of nine students sent abroad by the Japanese government to gain knowledge and experience at military and other tertiary academies in Europe.[3]

Hong Kong offered an opportunity for late nineteenth-century Japanese travellers on their way to European destinations to enjoy what might well be their last Japanese-style restaurant meal for months or even years. Mori was of sufficient social standing to receive an invitation to dine at the Japanese Consulate. He opted to return to his ship to sleep as Hong Kong had a reputation for robbers, though he possibly also wished to spare the expense. An unfavourable exchange rate for the yen made hotel stays expensive.[4]

Mori Ōgai became one of the Meiji era's most celebrated writers. His contemporary, the acclaimed novelist NATSUME Sōseki (夏目漱石; 1867–1916), passed through Hong Kong too.[5] He stopped over in the city in September 1900 on his way to London and enjoyed a meal of *tai*, or perch, sashimi, grilled fish, and miso soup at Tsuruya (鶴屋) inn on Des Voeux Road. He ended his dinner with a comforting bowl of *chazuke* (茶漬) – tea poured over cooked rice.[6] While he appreciated the food, the filthy conditions of the Japanese establishment repulsed him and, like Mori, he preferred to sleep in his cabin.[7]

However, more adventurous visitors needing a bed for the night turned to the Japanese boarding houses that served a clientele in search of a more familiar style of accommodation. At the lower end of the scale were the *geshuku-ya* (下宿屋) that provided cheap lodging for sailors and others on a tight budget; at the upper end were the *ryokan* (旅館).[8] Unlike in Japan, where they occupied a whole building, Hong Kong's *ryokan* were usually located on the upper floors of a property used for other commercial or residential purposes. Most *ryokan* incorporated Japanese furnishings, such as tatami mats, into their decor, and in some cases they supplied their guests with a steep-sided bathtub, known as a *furo* (風呂).

The operators of these establishments formed a key group within the early Japanese community in Hong Kong. In addition to providing a place to eat and stay, they acted as a rallying point both for Japanese visitors, sailors, and migrant workers passing through the colony, as well as for Japanese residents from the lower echelons of society. Several of them are buried, or have family members buried, in the Hong Kong Cemetery. Their graves are among the most distinctive, often adopting a flamboyant style of monument that makes them stand out from the more usual granite columns. This chapter sheds light on the lives of three prominent boarding house operators: ŌTAKA Saichi (大髙佐市), the manager of Ōtaka Ryokan, who died in 1896; UETSUKI Kakuzō (植月覚三), the owner of the Tokyo Hotel and Sei Foo Row Annex; and MATSUBARA Jisaburō (松原治三郎), the owner of Matsubara Ryokan.

Tōyōkan at 13 Aberdeen Street

Boarding house owners were among the first Japanese residents in Hong Kong. By 1888 there were four, including NISHIYAMA Yūzō (西山由造), who opened a *ryokan* and chinaware store in Wellington Street in 1887, and YOKOSE Yōkichi (横瀬要吉).[9]

Originally from Nagasaki, Yokose and his wife, Kato, were operating a *geshuku-ya* at 13 Aberdeen Street in the mid-1880s, which by 1887 had become a well-established *ryokan* called Tōyōkan.[10] Tōyōkan made an appearance in the memoirs of MURAOKA Iheiji (村岡伊平治; 1867–1942 [assumed]), who claimed to have stayed there for two months after his arrival in the city in December 1885. Muraoka is best known for his autobiography, a retelling of his life and, particularly, his role as a *zegen* (女衒) – or pimp – in the trafficking of Japanese prostitutes throughout Asia. He claimed he was regarded as a 'Godfather'-like figure in Shanghai, Singapore, and Manila, where he oversaw a network of brothels. Early on, he boasted that he only employed school dropouts and petty criminals as associates or to manage his interests, as the nature of his business was too lowly for men with education.[11]

Though scholars have challenged the veracity of Muraoka's account and argued that he embellished and misremembered many of the events he mentioned, the lack of alternative materials and the fact that some details can be verified mean that his name inevitably appears in discussions of Japanese prostitution in the late nineteenth and early twentieth centuries.[12]

Muraoka wrote that he was leading a meagre existence as a fish and vegetable peddler when he decided to leave Japan as an eighteen year old and make his fortune overseas. He travelled to Hong Kong with the intention of opening a shop with his two companions. He was impressed by the city at first: 'I was completely overwhelmed by this foreign place. As I walked around the pier, I observed majestic five-storied buildings. A sign read "Tōyō-kan (東洋館)". Chinese people occupied the first and second storeys and the hotel was on the third. There was another hotel called "Ōtaka-kan" but I chose "Tōyō-kan".'[13]

Muraoka quickly realised his naivety in believing he could afford to open a shop with the small amount of money he and his two acolytes had brought with them and they were soon down to their last couple of yen. Despite pleading with the boarding house owner to be allowed to stay until more money arrived from home, they were beaten, thrown out of Tōyōkan, and ended up camping on the Peak before seeking help from the Japanese Consulate. The consul secured accommodation for the three of them at a boarding house for sailors in Tai Ping Shan Street (太平山街) 'run by a Jew who arranges crew members for ships'. Thirty-six sailors, including ten Japanese, were lodging there when they arrived, and Muraoka commented on their rough and violent behaviour. Unable to find work, Muraoka claimed to have left Hong Kong in March 1886 as a deckhand on a British sailing ship.[14]

Ōtaka Ryokan at 21 Praya Central

Though Muraoka mentioned Ōtaka Ryokan (大高旅館) in the account of his 1885 stay in Hong Kong, the name did not appear in any official records until 1889, when it featured in a list of twelve Japanese establishments contracted to provide food and other supplies to a fleet of visiting Japanese ships.[15] By 1890, Ōtaka Ryokan was located on the third floor of 21 Praya Central (today's Des Voeux Road Central) and under the management of Ōtaka Saichi (大高佐市). HONDA Seiroku (本多静六), a twenty-three-year-old student heading to the Royal Saxon Academy of Forestry near Dresden in Germany, ate lunch there during his one-night stopover in the city in April 1890. Honda was accompanied by several of his shipmates, as well as by a student based at the Japanese Consulate in Canton [Guangzhou], SAWANO Kakutarō (澤野格太郎), who just happened to be in Hong Kong at that time.[16]

Honda describes his experience at Ōtaka Ryokan as follows: 'The hotel was on the third floor with exposed roof joists and was not well kept. But since there were no other Japanese hotels in town, we decided to have a break there . . . [The menu included] chicken hot pot, sashimi, prawns, simmered fish, broiled fish with *teriyaki* sauce, soup, and savoury egg custard. After our meal, however, it struck me how dirty the place was, and the toilet was so filthy that I felt nauseous.'[17]

After lunch, Honda made use of his time in the city to tour sites relevant to his discipline. He appreciated the city's Botanic Gardens, writing that they were 'created in a good natural environment, using the latest knowledge'. He found the layout and plant allocation of particular interest and marvelled at the colourful flowers, unfamiliar species of fern, and uncommonly tall banana and palm trees. However, a torrential downpour meant that he only got to see 'one percent of what [he] wanted to study'. Honda also took a dizzying ride on the recently opened Peak Tram, but the rain deprived him of the stunning view that he was hoping for.[18]

Honda highlighted the state of the toilet once again in the account of his evening meal on the same day, at a popular Chinese restaurant on Queen's Road this time, the Heng Fa Lou (杏花樓), which he stated to be one of Hong Kong's best.[19] His description of the Chinese eatery, though likely skewed by perceived class and ethnic superiorities, nevertheless provides a vivid image of what dining out might entail in the final decades of the nineteenth century.

> Our waiter was a boy in stained clothing and [when he served us] he stuck his finger well inside my rice bowl leaving a visible black fingerprint. He had a printed tea towel that he employed to wipe dirty dishes that were then immediately reused to serve food

Boarding House and Restaurant Operators 43

to other customers, without any washing up involved. The chopsticks were made of ivory, but had not been changed since the restaurant's opening, which meant that their ends were worn down and blackened, not unlike an old person's teeth. The toilet and kitchen were in the same place; staff urinated under the sink, which was very unhygienic and left a foul odour. Waiters topped up unfinished appetizers and served them to other tables in full view of the diners.[20]

Following their meal, Honda and his companions went back to their ship to sleep. He sailed the next day. Honda returned to Japan in 1892 and became a famous landscape architect. He is known for his designs for Tokyo's Hibiya Park (日比谷公園) and the forest surrounding the capital's Meiji Shrine.[21]

Ōtaka Saichi passed away five years after Honda's visit. He died of emphysema at the Government Civil Hospital on April 24, 1896, aged thirty-nine.[22] His gravestone is 2.4 metres tall and includes a grey marble plate with a fairly simple afterlife name that bears the characters for 'taka' and 'light' (髙光信士). The plate may have been added later, once a Japanese Buddhist priest had provided the afterlife name. Ōtaka Yoichi (與市) and Ōtaka Saburō (三郎, meaning 'third son') are recorded as the erectors of

Figure 3.1: Heng Fa Lou in 1869. The Chinese restaurant was popular with Japanese visitors and residents. (Photograph by John Thomson. Source: Wellcome Collection.)

Saichi's grave.[23] The monument's height and distinctive design indicate that Ōtaka Saichi enjoyed both wealth and power among the boarding house owner community.

Matsubara Ryokan at 18 Connaught Road

Located at 18 Connaught Road on the Central waterfront, Matsubara Ryokan (松原旅館) opened its doors in 1905 under the management of Matsubara Jisaburō.

The *ryokan*'s target clientele were the Japanese migrant workers heading to northern Australia to work as divers in the lucrative pearl-shell industry.[24] Their main destination was Thursday Island, one of 274 islands that lie between the tip of the Australian state of Queensland and Papua New Guinea in the Torres Strait. The Japanese government's Tariff Convention of 1866 made it possible for foreign ships to employ Japanese crewmen. The first Japanese man recorded as working in the Australian pearling industry was NONAMI Kojirō (野波小次郎) from Shimane (島根). Initially employed by a British commercial vessel in Yokohama, Nonami eventually found his way to the Torres Strait, where he joined the crew of a pearling 'lugger', a small sailing ship typically

Figure 3.2: A Japanese pearl diver and crew in the waters off Thursday Island. The original image appeared in Watanabe Kanjūrō's report on his 1893 visit to Australia for the Foreign Ministry. (Source: 外務省通商局第二課 [Section 2 of the International Trade Bureau, Foreign Ministry], 1894, 297.)

Boarding House and Restaurant Operators 45

staffed by two or three divers, tenders to operate the air pumps, a cook, an engineer, and a couple of sailing crew.[25]

Nonami was followed by a handful of Japanese sailors, whose excellent performance as divers encouraged the pearling companies to engage in more aggressive recruitment practices. One tactic used by the agents Gibb, Livingstone and Company in Hong Kong was to engage boarding house owners as 'crimps' to procure impoverished Japanese sailors. Historian David Sissons explains that, in 1883, 'there were about fifteen or sixteen Japanese recruited in Hong Kong to work as pumpers on the Thursday Island luggers on eighteen-month contracts'. As the number of crewmen needed increased, companies began recruiting in Japan directly, and by the time the industry reached its peak in 1913, it had 574 Japanese indentured labourers working out of Thursday Island.[26]

Risking his life to dive for pearls was a fate that INOUE Teijirō (井上貞治郎; 1881–1963) narrowly escaped when he stayed at the Matsubara Ryokan in 1909. Born in Himeji (姫路), Hyōgo prefecture, Inoue led a nomadic existence for fourteen years, travelling both within Japan and to other parts of Asia. In 1909, he found himself penniless in Shanghai and, after an illicit affair, fled to Hong Kong. Not having any official travel documents, he made his way to Kowloon aboard a 'coolie' ship, the *Guangda* (廣大号). Also on board were several Japanese labourers heading for Western Australia, a group of Chinese low-wage workers, as well as a human trafficker from Niigata, BANDAI Satarō (阪大佐太郎), and the young woman accompanying him, a *karayuki-san*. From Kowloon, Inoue paid 20 sen for a boat to Hong Kong Island, where he was met on the pier by a group of *ryokan* staff competing for customers. He chose the first name he could make out from the crowd of banners: Matsubara Ryokan.

Despite not having enough money for even one night, Inoue asked for a mid-range room and behaved as if he were a wealthy man. However, the staff were not so easily fooled and were soon demanding payment and threatening to hand him over to the Japanese Consulate. Inoue then offered himself up to pay for his stay. In an account of his life published by the *Nikkei* newspaper, Inoue claimed that:

> The manager did not say anything at the time, but later that day he told me that I would be sent to Western Australia to dive for pearls. The company is a British operation and my contract will be on an annual basis. I was ready to accept this, but that evening, while bathing, I told a man that I would be leaving the next day on a French ship bound for Western Australia. The man was alarmed and told me not to go. He said that I would face harsh treatment under the British and would have to dive deep for shells. I would spend the first year on the ship without going ashore, so as to prevent me and other crewmembers from fleeing. He added that three out of every ten divers died on the job.[27]

Deeply shaken, Inoue returned to his room and decided there and then that it was time for him to return to Japan. In desperation, he threw himself on the mercy of the human trafficker, Bandai, who, by chance, was staying in the room adjoining his own and whose voice he had heard through the thick paper *fusuma* screen. Incredibly, Bandai agreed to help him and paid for both his stay at the *ryokan* (60 to 70 yen) and a third-class cabin aboard the *Hakata Maru* to Yokohama (22.5 yen). They departed Hong Kong on April 3, 1909, and travelled together as far as Tokyo, where Bandai left Inoue with 10 sen in his pocket. With this money, Inoue decided to start a new, respectable life, and he went on to become a leading corrugated board manufacturer. The highly successful packaging company he established in 1920 still operates today under the name Rengo (レンゴー). In 1957, Inoue visited Niigata to search for his benefactor and repay his kindness to him, but since Bandai was most likely a false name, he was unable to find any trace of him. Instead, he 'prayed for the kind villain' at the famous Eiheiji temple (永平寺) in Fukui prefecture.[28]

Students of the Tōa Dōbun Shoin (東亜同文書院; East Asia Common Culture Academy) in Shanghai were among other frequent guests at the Matsubara Ryokan. Inaugurated on May 26, 1901, the Shanghai Academy was an offshoot of the semi-governmental Tōa Dōbunkai (東亜同文會; East Asia Common Culture Association). Founded three years earlier in Tokyo and covertly funded by the Ministry of Foreign Affairs, the association's stated aims included enhancing Sino-Japanese relations, promoting trade, and countering Western ambitions in the area. Students at the Tōa Dōbun Shoin received training in both the English and Chinese languages, as well as in business practices and research methods, and were required to undertake extensive fieldwork throughout China. The students produced investigative reports that were channelled to several Japanese government departments, and a number of the academy's graduates went on to serve in Japan's intelligence services.[29] These field trips, sometimes referred to as *dai ryokō* (大旅行) or 'Big Trip' in the tradition of the 'Grand Tour', often took the students to Hong Kong, and their reports mentioned their accommodation, in the form of a large, shared tatami room, at the Matsubara Ryokan.[30]

Matsubara Jisaburō died on March 7, 1918, aged fifty-four. His wife, Yasu, survived him, though it is unclear whether she took any part in the running of the hotel after his death.[31]

Tokyo Hotel at 38A Connaught Road Central

The Tokyo Hotel and Sei Foo Row Annex (清風樓) were situated on Connaught Road Central and operated under the proprietorship of UETSUKI Kakuzō (b. 1874) in the first two decades of the twentieth century. The Tokyo Hotel was located at 38A Connaught Road Central, on the corner of Pottinger Street. The Sei Foo Row, which functioned as both a restaurant and, on occasion, a *ryokan*, was in the adjacent building, facing the harbour. Sei Foo Row, a transliteration of the Japanese for 'cool breeze', made its first appearance as a restaurant on a list of Japanese businesses in 1901.[32]

MAKIYAMA Eiji (槇山榮次; 1867–1933) spent the night of December 18, 1905, at the Sei Foo Row when his Genoa-bound ship called into Hong Kong. The thirty-eight-year-old lecturer describes his accommodation as follows: 'The boarding house is on the fourth floor. Sei Foo Row, or "cool breeze", and a fourth floor room both sound attractive, but in reality this is a very small *ryokan*, occupying merely a corner of a Western-style building.'[33] Makiyama had difficulties with some of the Western-style facilities, failing to realise at first that the bathroom door had to be pulled rather than pushed. Nevertheless, he found the hotel's staff friendly and enjoyed his lunch of *kabayaki*, or grilled fish with teriyaki sauce.[34]

Both establishments, along with Uetsuki himself, who arrived in Hong Kong after his dishonourable discharge from the Japanese army's intelligence services in 1898,

Boarding House and Restaurant Operators

featured frequently in published applications for liquor licences.[35] This annual process was a discriminatory one, with the more liberal 'publican's licence' largely the preserve of Hong Kong's European or American hotel operators. Chinese establishments, meanwhile, had to apply for a 'Chinese restaurant licence', which permitted the retail of 'intoxicating liquors' to 'persons of Chinese race only'.[36] Japanese applications presented something of a conundrum, since they belonged to neither of these groupings, and boarding house owners like Uetsuki had no choice but to petition for a more restrictive 'adjunct licence', which meant spirits could only be served with food and did not permit the keeping of a public bar open to customers of any nationality who just wanted to come in for a drink.

The April 8, 1908, edition of the *Hongkong Daily Press* carried a report on Uetsuki's submission for 'an adjunct licence to sell by retail intoxicating liquors on premises numbered 36 and 37, Connaught road Central under the sign of "Sei Foo Row"'. The account detailed the reasons why the application should be granted, as put forward by Uetsuki's solicitor, Matthew Stephens.

> Mr. M.J.D. Stephens . . . pointed out that there was no Japanese hotel in the Colony where the Japanese could get their sake. It was only lately that [the] Japanese had taken to doing business in foreign countries and a Japanese hotel was a necessity. In Japan, he remarked, Europeans were allowed to conduct hotels. They were not expected to go outside for their wines, and Mr. Stephens thought it should be reciprocal. The application was made in order to cater for the Japanese, who would feel when they were in their own hotel that they were guarded from trouble. The Japanese clerks in the city also would prefer to be in a hotel of their own rather than go to others.

Members of the Licensing Board were clearly perplexed as to how to proceed, since the relevant ordinance made no provision for Japanese hotels; one even asked whether they should 'invent a new licence for Japanese'. Nevertheless, despite some objection, the Sei Foo Row was finally granted an adjunct licence to sell sake and Japanese beer.[37] However, when Uetsuki submitted an application for a publican's licence for the Tokyo Hotel in 1911, which would have permitted him to serve alcohol to any member of the public without food or accommodation, it was rejected.[38]

In contrast to Makiyama, MIYAKE Kokki (三宅克己; 1874–1954), who stopped over in Hong Kong in 1910 while on his way to study watercolour painting in Europe, was far from impressed by the quality of Sei Foo Row's culinary offerings. He reports in his diary:

> There are many Japanese *ryokans* and restaurants in Hong Kong, all of them overpriced. At Sei Foo Row, [I and my companions] ordered two *soba* buckwheat noodle dishes, one with tempura and another with duck and leek. The establishment is well known and dubbed 'the best Japanese restaurant in town.' The food tasted horrible, more like the unrefined fare served in Itabashi, Senju, and Yodobashi on the outskirts of Tokyo. As we stood up to leave, we all regretted having eaten there. The noodles were totally overpriced at 37 sen a bowl. We, who are generally adventurous types, looked at each other in dismay.[39]

Miyake, like many of his compatriots, made good use of his stopover in the city to purchase a wicker chair so as to enjoy the fresh air on deck during his long sea voyage to London.[40]

The Tokyo Hotel was evidently offering its customers the services of geisha (芸者), along with meals and lodging. In a 1913 submission for the renewal of his adjunct licence, Uetsuki was taken to task by members of the Licensing Board for keeping five 'geisha' in the annex to the hotel in which he, his wife, and their servants lived. The chairman put the following questions to him: 'Did you ask anybody whether it was considered proper to have geisha girls at all connected with an hotel in Hongkong? Does it occur to you that Hongkong [is] a British colony and that manners and customs may be different here; did you ask anyone, before you got the geisha girls, to go and stay there, whether it was a proper thing to do?'[41] Uetsuki was unable to respond and an interpreter was called. It seems, however, that the liquor licence was eventually granted.

Uetsuki employed the five women as geisha, meaning that their primary function was to supply dinner-time entertainment. Indeed, a 1913 census conducted by the Japanese Consulate counted thirteen geisha and 155 prostitutes among the 1,189 residents.[42] The women mentioned in the article were most likely from the lower echelons of the geisha hierarchy. Comparatively less sophisticated and proficient than their more famous contemporaries in Kyoto or Tokyo, they may have provided sexual services to selected guests along with pouring sake and playing the *shamisen*.

Uetsuki Kakuzō died on February 26, 1918, aged forty-five. Several of his family members are buried in the Hong Kong Cemetery as well. His widow, Yoneko (米子), a former geisha from Tsuyama, Okayama (岡山県津山), took over the running of the business after his death.[43]

Figure 3.3: Uetsuki Yoneko features in a 1926 ad for the Tokyo Hotel. She took over the running of the hotel following the death of her husband, Kakuzō, who died in the 1918 Happy Valley Racecourse fire. (Source: Nippon Yusen Kaisha, *Glimpses of the East*, 1925–1927.)

Boarding House Owners and the Traffic of *Karayuki-san*

In the late nineteenth century, Hong Kong was not only a destination for *karayuki-san*, as explored in the previous chapter, but also a major transit point for their traffic to other parts of the British Empire. An 1896 article in the *Japan Weekly Mail* gives statistics for the numbers and incomes of 'Japanese women who are living a life of shame' in Hong Kong (one hundred women earning 100 yen each a month), and separate locations in the region. '[These women] are smuggled under various ingenious devices on board foreign steamers and generally go first to Hongkong where they find agents engaged in this special line who are ready to provide them with the means of subsistence. They are all required to learn English, and after a short stay drift southward to Singapore, Penang, Australia, and India.'[44]

Though the article implies that these women had some agency in their movement from one country to another, this was unlikely, and a whole network of procurers, sailors, and corrupt harbour and petty officials benefitted from their traffic. Furthermore, though Hong Kong was initially the main point of transit for prostitutes to different parts of Asia and Australia, it gradually relinquished that role to Singapore from the late 1880s onwards.[45]

Working with procurers and pimps such as Muraoka, Hong Kong's Japanese boarding house owners were instrumental in facilitating the *karayuki-san*'s transit through the city and grew rich on the proceeds of their sale to brothel owners overseas. Their involvement went from providing a place to stay for a few days or weeks and helping to procure fake passports to escorting the women to their ultimate destinations.[46]

The name 'Matsubara' appeared in a statement given by HASHIMOTO Usa to the Government Resident for Queensland. In it, Usa detailed her journey from Nagasaki to Thursday Island in the summer of 1897. She left her home without a passport and with the intention of joining her sister in Singapore. A procurer arranged for her and ten other young women to travel to Shanghai and then Hong Kong, where they arrived on July 13, 1897. They were taken to a boarding house run by Ōtaka Yoichi, where Usa was informed that it was impossible for her to enter Singapore without a passport.[47] Distraught, she continued:

> Otaka the keeper of the lodging house told me that Thursday Island in Australia was a very good place to make money, and that I could freely land there without passport. He strongly advised me to go to Thursday Island. I followed his advice thinking that in doing so I might find an opportunity to get afterwards to my sister at Singapore. So I boldly decided to go to Thursday Island, and was accompanied there by Matsubara from Otaka's lodging House. We arrived at Thursday Island on the 11th day of September. There were other women with Matsubara whom he brought to sell along with me. Matsubara is not himself the keeper of a brothel.

Usa added that she entered into an agreement with the brothel keeper on Thursday Island to repay him the sum of 100 pounds sterling from her earnings. This was the amount she believed he paid Matsubara for her passage and expenses.[48]

Without a first name, we cannot be entirely sure that this was the same Matsubara Jisaburō who managed the Matsubara Ryokan. However, no one else with that surname was recorded as residing in Hong Kong at that time, and it is plausible that he worked for another boarding house before he started his own.[49] As mentioned earlier in this chapter, the original proprietor of Ōtaka Ryokan, Ōtaka Saichi, died in 1896. Ōtaka Yoichi, who paid to erect his grave, was possibly an associate, a relative, or a member of the same crime 'family', based in Nagasaki but travelling regularly to Hong Kong to oversee the *ryokan* and its involvement in the traffic of *karayuki-san*.

As further evidence of the boarding house owners' connections to the criminal underworld of human trafficking, Ōtaka Yoichi makes an appearance in Muraoka Iheiji's autobiographical account.[50] Muraoka claimed that while based in Manila in early 1906, he came to Hong Kong to mediate between two rival gangs, one based in Shimonoseki, Yamaguchi prefecture (山口県下関), headed by a man named SUZUKI (鈴木), and another based in Nagasaki headed by Ōtaka Yoichi. The gangs were fighting over territory in Hong Kong and the situation had escalated after one of Ōtaka's men, ARAKI (荒木), murdered one of Suzuki's subordinates. The murderer had been jailed, and Suzuki's men had taken over Ōtaka's operations, setting the scene for a violent showdown. Muraoka boasted that he had successfully negotiated an agreement between the two parties: Ōtaka was to control the traffic of women departing from Kyushu and Shanghai and Suzuki would handle those departing from the main island of Japan.[51]

While the English-language press made no mention of the 1906 gang war, a case involving another man named ARAKI featured heavily the following year. In April 1907, ARAKI Taizo brought three *karayuki-san* to the Yamato-kan (大和館), a boarding house in Central, and was subsequently stabbed to death by four Japanese men. The ensuing trial attracted much attention and was attended by Japanese, Chinese, and European spectators. During the proceedings, the prosecution asserted that the occupation of both the deceased and his assailants was 'bringing Japanese women into the colony'.[52] Muraoka's and the court's accounts both testify to the fact that, by the early twentieth century, the traffic of *karayuki-san* was very much in the hands of organised crime and could not have operated without the complicity of boarding house owners like Ōtaka and Matsubara.[53]

The Japanese Benevolent Society

Matsubara and Uetsuki were key members of the Japanese Benevolent Society (日本人慈善會). Established in Hong Kong in 1890, the society's original mission was to provide assistance for the treatment of the sick and burial of the destitute.[54] At least forty-eight of the identifiable Japanese graves in the Hong Kong Cemetery were erected by the society between 1892 and 1910, with many belonging to *karayuki-san*. It is probable that the society's members were all involved with prostitution in some way, either as boarding house, brothel, or 'café' managers, or as small traders like kimono and porcelain dealers, whose business depended largely on *karayuki-san* as customers. Looked down upon by Japanese residents involved in more respectable enterprises and needing a more organised means of resolving issues such as the burial of penniless, indebted prostitutes, they set up their own association.

Starting in 1909, approximately 40 per cent of the Benevolent Society's revenue came from horse-racing-related activities. The society's booth at the 'Derby Day' horse races in Happy Valley was a particularly lucrative source of funds.[55] This annual event drew 10,000 spectators.[56] The booths, which the Department of Public Works auctioned

Figure 3.4: A beach outing organised by a youth society affiliated with the Japanese Benevolent Society, circa 1911. The group of men includes boarding house operators and tradespeople. (Source: 『香港青年』 [Hong Kong Youth], vol. 7, 1911 in 濱下・李 監修 [Hamashita and Lee, eds.], 2013.)

Figure 3.5: Matsheds at the Happy Valley Racecourse, circa 1910. The row of Japanese flags (centre right of the photograph) indicates the location of the matshed operated by the Japanese Benevolent Society. (Source: Hong Kong Museum of History, MHP1968.89.)

off each year, were temporary structures, or matsheds, made of bamboo and palm leaf matting. They supplemented the existing permanent grandstand that was predominantly open to members of the Hong Kong Jockey Club, the colonial elite, and other local dignitaries. Derby Day was one of the few events on the city's social calendar that brought together people from different classes and ethnic backgrounds. However, the majority of the matsheds were leased by members of the middle and lower classes, including Chinese merchants, Portuguese clerks and printers, and various business owners, such as those involved in the Japanese Benevolent Society.[57]

The society's Mutual Aid branch, which provided financial assistance to the sick for treatment or return to Japan, to pregnant women for delivery fees, and for funeral expenses, had fifty-three members in 1917, including Matsubara, who was its chief accountant, and Uetsuki.[58]

Ōtani Kōzui and the Nishi Hongwanji

In 1917, the Japanese Benevolent Society's office was located at the Hongwanji Mission Centre in Hong Kong.[59] Jyōdoshinshū Hongwanji (浄土真宗本願寺), commonly known as Nishi Hongwanji (西本願寺), was, and remains, one of the largest and most influential schools of Buddhism in Japan, and it facilitated the establishment of several Japanese overseas resident associations. Indeed, ŌTANI Kōzui (大谷光瑞; 1876–1948), the twenty-second abbot of the Jyōdoshinshū Hongwanji, from 1903 until his enforced abdication in 1914, travelled to different parts of Asia, including Hong Kong.

In 1868, the newly installed Meiji government issued a series of decrees ordering the dissociation of Shintō and Buddhism, which negatively impacted Japanese Buddhists. This, together with a desire to demonstrate that Buddhism was the equal of other religions and to respond to the sudden influx of Christian missionaries, prompted Ōtani's father, the twenty-first abbot, to institute a number of much needed reforms. He reviewed the Nishi Hongwanji organisational structure, updated the educational system to include the study of geography and English, and encouraged overseas travel to learn from diverse faiths and philosophical traditions and to promote a more modern image of Japanese Buddhism.[60]

Ōtani received both traditional Buddhist and modern educations. He shared his father's outlook and travelled widely. He spent two and a half years in London, arriving in the city in March 1900. During his stay, he published an account of his travels in China and was consequently made a Fellow of the Royal Geographical Society. In Japan, he is best known for the three expeditions along the Silk Road that he organised and financed between 1902 and 1914, with the purpose of excavating Buddhist sites and collecting archaeological material.[61]

Hong Kong's Hongwanji centre officially opened in February 1907, and the Nishi Hongwanji headquarters in Kyoto funded the sending of a priest to the city in 1909, 1910, and 1911. However, as early as 1900, a Hongwanji priest, TAKADA Seigan (髙田栖岸), was engaged in missionary work in Hong Kong.[62] He is credited with starting a small operation at 117 Wanchai Road where he taught history and the philosophy of Mencius to children. This would later evolve into a Japanese primary school, the management of which was assumed by the Japanese Benevolent Society in 1911.[63]

Keen to spread the Nishi Hongwanji message and recruit followers, Ōtani Kōzui actively supported the setting up of Japanese overseas resident associations and the establishment of temples. His wife, Kazuko (大谷籌子; 1882–1911) assisted him in these endeavours. During a trip to Hong Kong in 1899, he encouraged the setting up of a women's association and the group was launched the following year with forty-eight members, all of whom were involved in lower-class occupations.[64] Ōtani's donation of 500 dollars made during the same visit helped finance the creation of the city's Nippon Club (日本倶楽部) to serve upper-class Japanese residents.[65] Originally developed from Yamato Kai (大和會), a Japanese association founded by two company executives in 1903, the Nippon Club was officially established in 1905.[66] Its Ice House Street premises featured games rooms and dining and reading facilities. The club organised numerous social and sports activities, with tennis playing especially popular as a mark of elite status.[67]

The Nippon Club was very much separate from the Benevolent Society. Its early membership was confined to government employees, bank and shipping executives, as well as the managers of the city's leading commercial houses. Though Matsubara's food and beverage industry skills would eventually see him put in charge of the club's in-house restaurant, his involvement was as a catering contractor rather than a member.[68]

Japanese Crematorium in So Kon Po

Members of the Japanese Benevolent Society and the Nishi Hongwanji came together in the 1910s to establish a crematorium to serve Hong Kong's growing Japanese resident and transient population, with an estimated twenty-five to thirty deaths per year.[69] The majority of the early Japanese graves in the Hong Kong Cemetery contain bones, as there was no other respectful means of disposing of the corpses of the deceased. A crematorium enabled relatives to carry the ashes of their departed loved ones back to their hometowns in Japan.

Japanese Buddhism advocated cremation, which it saw as purifying the body of the deceased, and the Nishi Hongwanji had already helped fund the construction of modern cremation facilities in Kyoto in 1877.[70] However, Confucians and the members of several Christian faiths, Catholics in particular, were vocal opponents of this practice.[71] In Hong Kong, conditions rarely permitted the return of corpses to Japan and this meant that many families had to leave their dead behind in graves they were unlikely to ever visit again. Unkempt monuments were left vulnerable to the elements and remains risked removal to an ossuary.

The Japanese Consulate made a formal application to the Hong Kong government for a plot of land on which to build a crematorium in 1910.[72] The following year, the colonial administration agreed to grant a lot of 30,000 square feet in So Kon Po (掃桿埔) to the 'Japanese Consul for the Japanese Community as a site for a Crematorium' with a seventy-five-year lease.[73] The site, largely surrounded by grasslands at the time, was located near what, in 1929, would become the Tung Wah Eastern Hospital in Causeway Bay. A cow shed had to be removed to accommodate the approach road to the crematorium. Though the submission was made through the Japanese Consulate, four of the signatories on the lease were affiliated with the Benevolent Society and Nishi Hongwanji, including Matsubara and MAJIMA Keinosuke (馬島珪之助), a medical practitioner who operated a Wan Chai clinic serving members of the Japanese community, particularly *karayuki-san*.[74]

The Japanese crematorium was built at a cost of 4,000 dollars and opened in 1912. The *Hongkong Telegraph* offers a brief description of its appearance: 'A portion of the hillside has been levelled and a handsome wall with ornamental ironwork gates has been erected on the north side of the piece of land set aside for the crematorium. The furnace is in the south west corner and though not at present complete, has the fire box in position and the tray for conveying the remains into the furnace proper. Draught is obtained downward and the fumes are subsequently carried away through a short chimney.'[75]

Since existing laws 'did not provide adequately for the control of this method of disposing of the dead or for the regulation of Crematoria', the Sanitary Board had to draft and approve a special bill for this purpose.[76] Twenty-nine cremations took place in 1916–1917, with two carried out free of charge and two for 'foreigners', that is, non-Japanese.[77] Following the opening of the crematorium, the number of Japanese buried in the Hong Kong Cemetery showed a marked decrease. The average age of those interred changed too, with many of the identifiable graves after 1912 belonging to stillborn babies and very young children.[78]

The Benevolent Society and Nishi Hongwanji had ambitions beyond the crematorium. The Nishi Hongwanji premises at 117 Wanchai Road consisted of a few rented rooms in a residential property.[79] On December 16, 1911, the acting Japanese consul general submitted a request for a second lot on which to build a Buddhist temple. In his letter, he mentions that the community 'has raised about dollars thirty thousand ($30,000), one third of which amount was contributed by the Chief Temple of "Hon-Gwan-Ji" in Kyoto, Japan. . . . The plan of the building was designed by the Dr. C. Ito, the most famous architect in Japan. It combines the architectural ideas of Europe and Asia, especially India, and is planned so as to withstand the strongest typhoon [in] South China.'[80]

The consulate was informed of the success of its application on May 30, 1912. The government granted a second lot of 75,170 square feet as a site for a Buddhist temple for a term of seventy-five years and at a nominal rent of 1 dollar per year.[81] The area was located just uphill from the Japanese crematorium. The Nishi Hongwanji, working with a close collaborator of Ōtani, the renowned architect ITŌ Chūta (伊東忠太; 1867–1954), did indeed draw up the plans for a Hong Kong Betsuin (香港別院; branch temple).[82]

However, the funds collected proved insufficient and the temple was never completed. The consulate had to return the plot to the Crown, though the Nishi Hongwanji continued to perform ceremonies and death rituals at the crematorium.

Happy Valley Racecourse Fire

Matsubara and Uetsuki perished in what remains one of Hong Kong's worst human-made disasters, the Happy Valley Racecourse fire of February 26, 1918. The disaster left over 600 people dead, many burnt beyond any formal identification, including at least thirteen members of the Japanese community.[83] The Japanese Benevolent Society had successfully bid 1,280 dollars for booth no. 15 and had a two-floor plus basement

Figure 3.6: Count Ōtani Kōzui (seated) attends a groundbreaking ceremony with members of Hong Kong's Japanese community during a stopover in June 1915. From left: Matsumoto Jyūrō (Matsumoto Trading), Aoi Matsutarō (Daibutsu Trading), Matsubara Jisaburō (Matsubara *ryokan*), Dobashi Hisakichi (Dobashi Trading), Gōhara Kinjirō (Gōhara Trading), Kusumoto Taketoshi (NYK General Manager), Kuchiba Yoshinori (Hongwanji priest), Majima Keinosuke (medical doctor), Ōhashi Renzō (interpreter), Yokose Kyoshi (Tōyōkan), Uetsuki Kakuzō (Tokyo Hotel), Era Hikotarō (photographer), and Arakawa Tadaaki (Arakawa Trading). (Source: 『大陽』 [Taiyō], vol. 6, 1915.)

Figure 3.7: The Happy Valley Racecourse fire of February 26, 1918, left over 600 people dead, including at least thirteen members of the Japanese community. (Source: Frank Fischbeck Collection, The University of Hong Kong Libraries.)

matshed erected from which it sold sweepstakes tickets. Its matshed could hold up to 200 people at any one time.[84] Due to unseasonably dry weather that February, the contractor responsible for putting up the nineteen matsheds had been unable to sink the support poles firmly into the ground, a contributing factor to the sudden collapse of the comparatively flimsy structures just before the start of the first race after tiffin, or lunch, at around 3 p.m.[85] Many of the booths offered refreshments such as hot tea and had rudimentary charcoal stoves, or chatties, for the purpose of boiling water. The falling poles and matting not only trapped the booths' visitors but also rapidly caught fire, burning those inside to death or causing them to suffocate from the fumes.

The Japanese stand had around 150 guests at the time of its collapse, with those in the first row of seats sustaining serious injuries. Among the matshed's occupants was a large number of women, most likely *karayuki-san* and geisha rather than the wives or relatives of male patrons, but very few children. In his description of the scene, K. Nakagawa, a lieutenant in the Imperial Japanese Army, states that 'Mr. Uetsuki was sitting at the counter for receiving bets along with Mr. G. Matsubara at the time of the collapse. Mr. Uetsuki was pinned between the counter and wall and could not be extricated.'[86]

Boarding House and Restaurant Operators

Other Japanese casualties mentioned in the press included 'Mr. Kitashima, the hairdresser of Hongkong Hotel' and Mr Z. Fukuda, an employee of Mitsui Bussan Kaisha, who was the guest of a shed erected by the Portuguese Xavier family.[87] Nakagawa explained that the Japanese Benevolent Society flag had been recovered from the counter and hoisted to serve as a rallying point for the injured members of the Japanese community and those seeking information on missing friends. One of the many rumours circulating shortly after the disaster was that five Chinese robbers had surrounded Matsubara just before the matshed collapsed.[88]

The colonial government opened an enquiry into the tragedy on March 7, 1918. While no criminal negligence was attributed, the enquiry highlighted the Department of Public Works' lack of oversight of the matshed construction process, the insufficient police presence, and the inadequacy of firefighting provisions at the site.[89] As a result of the fire, the governor, Sir Francis Henry May, permanently banned matsheds from the racecourse and ordered the building of permanent stands.[90]

Uetsuki's funeral was held on February 28 and his body cremated at the So Kon Po crematorium.[91] Matsubara died of his injuries on March 7, 1918, at Majima Keinosuke's clinic in Wan Chai. His age is engraved on his headstone – fifty-four years old. Both men's gravestones are testaments to their wealth. Uetsuki's is a white marble affair with an inscription that claims his services were recognised by the Japanese government

Figure 3.8: The grave of Matsubara Jisaburō includes an incense burner and two flower holders. It was probably made in Japan and shipped to Hong Kong. (Photo credit: Miyuki Kume.)

Figure 3.9: The Memorial to Ten Thousand Souls was erected to commemorate the victims of the 1918 Happy Valley fire. (Photo credit: Miyuki Kume.)

with a medal of honour. Matsubara's is unlike any other in the cemetery, with distinctive Japanese Buddhist features that suggest it was manufactured in Japan and then shipped to Hong Kong.

On February 26, 1919, the Japanese Benevolent Society unveiled a grand monument dedicated to all the victims of the fire. The tall rectangular pillar is shaped like an obelisk and engraved on one side with three characters written in the style of an ancient Chinese seal. The calligraphic inscription, which can be translated as 'memorial to ten thousand souls', is the work of Ōtani Kōzui. Initially situated next to the crematorium, it was moved to its present location in the Japanese section of the Hong Kong Cemetery in 1982.[92]

Good Food in Bad Company? A Taste of Home on the Hong Kong Waterfront

A Japanese Foreign Ministry handbook on Hong Kong published in the same year as the Happy Valley Racecourse fire listed ten Japanese-style boarding houses. Room prices ranged from 1.5 dollars per night for a third-class room at a third-rate *ryokan* to 6 dollars per night for a first-class room at a first-rate *ryokan*.[93] A list of nineteen establishments applying for liquor licences in October 1919 also included ten Japanese hotels and restaurants, testifying to a growing demand for their services. Along with the more upmarket *ryokan* in Central, such as the Tokyo Hotel, the list included a couple of 'houses' in Kowloon and several more in Wan Chai.[94] Indeed, in an earlier application for a licence for one establishment in Wan Chai, its female manager, ISHIYAMA Sei

Boarding House and Restaurant Operators 59

(石山セイ), claimed that it was needed to cater to the 1,500 Japanese living in the area.[95]

Table 3.1: List of Japanese liquor licence applicants in October 1919

Applicant	Sign of House	Address
Mrs Yoneko Uyetsuki	Tokyo Hotel	36, 37, 38A, and 38B, Pottinger Street
Isekichi Seki	Chitose Hotel	6, 7, and 8 Hau Fung Lane [Wan Chai]
Juhachi Tada	Kowloon Tei	39, Peking Road, Kowloon
Tokutaro Miyajima	Suehiro Hotel	45, Haiphong Road, Kowloon
Tokutaro Ishiyama	Iroha Hotel	1 Haufung Lane, Wan Chai
Sohichi Yoshizawa	Yoshizawa Tokuhachi	35, 36, and 37 Praya East
Mrs Yone Namura	Harunoya Hotel	22, 23, and 24 Praya East
Joe Yamakawa	–	47, Praya East, Ground and 1st floors
Yoshitaro Futami	–	1, Spring Garden Lane, Ground floor
Ikuzo Nomura	Shokudoraku	7, Cross Street [Wan Chai]

Source: *South China Morning Post*, October 27, 1919, 4. Names appear as in the original article.

These establishments were visited by predominantly Japanese patrons from different social strata. Upper-class Japanese eager for a taste of home were left with no choice but to interact with people they would have considered unsavoury in Japan at these waterfront *ryokan*. However, the boarding houses' association with human trafficking and other criminal enterprises meant that their owners were not accepted within the higher circles of Japanese society in Hong Kong. Someone of the stature of Natsume Sōseki might dine at their restaurants, and they might be acknowledged for their charitable services, yet men like Ōtaka, Matsubara, and Uetsuki still remained on the fringes of what was considered respectable society. Though there was some crossover within this community of two halves, its members remained divided, with their own, separate social clubs and business associations. As mentioned earlier in the chapter, the opening of the crematorium made it possible for people to carry the ashes of deceased loved ones back to Japan. Yet Uetsuki's and Matsubara's families both elected to erect prominent graves in Hong Kong instead. They stand as ostentatious displays of their financial success and an appeal for the recognition that their questionable activities denied them in Japan.

4

A Japanese Ship in Victoria Harbour

That we should have here in this harbour a noble vessel, fitted with every comfort which passenger or heart could desire, belonging to a power but the other day little known in the world, [shows] the wonderful force and progress of civilisation.[1]

[Toast by barrister Thomas Hayllar aboard the *Niigata Maru* on November 13, 1879]

A guest representing Hong Kong's Attorney General made this observation at the luncheon, or tiffin, organised by the Mitsubishi Mail Steamship Company to mark the launch of Japan's first commercial service between Yokohama and the city in 1879. The firm's recently arrived Hong Kong office general manager, HONDA Masajirō (本田政次郎), officiated at the event.[2] Born in Nagasaki and of commoner stock, Honda had gained extensive experience in shipping matters during previous postings in Shanghai and Yokohama and provided interpreting services during a stint in Tokyo. Despite Mitsubishi's confidence in his management and linguistic abilities, he was, nevertheless, clearly uncomfortable with the English language. While some of the assembled dignitaries, including Hayllar, delivered eloquent toasts, Honda reportedly uttered just one sentence: 'Gentlemen, *macotoni arigato*' (I am really obliged to you).[3]

The Japanese ship's presence in Victoria Harbour was a significant milestone for both Mitsubishi and the country. As an island nation, shipping was vital to Japan's international ambitions and quest to rival the Western powers that had largely dictated the terms of its engagement with the global economy so far. For IWASAKI Yatarō (岩崎彌太郎; 1835–1885), Mitsubishi's founder, the new route was a further step in the realisation of his vision to criss-cross the globe with Japanese lines.[4]

Iwasaki Yatarō and the Mitsubishi Mail Steamship Company

The origins of the Mitsubishi Mail Steamship Company can be traced back to the final years of the Tokugawa regime. The commercial treaties that the *bakufu* signed with the United States, Britain, France, Holland, and Russia in the 1850s formally established Japan's first treaty ports. Hakodate, Niigata, Yokohama, Kobe, and Nagasaki joined a network that already connected major Chinese treaty ports such as Shanghai, Xiamen, Tianjin, and Guangzhou (上海, 厦門, 天津, 広州), as well as the British colony of Hong Kong.[5] The opening of the country brought with it greater vulnerability to the commercial ambitions of established European and American powers and the realisation that Japan needed to urgently upgrade its shipping capabilities to compete with the foreign steamship companies that monopolised global trade routes, such as the Peninsular and Oriental Steam Navigation Company (P&O) and the Pacific Mail Steamship Company.

In the late 1860s, both the *bakufu* and several of the more internationally minded domains, including Tosa (土佐, later Kōchi prefecture 高知県), purchased a number of mostly second-hand ships and established agencies to oversee marine defence and commercial development.[6] It was at one of these agencies that Iwasaki Yatarō, the eventual founder of Mitsubishi, first developed his entrepreneurial ideas and skills. In 1868, Iwasaki's domain, Tosa, sent him as a representative to Nagasaki, where he further enhanced his expertise in trade and shipping activities. In 1870, shortly after the overthrow of the shogunate, part of the agency was set up as a separate firm, Tsukumo Shōkai (九十九商會; Tsukumo Trading Firm), before becoming independent from the domain in 1872.[7]

In 1873, under Iwasaki Yatarō's leadership and with the financial and political backing of the new Meiji government, the company was renamed Mitsubishi Shōkai (三菱商會) and adopted its now distinctive three-diamond crest, which was a blend of the Tosa and Iwasaki emblems. Shipping was Mitsubishi's largest enterprise in the early 1870s, though it was also active in other areas, particularly mining with its purchase of the profitable Yoshioka copper mine (吉岡銅山) in 1873.[8] A lack of suitable ships meant that the firm initially focused on Japanese coastal shipping, despite its desire to expand into international routes. The Meiji government's 1874 Taiwan Expedition finally enabled it to do so.

The murder of over fifty shipwrecked Japanese sailors on the southern coast of Taiwan in late 1871 provided the Meiji government with the pretext to lead a punitive expedition to the island in 1874. By necessity rather than choice, Mitsubishi was awarded the military transport contract for the seven-month operation. The government purchased thirteen steamships capable of covering the longer distances required – though only ten were actually delivered prior to the end of 1874 – and entrusted Mitsubishi with their management. The terms of the contract were primarily concerned with the carriage of munitions and troops, yet they do not appear to have excluded the use of these ships for mercantile purposes. Ultimately, this investment in larger craft is what made it possible for the rebranded Mitsubishi Mail Steamship Company (郵便汽船三菱會社; Yūbin Kisen Mitsubishi Kaisha) to launch Japan's first overseas commercial shipping service with the opening of the Yokohama to Shanghai line on February 3, 1875.[9]

The Shanghai line initially did not fare well and faced stiff competition from the American Pacific Mail Company. Mitsubishi ultimately emerged victorious from this encounter when it purchased the line and the four ships serving it from Pacific Mail eight months later. This victory was short-lived, with P&O establishing its own Hong Kong–Shanghai–Yokohama service in 1876. However, with the support of the Japanese government, Mitsubishi was able to see off its British rival and plan for the expansion of its international routes. In October 1879, the company launched its fortnightly service between Yokohama and Hong Kong, via Kobe.[10]

Yokohama to Hong Kong Line

The Hong Kong route was started with two of the ships purchased from P&O for the Taiwan Expedition, the *Niigata Maru* (新潟丸), captained by British-born Wilson Walker (1845–1914), and *Takasago Maru* (高砂丸), captained by another Englishman, Christopher Young.[11] Born in Maryport in 1845, Walker served on ships in Britain before making his way to East Asia in 1867. He worked for Nagasaki-based Scottish businessman Thomas Blake Glover until the collapse of Glover & Co. in 1869. Following a brief sojourn in England, Walker returned to Japan in 1870 and was offered a position by Iwasaki Yatarō, first for the Tosa domain and later for Mitsubishi.

Prior to their use on the new line, Mitsubishi had sent both vessels to the Scottish shipbuilding company Lobnitz & Co. Ltd. in Renfrew on the River Clyde for refitting with new boilers and engines. The *Niigata Maru* made quite an impression as it sailed down the Thames in the summer of 1877. An article detailing the ship's arrival was published in newspapers across Britain, including the following:

> A fine ship, called the Niigata Maru, Captain Walker, has arrived in the Thames from Japan. This is the first vessel bearing the Japanese flag which has entered the port of London. Though built as a steamer, she has made this long passage round the Cape under sail, occupying 141 days. The crew consists of thirty-four men, all of whom, with three or four exceptions, are Japanese. The Niigata Maru brings a cargo of about 1600 tons, chiefly rice, and is likely to be the first of a series of regular traders.[12]

The ships' crews included several students from the Mitsubishi Nautical College (三菱商船學校; Mitsubishi Shōsen Gakkō), which Iwasaki Yatarō had established in 1875.[13] They were to complete their training during the long sea voyage and the year or so spent in Scotland.[14] Though Captain Walker was reportedly impressed by the Japanese sailors' performance, their stay was not entirely uneventful.[15] One Japanese crewmember aboard the *Takasago Maru* ended up in a local Scottish court, accused of wilfully neglecting his duty and of disobeying his captain's commands. He had asked for a 3 pound advance on his salary to buy clothes. His request was refused and he consequently stopped working, with other members of the crew following suit.[16]

Table 4.1: Lobnitz & Co. financial records – balance April 17, 1879

Yard Number	Name of Job	Grand Total of Charges	Net Prices Charged or Received	Loss or Commissions Paid
No. 167–8	S.S. Niigata Maru	£63,545 18s 10d	£25,250	£4,264 6d
	S.S. Takasago Maru		£15,358 1s 1d	
			£18,673 17s 3d	

Breakdown of total charges:	
This year's materials less credits:	£36,772 7s 3d
This year's wages:	£21,040 9s 5d
This year's charges:	£5,733 2s 2d

Source: National Records of Scotland and University of Glasgow Archives and Special Collections, Lobnitz & Co Ltd collection, GB248 UCS 004/4/6. s = shilling; d = pence.

A Japanese Ship in Victoria Harbour   63

The cost of the refit for both ships came to over 63,000 pounds, with Mitsubishi securing a loan from the Japanese government to cover the amount.[17] The *Niigata Maru* finally returned to Yokohama in November 1878.[18]

On October 4, 1879, the *Niigata Maru*, captained by Walker, departed Yokohama on the inaugural sailing of the new line to Hong Kong. Among its passengers were ANDŌ Tarō (安藤太郎; 1846–1924), Japanese Consul to the city since 1874, and his wife, Fumiko (文子).[19] Andō was returning to Hong Kong after accompanying John Pope Hennessy and his family on a three-month trip to Japan. During his visit, which is discussed in Chapter 1, the consul had ensured that the Hong Kong governor was welcomed by the most senior members of the Japanese political and commercial establishments, including an audience with the Mikado himself.[20]

The Japanese ship *Niigata Maru* arrived in Hong Kong's Victoria Harbour on October 12, 1879, amid considerable fanfare. Eager to promote its business in the face of intense competition from P&O, Mitsubishi organised an onboard luncheon on November 13, during the service's third run. As mentioned earlier in this chapter,

Figure 4.1: A *Japan Punch* cartoon taking aim at the princely welcome afforded the governor by Japan's elite businessmen and politicians during his 'private' trip to the country. The cartoon also lampoons Pope Hennessy's popularity among Hong Kong's Chinese population and the animosity his behaviour aroused in the city's English-language press. (Source: *Japan Punch*, June 1879.)

Honda Masajirō, Mitsubishi's Hong Kong office general manager, was on hand to welcome some sixty guests, all men and mostly colonial officials and businesspeople. Honda was joined by another Mitsubishi agent, Henry John Howard Tripp, who had spent eleven years in the employ of P&O before joining the Japanese company.[21] A portion of the British Army's 27th Inniskillings Regimental Band played throughout the event, in a nod to Pope Hennessy's Irish roots. Along with toasts to 'The Queen' and '[His Majesty] the Mikado of Japan', glasses were raised to 'The Army and Navy', 'The Bar', 'The Merchants of Hongkong', and 'The Managers and Directors of the Company, and Success to the Company'.[22] These toasts were indicative of the respect accorded to this new entrant in the Hong Kong shipping market, with the governor's attendance no doubt secured by Andō as a gesture of gratitude for his chaperoning of Pope Hennessy around Japan.

Among the guests were several with strong ties to Japan. The Consul General for Portugal, José da Silva Loureiro, had previously served as the Portuguese Consul in Nagasaki.[23] Commander Archibald Lucius Douglas had spent almost three years in Japan from 1873 to 1875 as part of the Meiji government's mission to modernise the Japanese navy, during which time he had assumed direction of the Imperial Naval College in Tokyo.[24] In his speech of thanks on behalf of the navy, Douglas stated that 'he had the greater pleasure in thanking [the assembly] for the honour, in that he had himself taken part in the formation of the Japanese Navy'.[25]

Other dignitaries included the Consul of the United States, John Singleton Mosby, a former Confederate officer better known by his nickname 'Gray Ghost', which he had earned for his exploits as a cavalry scout during the American Civil War (1861–1865). Also attending were the superintendent of Victoria Gaol (prison), Malcolm Struan Tonnochy, and Phineas Ryrie, who would become the first chairman of the Hong Kong Jockey Club in 1884.[26]

The Japanese Consulate helped organise the event. In his response to the toast to the Mikado, Consul Andō expressed his hope that the new line would lead to the growth of mutual trade between Hong Kong and Japan.[27] Indeed, in a letter from Iwasaki Yatarō thanking Andō for his part in the success of the tiffin, the Mitsubishi president emphasised the role of the route in the development of Japan's international business aspirations and conveyed his fear of the damage to the company's, and even the country's, reputation should it fail.[28] Andō, in turn, conveyed the governor's approval of Mitsubishi's appointment of a Japanese man – Honda – as general manager in the colony, as other firms usually hired Westerners for this role. He believed the tiffin had done much to enhance the reputation of the Japanese in Hong Kong.[29] A few weeks after the gathering, Iwasaki Yatarō wrote personally to Pope Hennessy to express his appreciation for 'being present at the tiffin on board of the "Niigata Maru" and for the kindly sentiments [Pope Hennessy] there expressed toward [Iwasaki's] country and its enterprises'.[30]

The two ships serving the line, the *Niigata Maru* and *Takasago Maru*, had returned from Renfrew much improved and their updated interiors were reportedly popular with passengers, 'having, in addition to the advantage of the P. & O. roominess of olden days, all the modern improvements in fittings and appliances which the ingenuity and skill of the Clyde shipbuilders can supply'.[31] Indeed, the *China Mail* informed its readers that the *Takasago Maru*'s 'superior accommodation for the comfort of

Figure 4.2: A newspaper ad for the launch of the Mitsubishi Mail Steamship Company's Yokohama to Shanghai service in 1875. The firm reassigned two of the ships serving the route, the *Niigata Maru* and *Takasago Maru*, to its Hong Kong service in 1879. (Source: 『東京日日新聞』 [*Tokyo Nichinichi Shimbun*], May 25, 1875.)

Figure 4.3: Passenger fares from Hong Kong to Japan published in the January 1, 1880, issue of the *Hongkong Daily Press*.

passengers, – in the fine state rooms, spacious saloon, and extensive free space for promenade on deck, – afforded all the pleasures which passengers could desire'.[32]

Fares from Hong Kong to Yokohama cost 75 dollars for a cabin and 20 dollars in steerage. First-class fares for the same routing on P&O and the French shipping company Messageries Maritimes were slightly higher at 80 dollars; Pacific Mail, meanwhile, matched Mitsubishi's pricing.[33]

However, Mitsubishi's main interest was in freight rather than passengers. In 1879, freight represented close to 65 per cent and passengers just 20 per cent of the company's total income.[34] Commenting on the importance of cargo, a December 1879 article in the *China Mail* mentions that 'on the last trip of the *Niigata-maru*, articles of Japanese produce to the value of ninety thousand yen were shipped for Hongkong; and by other recent departures large quantities of native goods of a proportionate value, have been sent away'. Much of this produce was exported to China through Hong Kong, with the additional capacity and increased demand driving up the prices of dried mushrooms and seafood in Osaka by 30 per cent.[35] Tripp's reports to Mitsubishi's Yokohama and Tokyo offices reveal the variety of cargo transported on the line. Freight carried to Japan included sugar, Manila rope, and yarn. Camphor, raw silk, and copper travelled in the opposite direction, much of it coming to Hong Kong for transshipment to European destinations and India.[36]

The carriage of freight came with its own issues, as evidenced by correspondence between the company and Captain Walker during the early days of the Hong Kong service. Several letters relate to claims made against Mitsubishi for damaged cargo. One mentions 296.90 dollars paid out for ninety-one bags of sugar ruined by oil leaking through the decks of the *Niigata Maru* during the voyage home.[37] The increasing number of claims led Mitsubishi to institute a policy requiring whichever crew member was at fault to cover one-half of the compensation costs.[38]

Japan's marine insurance industry was in the early stages of its development in the 1870s, with the market dominated by foreign insurers, such as Jardine Matheson & Co., who represented the Canton Marine Insurance Company in Yokohama.[39] However, as in all other areas related to trade and military expertise, the Meiji government was keen to lessen its reliance on foreign know-how and establish its own institutions. In the same year as the start of its Hong Kong service, Mitsubishi took a stake in Japan's first insurance company, the Tokio Marine Insurance Company, which was formally launched on August 1, 1879.[40]

Crew numbers for the *Niigata Maru* and *Takasago Maru* in 1880 totalled seventy-five per vessel. Onboard occupations included first- and second-class sailors, oilmen, coalmen, watchmen, painters, and pilots.[41] Mitsubishi employed a stewardess only as needed, to attend to 'lady passenger[s] from Hongkong'.[42] The nationality of the crew was diverse, with European captains and pursers, and Chinese or Japanese carpenters, stewards, and chefs. The ships had six chefs each, four Chinese and two Japanese, with one of the Japanese chefs catering to first-class passengers. Separately, two cooks per ship prepared the meals for the crew.

While Mitsubishi was making great strides in training up Japanese personnel for its growing shipping concerns, the company still relied extensively on foreign expertise, particularly in the more senior positions. The list of thirty-six ship commanders posted under Mitsubishi's Tokyo entry in the 1879 *Chronicle & Directory* included two Japanese names, while that of the twenty-nine chief engineers had none.[43]

Captains were paid per voyage – which in the case of the Yokohama to Hong Kong route took nine days in each direction – averaging between 1,900 and 2,200 yen each time, with an additional 50 yen pilotage allowance.[44] This was a handsome sum when compared with the monthly maximum of 500 yen made by Mitsubishi's Japanese employees.[45] The pay for less skilled sailors was divided into two categories, first and second class, and was dependent on an individual's experience and ability. A first-class ordinary seaman might earn 11 yen per trip.[46] Finding and retaining quality crew was clearly a challenge, though correspondence from senior Mitsubishi executives reveals that they were keen to hire Japanese over European or Chinese seamen wherever possible. In a letter sent shortly before the launch of the Hong Kong service, for example, the company advised Walker that it intended to 'do away with the Chinese Oilers on board [his] command' and was looking for 'some good Japanese to replace them'.[47]

Honda Masajirō: Mitsubishi's First General Manager in Hong Kong

Born in Nagasaki in the mid-1840s, Honda was of commoner rather than *samurai* stock. He joined Tsukumo Shōkai as a salesman in Osaka in 1870 and was leading a team of ten when the company became independent from the Tosa domain two years later. Honda suffered from ill health and was put on paid, extended sick leave for twenty months before returning to the position of sales clerk at the renamed Mitsubishi Shōkai's Nagasaki branch in August 1874. Mitsubishi's support during this period demonstrates how much it valued his shipping expertise. Honda was involved

Figure 4.4: Iwasaki Yatarō (first row, second from left) and Mitsubishi executives, circa 1877. Honda Masajirō is in the back row, directly behind Iwasaki. (Source: The Mitsubishi Archives.)

in the launch of the Yokohama to Shanghai line in early 1875 and worked as a shipping clerk and cashier at Mitsubishi's office on the Bund. By the end of 1876, he was back in Tokyo where he headed up the Procurement Department and provided interpretation services.[48] In December 1878, Honda took on the post of general manager of the firm's Yokohama branch, likely in preparation for his future leadership role in Hong Kong.[49]

Honda arrived in the city aboard a Messageries Maritimes ship on September 27, 1879, barely a week before the launch of the service.[50] He came without his family and resided in a room above the Mitsubishi offices at 6 Queen's Road.[51] As explained by Honda himself in a company report sent a couple of months after his arrival, this was a common arrangement for newly established Japanese enterprises in Hong Kong. Another distinguishing feature of his posting was that, for the first time, he was paid in silver dollars rather than yen. As Hong Kong general manager, he received a monthly salary of 125 dollars, which increased to 130 dollars after the start of the service.[52]

Honda devoted the majority of his first, handwritten report to Mitsubishi headquarters, drafted in November or December 1879, to his impressions of the city rather than a detailed evaluation of the business environment. He was impressed by the number of large ships the harbour accommodated and appreciated Hong Kong's status as a free port, with only a 10-dollar lighthouse tax required for every 1,000 tons of cargo carried. He describes the area surrounding Queen's Road where the Mitsubishi office was located, not far from the five-storey Hongkong Hotel and General Post Office, the two tallest buildings in the city at that time.

> If you turn left at the hotel and walk half a block, you will see the telegraph office on your left and the beautiful three-storey building sporting the Mitsubishi Mail Steamship Company's signage in Chinese characters on your right. The office occupies the ground floor and the top floor serves as the residence for the general manager, etc. The second floor belongs to an unconnected family. Next door to the right are the premises of Kōgyō Shōkai (廣業商會), with the third floor also reserved for living quarters. This is a common practice in this port. . . . Other than our own, the most famous Japanese companies in town are Mitsui Bussan Kaisha (三井物産會社) and Kōgyō Shōkai. As to the number of Japanese residents here, I hear that there are around thirty.[53]

Descriptions of Hong Kong's major tourist attractions, including City Hall and Dent's Fountain, the Botanic Gardens, and the Peak, follow.[54] Honda was taken with the imposing colonial architecture, efficient policing, and well-maintained streets, which were brilliantly lit by gaslight at night. He was also impressed by the abundance of greenery and exotic birds he encountered in the Botanic Gardens. By contrast, he was critical of the largely Chinese areas of the city to the west of the Praya, which he found crowded, filthy, and smelly, with food stalls on every street corner, and was disgusted by people eating as they walked. He was particularly shocked by the widespread consumption of opium among the Chinese population and the lack of any attempt by the Chinese government to control this trade.

Honda's remarks on the number of ships in the harbour, the city's status as a free port, and its policing arrangements echo those of the noted Victorian traveller Isabella Bird (1831–1904). Bird sojourned for a couple of weeks in Hong Kong after spending seven months in Japan, arriving on December 26, 1878.[55] In her account of her travels in the region, *The Golden Chersonese and the Way Thither*, which was first published in 1883, Bird referred to the city's 'magnificent harbour' as 'the naval and commercial

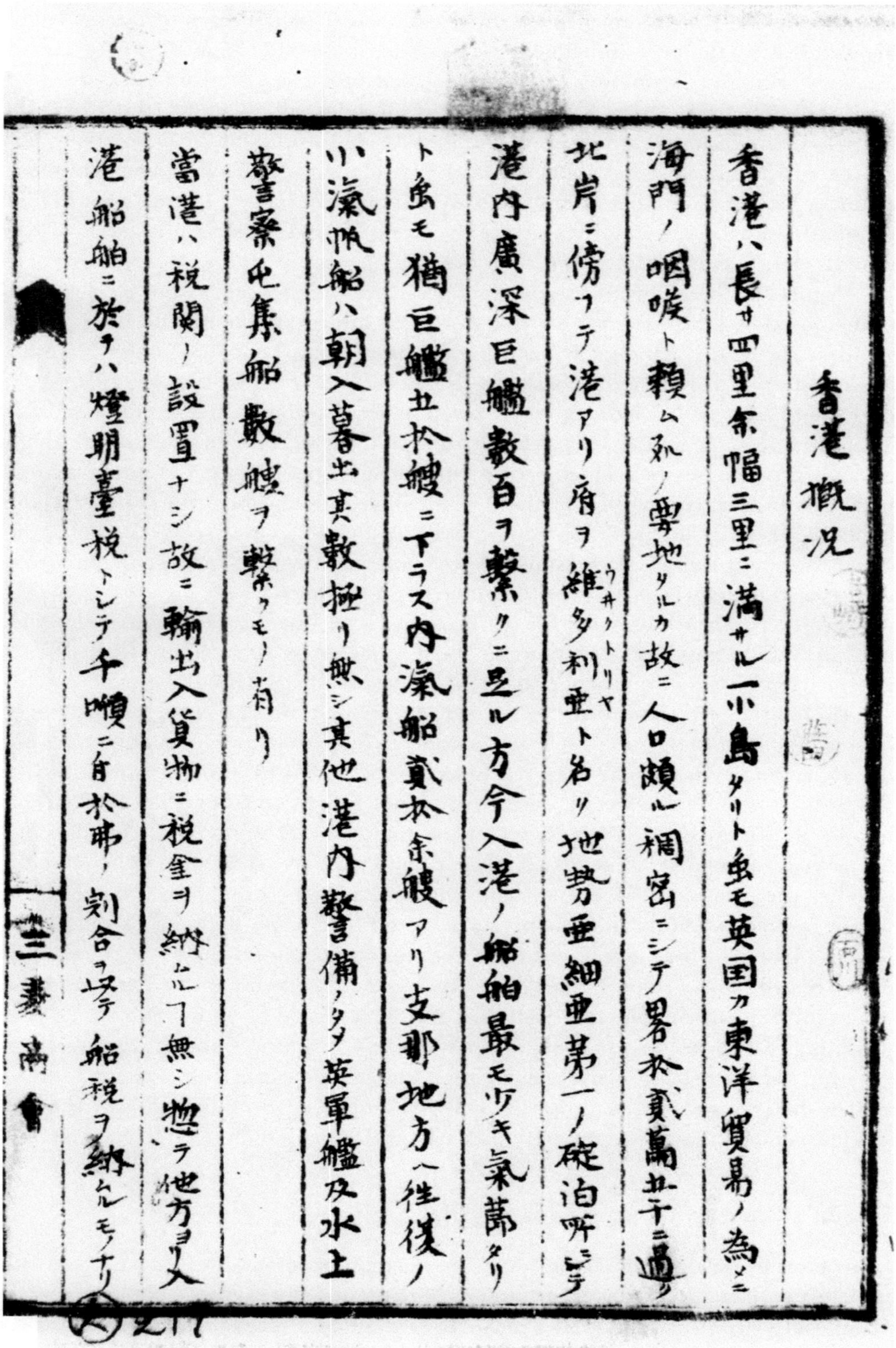

香港概況

香港ハ長サ四里余幅三里ニ満サル一小島タリト雖モ英国カ東洋貿易ノ為メニ

海門ノ咽喉ト頼ムヘキノ要地タルカ故ニ人口頗ル稠密ニシテ署ハ貳萬五十二ニ過キス

北岸ニ傍フテ港アリ府ヲ維多利亜ト名リ地勢亜細亜第一ノ碇泊所ニテ

港内廣深巨艦數百ヲ繋クニ足ル方今入港ノ船舶最モ少キ氣萬タリ

トモ猶巨艦立於艘ニ下ラス内港船貳本余艘アリ支那地方ハ性後ノ

小蒸帆船ハ朝入暮出真敷挽リ無シ真他港内警備ノタ英軍艦及水上

警言察屯集船數艘ヲ繋クモノ有リ

當港ハ税関ノ設置ナシ故ニ輸出入貨物ニ税金ヲ納ルニ無シ惣テ他方ヨリ入

港船舶ニ於テハ燈明臺税ヽシテ千噸ニ付於弗ノ割合ヲ以テ船税ヲ納ルモノナリ

Figure 4.5: A page from Honda Masajirō's first report on Hong Kong written shortly after his arrival in 1879. (Source: The Mitsubishi Archives.)

terminus of the Suez Canal'. To the three and a half million tons of freight entering and leaving the port annually 'must be added thousands of smaller native boats
of every build and rig trading to Hongkong, not only from the Chinese coasts and
rivers, but from Siam, Japan, and Cochin China. Besides the "P. and O," the *Messageries
Maritimes*, the Pacific Mail Company, the Eastern and Australian Mail Company, the
Japanese "Mitsu Bichi" [sic.] Mail Company, etc., all regular mail lines, it has a number
of lines of steamers trading to England, America, and Germany.'[56] Bird's inclusion of
Mitsubishi was obviously a mistake, since the Hong Kong service did not start until ten
months after her visit.[57]

Honda concluded his seven-page report with a brief mention of the good reputation enjoyed by Japanese coal in Hong Kong and hinted at potential business opportunities. He wrote that coal from the Takashima mine (高島炭鉱) near Nagasaki
was cheaper than Australian coal and, therefore, preferred by suppliers.[58] Indeed,
coal would become a major source of revenue for Mitsubishi after it purchased the
Takashima mine in spring 1881. The first mine in Japan to be mechanised through
the efforts of the Nagasaki-based Scottish merchant Thomas Blake Glover, Takashima
had been briefly nationalised by the new Meiji government before passing into the
hands of the politician GOTŌ Shōjirō (後藤象二郎). Gotō's purchase was funded by the
British company Jardine Matheson & Co. and, after a series of calamities, the firm sold
its shares to Iwasaki, who returned the mine to profitability.[59]

Jardine continued as agent for the mine in Hong Kong for a year after the sale,
until Mitsubishi appointed its shipping agent to take over the role in March 1882.[60]
Letters from Tripp to the manager of the Takashima colliery, KAWADA Koichirō (川田
小一郎; 1836–1896), sent during the first year of his appointment, detail the challenges
of convincing customers to purchase its product. Takashima's main competitors were
Australian and Welsh, widely referred to as Cardiff, coal, with the latter preferred by
the British naval establishment, despite its higher freight costs. In April 1883, Welsh
lump coal was priced at 10–10.25 dollars per ton, Australian at 6.25–6.75 dollars per
ton, and Takashima at 5.60–5.90 dollars per ton. Prices also fluctuated depending on
whether the coal was sold directly from the ship or from a godown, or warehouse.
Tripp gradually won over new clients, such as the China Sugar Refining Company.[61]

The letters further hint at efforts to counter competition from lower-priced coal
dust from the Miike mines (三池炭鉱). The Japanese government had acquired the
mines in 1873 and appointed Mitsui Bussan Kaisha as sole agent in 1876. Miike coal
was largely sold to customers in Shanghai in the 1870s, but there was clearly interest in
entering the Hong Kong market. In addition to selling its coal, Tripp sometimes dealt
with ad hoc requests for items for the colliery. Indeed, one of his first tasks as agent
was the acquisition of a fireproof Milner's safe, which he duly shipped to Nagasaki.[62]

Honda's Death

Honda was living alone in Hong Kong. His situation prompted Consul Andō to write
to both Yatarō and his younger brother, IWASAKI Yanosuke (岩崎彌之助; 1851–1908),
Mitsubishi's vice president, in December 1879 to suggest that Honda's family be permitted to join him. Andō argued that Honda was in the city for the long term and fully
committed to making the new line a success; having his loved ones with him would

A Japanese Ship in Victoria Harbour 71

only provide further impetus to do well.[63] The Iwasakis concurred and Honda's wife, Sato (左登), and ten-year-old son, Fukujirō (福治郎), travelled to the city, arriving on March 1, 1880.[64] Though this reunion lifted his spirits, Honda's health deteriorated and he passed away from consumption on November 2, 1880, aged thirty-five.[65]

The last few weeks of Honda's life are detailed in a report submitted by KANDA Aijirō (神田愛次郎), an office manager aboard the *Sumida Maru* (隅田丸), to Mitsubishi president Iwasaki Yatarō, dated October 29, 1880.[66] Following the arrival of the *Sumida Maru* in Hong Kong on October 24, Kanda received an urgent update on Honda's medical condition. Honda had travelled to the Guangzhou area in early October to recuperate, and Mitsubishi had hoped that his health was sufficiently improved for him to return to Kobe aboard the *Sumida Maru* when it departed Hong Kong on October 30. However, Kanda found Honda vomiting blood and in no state to make the trip. Following a discussion between Tripp and the Dutch captain of the *Sumida Maru*, H. Hubenet, they sought permission from Mitsubishi headquarters for Kanda to remain in Hong Kong and monitor Honda's situation in the hope that his condition might allow his transfer to Kobe in the future. Honda's wife Sato was grateful for his presence as she did not speak any English and could not communicate with the doctors and others assisting her husband.[67]

Commenting on Honda's medical treatment, Kanda advised that Consul Andō and Tripp had ensured that he was receiving the best available care. This included giving him milk, a beverage that few Japanese were accustomed to drinking, to try and boost his strength.[68] A private physician, Dr Richard O'Brien, assisted by his colleague, Dr William Hartigan, visited Honda at least three times a day and were on call day and night should their services be required. Honda's wife and servants remained constantly at his side to provide comfort and support. Despite their efforts, Honda succumbed to his illness and a telegram was sent to Mitsubishi headquarters with the news of his death.[69] Iwasaki Yatarō immediately ordered his Hong Kong staff to do their utmost with regard to his funeral arrangements and had all the firm's ships fly the Mitsubishi house flag at half-mast in Honda's honour.[70]

Local English-language newspapers also carried announcements of his passing:

> We regret to have to record the death of Mr. Honda, the Japanese agent of the Mitsu Bishi Company at this port [of Hong Kong], which took place last night. The deceased died at the early age of thirty-five. Mr. Honda has not enjoyed good health here since his arrival about a year ago; and he had shown symptoms for several months back of rapid consumption; so that his death was not by any means a surprise to his friends. He was a Japanese gentleman of a very quiet disposition, who earned the respect and esteem of all with whom he had to deal. Lately he has been but little seen in business circles; but he will be remembered by many as one of the most amiable representatives of his nation that has ever resided in this Colony.[71]

The company's original intention was for Honda to be buried in Hong Kong. However, his brothers informed Mitsubishi that Honda's distraught mother, who was over seventy years old, very much wanted his remains returned to Japan so that he could be interred in the family grave in Nagasaki.[72]

Mitsubishi covered the costs of Honda's treatment in Hong Kong as well as the repatriation of his embalmed body to Kobe, spending a total of 144.78 silver dollars. This included 5.85 dollars for nutritious milk to boost his strength, 46.17 dollars for

Figure 4.6: The grave of Honda Masajirō, the Mitsubishi Mail Steamship Company's first Hong Kong office general manager, who died in 1880. The Japan Seafarers Relief Association erected the monument over thirty years after his death. (Photo credit: Miyuki Kume.)

medicine, 54 dollars for a lidded coffin, and 1 dollar for his death certificate.[73] Though Honda was not buried in Happy Valley, an obelisk was later erected in his memory, which still stands today.[74]

To the great dismay of Mitsubishi executives, Honda's death was followed just six months later by that of his junior Hong Kong branch office colleague, MURAKAMI Hideshi (邨上秀士).[75] Murakami, who was originally from Ōita (大分) in Kyushu and had been in the city for only a year, passed away from remittent fever, or 'Hongkong fever', on June 8, 1881, at the age of twenty-one years and eight months.[76] The company covered the costs of Murakami's burial, totalling 261.63 yen (approximately 160 silver dollars). Unlike in Honda's case, Murakami's corpse was transferred to the Hong Kong Cemetery in a horse-drawn carriage and laid to rest there.[77]

> [Murakami's] funeral took place [on June 8, 1881], and amongst those taking part in it were the Japanese Consul, Mr Taro Ando; the Captain of the Company's steamer *Takasago Maru*, Captain Young; the Agent of the Company at Hongkong, Mr H. J. Tripp; the European and Japanese pursers of the *Takasago Maru*, and, we believe, all the Japanese residents in this Colony. The coffin was carried to the grave in the Protestant Cemetery by six sailors of the steamer. Every mark of respect was paid to the deceased, showing the high and respected position he had occupied in the minds of his compatriots.[78]

A Japanese Ship in Victoria Harbour

Japanese Seamen's Graves

Honda's and Murakami's are by no means the only monuments related to the shipping industry in the Hong Kong Cemetery. Indeed, many of the earliest identifiable graves belong to sailors. The Tariff Convention of 1866 permitted not only overseas travel and trade, but also employment on foreign ships. As new trading routes opened and both Japanese and foreign shipping concerns expanded, Asian seamen, who were cheaper to hire than their European or American counterparts, became very much in demand for rank-and-file positions. Japanese sailors competed with Chinese, Indian, Filipino, and Malay seafarers for jobs.[79]

In an effort to control their movements when ashore in Hong Kong, ordinary sailors were required to stay at designated boarding houses. The government issued licences for these establishments annually on the condition that they conform to strict guidelines, such as not selling alcohol and, later, as part of governmental efforts to curb the spread of venereal diseases, that they report on the health of their boarders. As discussed in the previous chapter, Japanese seamen were also the targets of a practice known as crimping, whereby unscrupulous individuals of various nationalities, among them Japanese boarding house owners, enlisted sailors through swindling or coercion.[80]

In the 1840s, charitable and other organisations emerged to assist seafarers in Hong Kong, including a sailor's hospital and, in 1861, a home. However, these provisions were mainly aimed at supporting European or American seamen.[81] Japanese sailors who found themselves down on their luck in Hong Kong had nowhere to turn to besides the Japanese Consulate. YOKOTE Umejirō (横手梅次郎) was one such unfortunate.

In an appeal for aid dated October 19, 1885, Yokote details how he ended up in the city, destitute and sick. Originally from Nagasaki, he volunteered and served aboard the Japanese navy's *Jingei* (迅鯨; *Swift Whale*) from December 1878 to April 1883. He then joined Mitsubishi as a crew member on the *Niigata Maru* for seven months. There followed a series of short-term jobs on foreign ships, sailing up and down the Chinese coast, with a brief stay in Tianjin, and to Japan. He eventually wound up in Xiamen, where he was living before coming to Hong Kong. He fell ill with chronic diarrhoea soon after his arrival and was in a serious condition at the time of his writing. Though it seems the consulate provided assistance, it came too late and Yokote died at the Government Civil Hospital on October 31. The consulate paid 20 dollars for his gravestone, a relatively reasonable amount when compared with that expended for Murakami's interment. Yokote's one-metre-tall obelisk sits directly behind the far taller monument to *karayuki-san* KIYA Saki (木谷佐喜) in the Hong Kong Cemetery. Certain Japanese visitors later remarked on this disparity in height with some distaste, shocked that a prostitute's grave marker should be grander than that of a former navy sailor.[82]

Life onboard Japanese commercial and military vessels, as well as foreign-owned ships, was tough and sickness was rife. SHIMIZU Masanosuke (清水政之助), a seaman from Wakayama (和歌山), near Osaka, serving aboard the Japanese naval corvette *Nissin*, died in Hong Kong of diarrhoea in 1879. In addition to his own grave, he was subsequently commemorated in a monument to seven seafarers erected by the Japan Seafarers Relief Association in the 1890s.[83] 'KAUSTIONI Oto', a fireman aboard the German-owned S.S. *Brutus*, also passed away from diarrhoea at the Government

Civil Hospital on September 9, 1881.[84] These are just two of the at least sixty Meiji-era Japanese seamen's graves in the Hong Kong Cemetery.[85]

Criss-crossing the Globe with Japanese Lines

From its very establishment, the Mitsubishi Mail Steamship Company faced competition from political and commercial rivals, such as Mitsui Bussan Kaisha, anxious to break its monopoly over military and commercial shipping and to find alternatives to the high rates it charged. The firm's early fortunes depended on government contracts and subsidies, and on whether politicians favourable to Iwasaki were in office. After several unsuccessful attempts, disenchanted merchants, with the backing of Iwasaki's political opponents, established the Kyōdo Un'yu Kaisha (共同運輸會社; Union Transport Company/KUK) in July 1882. Shareholders in the new company included the government, Mitsui, and the Tokio Marine Insurance Company.[86] Three years of intense competition followed, with the KUK and its newly acquired ships challenging Mitsubishi on established routes, driving down shipping rates. As a result, Mitsubishi cut back on some of its international lines, discontinuing the Hong Kong service in May 1884 after 119 voyages.[87]

The KUK and Mitsubishi encountered a further challenge in the form of the Osaka Shosen Kaisha (大阪商船會社; Osaka Mercantile S.S. Co., Ltd./OSK), an association of fifty-five individual shipowners with a complement of ninety-three ships, established on May 1, 1884. By this time, Mitsubishi's shipping income had fallen by almost 50 per cent and the KUK was failing to turn a profit. To resolve this counterproductive state of affairs, the government hosted a series of discussions between the KUK and Mitsubishi, which ultimately resulted in the merger of the two companies and the establishment of the Nippon Yusen Kaisha (日本郵船會社; Japan Mail Steamship Company/NYK) in October 1885.

The launch of the new firm came eight months after the death of Iwasaki Yatarō on February 7, 1885. In a handwritten memoir recounting his life in Japan, Wilson Walker praises the Mitsubishi founder for his vision and business acumen:

> It is not in my power to chronicle the strenuous times, the constant unremitting labour of Mr Iwasaki Yataro himself or of his two able Co Directors, Messrs Ishikawa [Shichizai] and Kawada [Koichirō], for on these three gentlemen the whole labour of organising this the first large business in Japan – it devolved on these men first to learn and devise, then to instruct subordinates, with no precedent to guide them, no shipping law, nothing, they just took hold of the raw material and have left the Nippon Yusen Kaisha behind them as a monument to their gigantic labour.[88]

Yatarō's younger brother Yanosuke succeeded him to the leadership of Mitsubishi. Though Mitsubishi remained involved in the NYK, with several of its executives taking key posts and twenty-nine of its steamships acquired by the new entity, it gradually moved away from shipping to concentrate on its other interests, including the Takashima and Yoshioka mines, as well as the Nagasaki shipyard, which it had leased from the government since 1884.

By the beginning of the twentieth century, both the NYK and OSK had established routes in and out of Hong Kong. NYK had services to Europe, India, Seattle in the United States, and Australia, via Thursday Island, that all passed through the city, while the OSK served Taiwan and ports on the eastern coast of China. They were joined by the period's third major Japanese shipping company, Toyo Kisen Kaisha (東洋汽船; Oriental Steamship Company), which had launched a mail service between Hong Kong and San Francisco in 1898.[89] Iwasaki Yatarō's vision of Japanese lines criss-crossing the globe had become reality.

As foreseen by Honda, Japanese coal was very much in demand in East Asia in the late nineteenth and early twentieth centuries. Stable supplies of coal and its by-products, such as coke, were needed to power growing military and commercial fleets and accounted for the bulk of Japan's exports to Hong Kong. An increase in the use of mechanised mining technology ensured Japanese mines could meet production targets. The generally lower price and acceptable quality of Japanese coal made it attractive to European and American shipping companies operating in the region. Between 1891 and 1895, Japanese coal made up close to 80 per cent of coal imports into Hong Kong, averaging 432,371 tons annually, versus just 30,196 tons for British (Cardiff) coal and 27,260 tons for Australian coal. The main sources of export coal in the 1870s and 1880s were Mitsubishi's Takashima mine and the Miike coal mines managed by Mitsui. The more abundant supplies of coal from the Chikuhō mines (筑豊炭田) near Moji (門司), now part of the city of Kitakyushu in Fukuoka prefecture, gradually replaced the more limited stocks of Takashima coal in the 1890s.[90]

The colonial government's annual records of the ships and their tonnage entering the Hong Kong harbour provide a clear picture of the huge growth of Japanese merchant shipping and of Japan's trade with the colony during this period. However, since Hong Kong was a free port, these tables do not reveal any information on the nature of the cargo carried; officials only reported on imports of opium and sugar, which constituted major sources of governmental revenue.

In 1872, just eight Japanese vessels entered Hong Kong, compared with 1,873 British ships.[91] The number rose to twenty-eight for 1880, following the start of Mitsubishi's Yokohama to Hong Kong service.[92] In 1901, 336 Japanese vessels with a total tonnage of 692,981 entered the colony and Japan was the point of departure for the highest number of all vessels – Japanese and foreign – coming into Hong Kong that year, after the 'Coast of China' and Macau.[93] Numbers dipped in 1904 and 1905, with many of the Japanese steamers requisitioned for the Russo-Japanese War.[94] Trade soon recovered and by 1912, the final year of the Meiji era, Japanese vessels entering Hong Kong outnumbered French steamers, coming fourth only to Chinese, British, and German craft.[95]

MIHARA Andrew Shigekichi (三原繁吉; 1862–1946?) served as NYK's manager in Hong Kong for ten years, from 1897 to 1907. Nagasaki-based journalist INOKUCHI Ushiji (井口丑二; 1871–1930) recalled meeting Mihara during his short stay in the colony in April 1899. NYK occupied the second floor of a building on the Central waterfront at the time and business was booming. The busy office employed several Japanese, as well as Chinese, Dutch, and Indian staff.[96]

Mihara was responsible for exploring new route opportunities during the crucial period following the end of the Russo-Japanese War, making exploratory trips to Bangkok and Yangon [Rangoon] in the latter part of 1905.[97] Unlike Honda, US- and Japan-educated Mihara was proficient in English and was posted to New York after his time in the colony.[98] Despite this linguistic advantage, life in Hong Kong remained challenging. When A. S. Mihara departed the city aboard the NYK's *Aki Maru* in September

Table 4.2: Number and nationality of vessels entering Hong Kong ports, 1872–1912

Year	Japanese	British	German	French	American	Chinese (incl. junks)	Other Foreign
1872	8	1,873	501	184	150	28,340	338
1880	28	2,073	246	114	139	24,075	126
1901	336	3,360	844	328	111	17,874	292
1904	51	5,099	862	484	78	18,462	525
1905	29	5,741	888	500	66	16,990	650
1912	592	5,462	637	496	70	13,799	632

Source: *Hong Kong Blue Book* for 1872, 1880, 1901, 1904, 1905, and 1912.

Figure 4.7: A sketch of the Hong Kong waterfront included in Inokuchi Ushiji's travelogue. (Source: 井口 [Inokuchi], 1904, 37.)

1907, he left behind the grave that he and his wife Masa had erected to the memory of their two infant sons in the Hong Kong Cemetery.[99]

Senior employees of established shipping and trading companies, like Honda and Mihara, belonged to the upper echelons of Japanese society in Hong Kong during the Meiji era. They represented the image of modernity and technological advancement that their government was so keen to project, in contrast to the prostitutes, boarding house operators, and associated small tradespeople that made up the other half of the Japanese community. However, not all within this elite group enjoyed the same status. The consul and executives of multinational enterprises, such as Mitsui Bussan Kaisha, Nippon Yusen Kaisha, and later the Yokohama Specie Bank, occupied the top-most positions in this hierarchy, while the managers of sizeable though less prestigious concerns sat slightly lower down the ladder.

5

A Developing International Business Elite

> It will be lonely living in a foreign place, far from home, but I am excited at the thought of competing with Europeans and Americans in a big international market and trying my luck.[1]
>
> [Ataka Yakichi describing his arrival in Hong Kong in 1895 in his memoirs]

The author of these words, ATAKA Yakichi (安宅彌吉; 1873–1949), arrived in Hong Kong in 1895 to work for the Osaka-based trading firm of Kusakabe & Co. He and other ambitious young Japanese like him who had received a more outward-looking education sought to take advantage of the burgeoning trade ties between Japan and Hong Kong to start their own operations or secure international postings. With the opening of the country, both newly established concerns, such as Mitsubishi, and commercial ventures of long standing, such as Mitsui Bussan Kaisha, were keen to expand overseas and guard against the American, European, and Chinese traders who were capitalising on the new economic opportunities offered by Japan's treaty ports. The Meiji government was intent on creating the expertise and networks necessary to compete with foreign interests and provided many of these Japanese companies with significant subsidies to help finance their growth. Three key types of enterprise led this expansion: shipping, with Mitsubishi and, later, Nippon Yusen Kaisha (NYK); trading, with Mitsui Bussan Kaisha; and banking, with the Yokohama Specie Bank (YSB).[2]

Japanese businesses operating in Hong Kong during the Meiji era were very much what historian Joshua A. Fogel terms 'multipurpose enterprises', engaging in the trade of a variety of different products in line with fluctuating demand, as well as acting as agents for different firms.[3] Their managers initially came from diverse backgrounds and had often spent time gaining experience in Nagasaki, Yokohama, or Shanghai before taking up their positions in Hong Kong. However, growing international operations increasingly looked to hire graduates with some form of tertiary education and, usually, of *samurai* lineage for managerial-level posts. The colony served as a stepping stone, with several high-flyers moving on to branches in Europe or the United States after their stints in the city.

These early executives had to deal with a complex environment, navigating between the Chinese and other foreign communities in the city. The Sino-Japanese War of 1894–1895 further complicated relations. The Treaty of Shimonoseki (下関条

約), which brought an end to the war, effectively ceded Taiwan to Japan and required China to pay an indemnity of 360,000,000 yen.[4] Chinese anger at the Qing government's acceptance of these terms festered over time, eventually coming to a head in 1908 with the *Tatsu Maru* affair (辰丸事件).

The colony's sanitary conditions in the late nineteenth century were poor and disease was rampant, with many company executives, such as Mitsubishi's first general manager in Hong Kong, electing to come alone. The city's hygiene gradually improved in the 1890s, however, and it became more common for Japanese expatriates to be accompanied by their families and raise their children in Hong Kong. Together with the consul and other senior diplomats, the Mitsui, NYK, and YSB executives formed the upper echelons of the Japanese community in the city: they established their own club, the Nippon Club, in 1905, featured on the colony's jury lists, and were guests at Hong Kong's main events on the social calendar.[5] The more regional nature of Kusakabe & Co.'s business meant that Ataka, despite coming from a similar social and educational background to the higher-ranked employees of larger operations, found himself on the fringes of this elite circle.

Hong Kong's First Japanese Firms

In 1869, the Meiji government formally incorporated the island of Ezo (蝦夷), home to the Ainu people, and renamed it Hokkaido (北海道).[6] The new regime quickly established a trade office and its head despatched an employee to Shanghai and then Hong Kong to investigate the market potential for marine produce, such as *konbu*, or kelp, as well as other dried seafood items popular with the Chinese. The report was favourable, stating that the government should ensure that it controlled the export of these foodstuffs rather than allow Chinese intermediaries to profit.[7]

The first Japanese trading firm to set up in Hong Kong was the Hokkaido-based, quasi-governmental entity Kōgyō Shōkai (廣業商會; Commercial Development Association). Started in 1876 under the leadership of Satsuma (薩摩; now part of Kagoshima prefecture) businessman KASANO Kumakichi (笠野熊吉; d. 1879), the enterprise specialised in the export of Hokkaido specialities, as well as matches and umbrellas.[8] Its Shanghai branch opened in August of the same year, followed soon by an operation in Hong Kong.[9]

Hong Kong Governor John Pope Hennessy visited Hokkaido during his three-month sojourn in Japan in the summer of 1879 and commented on the immense earning potential of the Hokkaido seafood industry. In a speech delivered in the port city of Hakodate (函館), he mentioned tasting 'well-cooked seaweeds' the previous evening, an experience he described as a 'not unpleasant sensation'. He went on to claim that 'before many years are past, the trade of Japan with China ought to be nearer to fifty millions than to ten millions of dollars, and your own contribution from Yesso [Hokkaido] six millions instead of $600,000'. Though the English-language press ridiculed Pope Hennessy's predictions, his words reinforced the Japanese government's conviction that there was money to be made.[10]

Kōgyō Shōkai enlisted KUSAKABE Heijirō (日下部平次郎; 1852–1899), who was already running his own trading business in Hong Kong, to help oversee its operations in the colony. Born in Tanba (丹波), a rural part of present-day Kyoto prefecture,

Kusakabe started his working life as a shop boy for a Chinese medicine wholesaler in Doshōmachi (道修町), Osaka, in the late 1860s.[11] Anxious to seek his fortune abroad, and with personal travel now possible, he allegedly stole money from his employer and escaped to Shanghai, where he picked up some English before eventually making his way to Hong Kong.[12] In 1877, realising the financial opportunities presented by the growing trade ties between the city and Osaka, Kusakabe established the Hong Kong branch of Kusakabe & Co. (日森洋行; romanised as Yat Sum), which sold Japanese chinaware and exported auction items to Japan.[13] He made up for his somewhat limited English with his confidence in his abilities, and Kōgyō Shōkai viewed his sales experience as an asset.

With its early successes in cornering the market for sales of dried seafood to China, Kōgyō Shōkai was a major player in the modernising Meiji economy, on a par with Mitsubishi and Mitsui. Kasano of Kōgyō Shōkai featured along with Iwasaki Yatarō of Mitsubishi (岩崎彌太郎), Masuda Takashi (益田孝) of Mitsui, and Shibusawa Eiichi (澁澤榮一) of Japan's First National Bank on an 1878 woodblock published in one of the leading Japanese newspapers of the time. The work portrays the country's four most prominent industrialists discussing relief efforts for the victims of the northern China drought-induced famine of 1876–1879.[14]

Figure 5.1: An 1878 woodblock portraying Japan's four most prominent industrialists discussing relief efforts for the victims of the northern China drought-induced famine. From left: Kasano Kumakichi of Kōgyō Shōkai, Masuda Takashi of Mitsui, Iwasaki Yatarō of Mitsubishi, and Shibusawa Eiichi of Japan's First National Bank. (Source: 朝野新聞 [*Chōya Shimbun*], March 18, 1878, Tokyo Metropolitan Library.)

The death of GODAI Tomoatsu (五代友厚; 1836–1885), the Satsuma entrepreneur who assumed leadership of Kōgyō Shōkai in 1879, and new financial policies unfavourable to the company led to its eventual closure in 1890.[15] Kusakabe & Co., meanwhile, maintained its operations in Osaka and Hong Kong.

A Young Entrepreneur in Hong Kong

Kusakabe was always on the lookout for enterprising young men who, like himself, were willing to try their luck abroad. Born in Kanazawa, Ishikawa prefecture (石川県金沢), Ataka Yakichi graduated from the Tokyo Higher Commercial School (東京商業學校; today's Hitotsubashi University) in 1895. Keen to start a career in international trade, he applied for various jobs before learning of an opportunity at Kusakabe & Co. in Hong Kong from one of his classmates. Against the objections of his professor at the school, who claimed that the company was too small and Hong Kong a death trap, rife with plague and malaria, Ataka made up his mind to accept the post. As general manager, he would earn a monthly salary of 25 yen, with meals and adequate accommodation provided. His remuneration was rather low when compared with the earnings of his counterparts at more prestigious firms.[16]

The twenty-two-year-old Ataka set out for Hong Kong in late October 1895.[17] The ship made a stopover in Shanghai, where Ataka met up with Yokohama Specie

Figure 5.2: A photograph of twenty-two-year-old Ataka Yakichi taken in 1895, shortly after his arrival in Hong Kong. (Source: 安宅産業社史編集室 編 [Ataka & Co. Corporate History Project, ed.], 1968, 24.)

Bank employee HIROTA Kōkichi (廣田耕吉), who was thrilled to see him as visitors from Japan were rare. Ataka and Hirota came from the same domain and had studied together at Kanazawa Vocational School (金澤專門學校).[18] Ataka left Shanghai on November 3 and sailed into the British colony on November 6.[19] Much like the Japanese students who had passed through the city thirty years before him, he was impressed by Hong Kong's modern infrastructure and imposing buildings, as well as its more recent transition to electric lighting. He wrote in his memoir that 'in Japan, they say that if you see Hong Kong, you have seen a part of Europe, and these reports are true'.[20]

In 1898, Kusakabe & Co. counted three employees in Hong Kong: Kusakabe, Ataka, and a teenage errand boy, HIROSE Matsujirō (廣瀬松次郎), who had joined the firm three years earlier, aged just fourteen. It now occupied premises in the busy thoroughfare of Queen's Road Central and had added the manufacturing of glassware and lampshades to its portfolio of commercial initiatives.[21] Ataka was key to expanding Kusakabe & Co.'s lucrative sugar trade. He built up his own network for purchasing raw sugar from Java and later developed a partnership with one of the most prominent Indonesian Chinese trading companies, Kian Gwan (建源號).[22]

Ataka and Hirose shared the same accommodation and a strong bond formed between them. They would set out together at 8 a.m., Ataka heading to the office and Hirose to a warehouse to pack sugar for shipping. Eight years his senior, Ataka took the teenager under his wing and taught him bookkeeping and English. The working day was long, ending at around 9 or 10 p.m., with no time left for leisure, and their salaries were too low to afford any luxuries.[23]

Hirose became ill with fever in May 1898 and a concerned Ataka had him admitted to hospital, only to discover that what he thought was a minor cold was actually the plague. Unable to visit Hirose at the quarantine facility where he was kept isolated, a distraught Ataka sent him a letter with his picture, but it was too late. His memoirs reveal the pain he felt at Hirose's death:

> Hirose was an intelligent boy, with a bright future ahead of him, so I taught him all I could. I was the only person he could count on and he worked hard. Yet, I could not visit him in his final hours. I could not even collect his body for burial. So I erected a gravestone in his memory in the Hong Kong Cemetery; this was the least I could do. . . . He sickened in a foreign land and his disease was fatal. He must have felt so alone and my heart still aches for him twenty years on.[24]

Hirose shares his imposing gravestone in the Hong Kong Cemetery with another Kusakabe & Co. employee, HORII Yasaburō (堀井彌三郎). Horii, originally from Shiga prefecture, came to Hong Kong in 1901.[25] He died of typhoid fever at the Peak Hospital on June 20, 1904, at the age of twenty-five. Ataka arranged for both his and Kusakabe's names to be inscribed on the single monument that honoured the two young men's lives.

Kusakabe, who resided mostly in Osaka, only visiting Hong Kong two to three times a year, passed away in October 1899. His son-in-law took over his affairs, rather incompetently, until his untimely death in 1904.[26] Ataka consequently established an independent company, though he retained 日森洋行/Yat Sum as his Hong Kong branch's name in Chinese.[27] Ataka & Co featured in the volume *Twentieth Century Impressions of Hong Kong, Shanghai, and Other Treaty Ports of China*, a 1908 compendium

A Developing International Business Elite

Figure 5.3: Ataka Yakichi erected the imposing grave of Kusakabe & Co. employees Hirose Matsujirō and Horii Yasaburō. The company's Chinese name, 日森洋行, is visible on the left-hand side of the photo. (Photo credit: Miyuki Kume.)

of the history, administration, industries, and commercial potential of various treaty ports and foreign settlements. The company's Hong Kong profile illustrates the 'multipurpose' nature of its activities:

> [Ataka & Co.] are largely interested in coal, yarn, sugar, rice, cotton, metals and practically every kind of Japanese and colonial merchandise, and control an irregular line of cargo steamers running between Hongkong, Japanese ports, Saigon [Ho Chi Minh City], Rangoon [Yangon], and Java. They are also the agents for the Japan Shipowners' Association, which has the charge of a fleet of over 130 vessels aggregating 300,000 tons; for the Nippon Marine Transport and Fire Insurance Co.; the Iwasaki Coal Mine; the Furukawa Coal Mine, and for the Omi Cotton Duck Co., of Japan, of whose canvas they sell very large quantities.[28]

Ataka & Co. and the *Tatsu Maru* Affair

On February 5, 1908, Qing officials boarded the Japanese ship *Tatsu Maru II* (第二辰丸) in the waters off the then Portuguese colony of Macau under suspicion of its purveying arms to anti-Qing revolutionaries in southern China. The ship, owned by Tatsuma Shōkai (辰馬商會), a member of the Japan Shipowners' Association, and captained by TERUMINE Hirokichi (照峰廣吉), had departed Kobe on January 26 with a cargo of coal, as well as marine and other products. Upon boarding the ship, the officials discovered at least 1,500 rifles and 40,000 rounds of ammunition. They proceeded to replace the Japanese flag with the Qing ensign and towed the ship to Whampoa, near present-day Guangzhou, where they placed the vessel and its cargo in custody.[29] Describing the scene in a letter to the ship's owner, Terumine wrote that 'no objection whatever would be listened to by the Chinese and should the steamer dare to weigh anchor or disobey their command the Chinese threatened to send her to the bottom in an instant. Under the situation [I] came to the final conclusion to follow the Chinese to Canton.'[30]

The Qing government's suspicions were not groundless. Japan had a large surplus of arms following the Russo-Japanese War of 1904–1905 and Japanese merchants found ready customers for them among anti-Qing revolutionaries in Guangdong. China and Portugal did not have a treaty clearly setting out territorial jurisdiction over the waters surrounding the Portuguese colony. This made Macau the preferred transshipment point for this arms trade.[31]

Nevertheless, the Japanese government responded with outrage to the boarding, stating that the arms had been shipped with all proper legal documentation by Awaya Shōkai (粟谷商會) in Osaka to a Macanese firm through the intermediary of Ataka & Co.[32] Furthermore, they claimed that the ship was not in Chinese territorial waters when it was boarded and that the removal of its Japanese flag was an insult. The incident led to intense and increasingly acrimonious negotiations between Tokyo and Beijing, with both sides relying on various documents and testimonies to justify their actions.[33] Journalists from around the world discussed the situation, advancing several suggestions to resolve the matter, such as appointing British and American intermediaries or referring the case to The Hague Arbitration Court.[34]

Ultimately, the Japanese government, threatening military action, put forward a five-point solution on March 13, 1908, which the Chinese government accepted two days later. The five conditions for a peaceful settlement, as reported in the March 14 issue of the London *Times*, included an apology and salute of the Japanese flag in the presence of the consul; the unconditional release of the vessel; payment of the cost of the arms under detention; China to investigate and take suitable measures against those responsible; and an indemnity for actual losses. As a conciliatory gesture, Japan undertook to cooperate in the task of preventing the smuggling of arms into China.[35]

Unfortunately, the agreement over the fate of the *Tatsu Maru* came too late for thirty-three-year-old Terumine Hirokichi. A native of Akō in Hyōgo prefecture (兵庫県 赤穂) who had previously served in the navy, Terumine was on his tenth voyage as the experienced captain of the *Tatsu Maru II*.[36] The climate of southern China did not suit him and he became sick, eventually passing away in Guangzhou from acute pneumonia on March 28, 1908. His body was conveyed to Hong Kong aboard the *Kiyo Maru* and he was interred in the Hong Kong Cemetery shortly thereafter.[37] Articles in the Japanese press announcing his death praised Terumine for his conduct throughout the crisis and claimed that he was planning to get married upon his return to Kobe.[38]

The *Tatsu Maru* incident took place in the context of extremely tense relations between Japan and China. Many Chinese were still angry at the terms of the Treaty of Shimonoseki, signed just thirteen years earlier, and the country's merchants faced increasing, and unwelcome, competition from the Japanese in the tea, sugar, silk, cotton yarn, and even porcelain export trade. In addition, the expansion of the Japanese commercial shipping fleet meant that Japanese trading firms could ship cargo directly to treaty ports in southern and northern China. They therefore relied less on Hong Kong as a transshipping centre, with local Chinese dealers losing out on this lucrative business.[39]

The Qing government's climbdown over the *Tatsu Maru* affair only exacerbated an already volatile situation, resulting in a call to boycott Japanese goods by Chinese merchants in Guangdong and Hong Kong. The boycott significantly impacted Japanese businesses, with exports to the colony down by 24 per cent in 1908 versus 1907.[40] A concerted attempt by Vice-Consul FUNATSU Tatsuichirō (船津辰一郎; 1873–1947) and major Japanese concerns, including Ataka & Co., to resolve the stand-off initially caused two days of rioting in early November 1908, which had to be put down by the police and British troops. However, the subsequent crackdown by the authorities and renewed efforts by the Japanese business community to mend ties were successful in bringing the boycott to a close by January 1909.[41] Commenting on the incident in his annual report, the colonial government's registrar general concluded that the 'Chinese passion for Japanese relishes' ultimately led to the movement's downfall.[42]

A prime example of Japanese attempts at rapprochement occurred on Saturday, July 17, 1909, aboard the Japanese navy cruiser *Otowa* (音羽). The vessel's senior officers held an 'at home' reception during its stay in the city, with a large number of Chinese merchants included in the invitation. Previously, important Japanese business and social occasions, such as Mitsubishi's 1879 tiffin, had but one or two prominent Chinese guests attending, if any. Japanese company representatives preferred to host separate gatherings for their Chinese counterparts. Hierarchy was maintained in the *Hongkong Telegraph*'s listing of the guests who attended the event, with European and American names appearing first, Chinese names last, and the Japanese in between – a reflection of their status in Hong Kong society. The same issue announced the promotion of Funatsu to full consul as a reward for his efforts both during and after the boycott.[43]

In the years after the *Tatsu Maru* affair, Ataka's business and family concerns increasingly kept him in Japan and he became too busy to travel to Hong Kong on a regular basis.[44] He eventually decided to sell Yat Sum to Kobe-based Suzuki & Co. (鈴木商店), one of the forerunners of today's Sojitz Corporation (双日).[45] From its headquarters in Osaka, Ataka & Co. would grow to become one of post–Second World War Japan's ten most prominent trading houses.[46]

Ataka is possibly best remembered outside Japan for his patronage of SUZUKI Teitarō Daisetsu (鈴木大拙, also known as D. T. Suzuki; 1870–1966). Ataka and Suzuki met while studying in Tokyo, where they lived in the same dormitory. A native of Kanazawa, Ishikawa prefecture, like Ataka, Suzuki was a scholar and author who introduced several generations of English speakers to Zen Buddhism. He spent eleven years in the United States, from 1897 to 1909, during which time he became fluent in English. Upon his return to Japan, and with the support of his American wife, Beatrice Erskine Lane, Suzuki launched *Eastern Buddhist*, Japan's first English-language journal on Buddhist studies. Towards the end of his life, he spent a number of years teaching at Columbia University, where his students included the composer John Cage and the author J. D. Salinger. Ataka supported Suzuki's endeavours throughout his life and financed many of his publications.[47]

Mitsui Bussan Kaisha

Mitsui Bussan Kaisha (三井; romanised as Sam Ching) opened its Hong Kong office in August 1878. Within a decade, it would become the city's largest and most prominent Japanese trading company. From the start of its operations in the colony, Mitsui looked to university-educated men from a *samurai* background to manage its interests. Unlike Kusakabe, who came from modest means, Mitsui's first lead agent, Saga-born SHUGYŌ Hiromichi (執行弘道; 1853–1927), was from an affluent family and had spent four years in the United States studying English and gaining expertise in foreign trade prior to coming to Hong Kong.[48]

The origins of the Mitsui Bussan Kaisha Trading Co. can be traced back to the seventeenth century. MITSUI Takatoshi (三井高利; 1622–1694) was born in Matsuzaka (松阪), in present-day Mie prefecture, and this was where he launched his first business, a small kimono store. In 1673, he moved to Edo to rejoin his brother and opened a successful drapery shop, Echigoya (越後屋; now better known as Mitsukoshi, 三越), and later a money exchange service.[49]

The Mitsui family and its, by then, considerable commercial interests weathered the upheaval of the Meiji Restoration, thanks, in part, to the foresight of entrepreneur MINOMURA Rizaemon (三野村利左衛門; 1821–1877), who advised its members to back the new regime. To limit the liability of the Mitsui holding company, Minomura restructured the firm to set up separate trading and banking entities in July 1876. He also looked outside the family to hire a new generation of forward-looking, university-educated managers, including MASUDA Takashi (益田孝; 1848–1938). Following discussions with INOUE Kaoru (井上馨; 1836–1915), a key figure in the new government, the Mitsui Bussan Kaisha Trading Co. was officially established in Tokyo with Masuda as operational president.[50]

Taking advantage of the Meiji government's new policy of openness and industrialisation, the company quickly expanded overseas, first to Shanghai and Paris, followed soon after by Hong Kong, New York, and London. Mitsui Bussan departed Hong Kong briefly in 1882, though it initially retained a presence in the territory through the agency of George R. Stevens & Co., a merchant house with its own line of ships to Australia.[51] The company reopened its Hong Kong office in 1886 to sell coal from the Miike mines (三池炭鉱), with which it had an exclusive sales contract.[52] Furthermore, Japan's Finance Minister ŌKUMA Shigenobu (大隈重信) was keen for Japan's first national bank, Daiichi Kokuritsu Ginkō (第一国立銀行), to have a presence in Hong Kong, and Mitsui already acted as agents for it in Shanghai.[53] Founded in 1873, the First National Bank was part of the country's efforts to modernise its fiscal system, with Mitsui providing some of the initial capital necessary for its establishment.[54]

FUKUHARA Eitarō (福原榮太郎) arrived in Hong Kong from Shanghai on February 16, 1886, to head the reopened Mitsui Bussan office.[55] Just twenty-six years old, he had attended Keio Gijuku (慶應義塾; later Keio University) and, like Shugyō, was one of the new breed of entrepreneurial executives prized by Minomura and Masuda.[56]

Born in 1862, Fukuhara was of *samurai* stock and a nephew of Inoue Kaoru.[57] He joined Mitsui Bussan in 1880 and spent time working in the Shanghai office before moving to Hong Kong.[58] Indeed, the Hong Kong office operated as a subdivision of the company's Shanghai operation when it was re-established in 1886 and Fukuhara reported to the manager there.[59]

The Hong Kong sub-branch prospered under Fukuhara's leadership. He extended the range of import items to Japanese-spun cotton yarn, paper, and rice and expanded the firm's trade in matches. However, its main business centred around the sale of Miike coal and coke – a coal by-product – to customers such as the French steamship line Messageries Maritimes and local enterprises including the Green Island Cement Company.[60]

The Miike coal mines, once Japan's largest, were located near the town of Omuta (大牟田) in Fukuoka prefecture, a short boat ride from Nagasaki. Nationalised by the Meiji government in 1873, Mitsui was appointed its sole agent in 1876. In April 1888, the mines were put up for sale and Mitsui outbid Mitsubishi by just 2,300 yen, acquiring them for 4,555,000 yen, a huge sum at the time.[61] Miike gradually replaced Mitsubishi's Takashima coal in the Hong Kong market during the late 1880s and early 1890s, going from 141,000 tons exported to the city in 1890 to 225,000 tons a mere three years later, in 1893.[62]

In recognition of his success, Fukuhara was promoted to general manager of the now stand-alone Hong Kong branch on April 30, 1892.[63] He and his wife Ei had welcomed a baby daughter, Kayo, at their home in Lower Mosque Terrace, near Caine Road in Mid-Levels, on January 5, 1892. Though Kayo was a common name at the time, the combination of characters used, '香世', was not. '香' is the first character in the Chinese name for Hong Kong '香港', and '世' means 'world'. While we can only speculate on their reasons for giving their daughter a name so connected with their situation, the choice was all the more poignant in that Kayo lived for less than five months, passing away from convulsions on May 28, 1892.

Figure 5.4: Fukuhara Kayo, the daughter of Mitsui's Hong Kong general manager, died aged five months on May 28, 1892. (Photo credit: Miyuki Kume.)

Figure 5.5: Hong Kong's Japanese elite gathered each year to celebrate the Emperor Meiji's birthday on November 3. This photograph of executives, associates, and their families was likely taken at Mitsui's mansion on MacDonnell Road around the turn of the century. (Source: Frank Fischbeck Collection, The University of Hong Kong Libraries.)

By the end of the century, Mitsui was by far the largest Japanese enterprise in Hong Kong, with over forty employees. In August 1896, with civil engineer Albert Denison (1860–1939) acting as intermediary, Mitsui purchased the 999-year lease for a plot of Crown land at 15–17 MacDonnell Road in Mid-Levels on which to build quarters for its senior staff members. A special condition of the sale was that only 'Buildings of the class of European Dwellings' could be erected on the site. The Mid-Levels area, though not as prestigious as the Peak, was already crowded with the stone mansions of wealthy merchants of different nationalities. Mitsui named its own imposing edifice after the company's Chinese romanised name, Sam Ching (三井).[64]

Mitsui was the first Japanese company to join the colony's pre-eminent, European-dominated commercial association, the Hong Kong General Chamber of Commerce, in 1894, with NYK and YSB following suit two years later.[65] Besides coal and cotton, Mitsui advertised its trade in railway materials, manure, opium, cigarettes, paper, and timber, among many other items.[66] By 1908, it had also added leather, brick, and beer manufacturers, as well as three insurance firms, including Tokio Marine Insurance Co., Limited, to the portfolio of companies it represented in the city.[67]

Kayo's gravestone still stands in a part of the Hong Kong Cemetery reserved for Japanese children. The two infant sons of NYK manager MIHARA Andrew Shigekichi (三原繁吉) and his wife, Masa, are buried nearby.[68] The Fukuhara family left Hong Kong, and Kayo's grave in Happy Valley, in 1893, the year following her death. After postings in London, Osaka, and Tokyo, Fukuhara was seconded to an affiliate of Mitsui Bussan, Onoda Cement (小野田セメント), where he served as president from 1906 to 1916.[69]

Figure 5.6: An advertisement for Mitsui Bussan Kaisha in Hong Kong featured in the *Chronicle & Directory* for 1908.

Yokohama Specie Bank

The Yokohama Specie Bank (横浜正金銀行) established its Hong Kong office on September 22, 1896, with Ataka's classmate at Kanazawa Vocational School, Hirota Kōkichi, among its first employees.[70] Like Fukuhara of Mitsui Bussan, Hirota had spent time gaining experience in Shanghai prior to his transfer. The advertisement announcing the start of YSB's operations in the city highlighted the bank's global ambitions: 'Drafts Granted on all the principal Places in Japan and China, and on the principal commercial centres in Europe, India and America and every Description of Exchange Business Transacted.'[71] Indeed, the bank was to play a crucial role in the Meiji government's drive to update Japan's banking and financial sectors in order to compete with Western powers on equal terms.

Prior to 1868, Japan had a quasi-banking system in place, but rice was still widely used for the payment of taxes, for example. The opening up of the country to overseas trade beyond a couple of its ports demanded that it rapidly institute a modern banking system in order to avoid falling victim to the unequal currency exchange practices that had already led to the depletion of the country's gold reserves during the final years of the Tokugawa shogunate.[72]

The Meiji government inherited a multitude of gold, silver, and copper coinage – or specie – along with a vast array of different banknotes, with almost every domain issuing their own version. Initiatives to standardise the Japanese currency included replacing the *ryō* (両) with the yen (円) in 1869 and the opening of the Osaka Mint in 1871.[73]

The Japanese Imperial Mint's machinery was, in fact, purchased from Hong Kong following the city's own failed attempt at limiting the number of currencies and proliferation of counterfeit coins in the territory. Established in 1866, the Hong Kong Mint was quickly deemed a failure and ceased all operations just two years later.[74] Japan saw its demise as an opportunity and purchased its machinery for 60,000 silver dollars, as well as the expertise of its engineers and architects, to set up its own facility in Osaka. Nagasaki-based Scottish merchant Thomas Blake Glover and Jardine Matheson & Co. acted as intermediaries for the sale, and Godai Tomoatsu of Kōgyō Shōkai, who was an official in Osaka prefecture at the time, played a key role in getting the Japanese government's go-ahead for the project.[75]

Initially, with the Mexican silver dollar recognised as the main form of payment in most treaty ports, the Meiji government had planned to base its new currency on the silver standard. However, after observing the transitioning of several major Western powers to gold, it nominally adopted the gold standard with an Imperial Ordinance in May 1871.[76] The modernisation of the banking system continued with the drafting of the National Bank Decree in 1872, the establishment of Japan's first national bank, Daiichi Kokuritsu Ginkō, in 1873, and the setting up of the Tokyo Stock Exchange in 1878.[77] Officials also made efforts to promote recognition of the yen overseas.

Hong Kong Governor John Pope Hennessy visited the Osaka Mint during his three-month trip to Japan in 1879. The governor of Osaka hosted a dinner in his honour on August 12, at which he was joined by the Japanese Consul to Hong Kong, ANDŌ Tarō (安藤太郎), and Godai Tomoatsu, then chairman of the Osaka Chamber of Commerce. Following an elaborate meal at a nearby hotel, the party adjourned for a firework display on the river in front of the mint.[78] Though his visit was officially a private one, Pope Hennessy was welcomed by a Japanese government eager to advocate for the acceptance of the Japanese yen as legal tender in Hong Kong.

Pope Hennessy's support and intense lobbying by Hong Kong's Chinese trading houses proved ineffective. One objection related to distrust of Japanese competence. An official in the Colonial Office pointed out in correspondence with the Hong Kong governor that the Japanese Mint was 'no longer under the superintendence of an European Officer and although the Empire of Japan [had] made great progress of late years [the British government had] no sufficient guarantee that the supply [of yen could] be adequately given or the standard of manufacture both in workmanship and purity [would] be maintained'.[79] The Lords of the Treasury in London ultimately decided against recognition of the Japanese yen in the British colony in June 1881.[80]

Notwithstanding the Meiji government's implementation of updated banking practices, a large amount of paper money, often in the form of inconvertible banknotes issued by both official and quasi-banking institutions, remained in circulation. This state of affairs led to the founding of the Yokohama Specie Bank, which opened its doors in February 1880. The YSB's primary task was to act as a collection point for silver and gold specie or bullion from both within and outside of Japan, which could then be circulated in a more controlled way and used as the basis for the country's paper currency.[81] Responsibility for the regulation of note-issuing fell to the country's new central bank – the Bank of Japan, founded in 1882.[82]

After some initial hiccups, YSB proved to be extremely successful in capitalising on Japanese exports of silk and tea, in particular, to secure a net import of specie through the use of discounted foreign bills of exchange. YSB collected payment for exports in foreign currency through the offices it had established in New York, San Francisco, London, and Lyons, which was a major European centre for the silk trade.[83] The London office – a branch from 1884 onwards – played a vital role in YSB's endeavours to remit specie to Japan. It was into YSB's London branch that China's indemnity of approximately 360,000,000 yen was paid in British pound sterling. It amounted to three times Japan's national revenue and was what finally enabled Japan to adopt the gold standard, both officially and in practice, on October 1, 1897. YSB was consequently permitted to open an account with the Bank of England in London, thereby signalling the Japanese bank's admission to the international banking arena and securing acknowledgement of Japan as a commercial rival on the world stage.[84]

Upon opening, YSB's Hong Kong office was located at 6 Praya Central (today's Des Voeux Road Central) and Ice House Street. By 1901, it had moved to the brand new, four-storey, fully electrified Prince's Building.[85] The city's Chinese merchants predominantly used silver for trade, and YSB played an important role in collecting and withdrawing Japanese silver specie from circulation through various financial transactions.[86] It then melted them into bullion, which could be used to buy gold for the Japanese government or sold on. With the value of silver prone to major fluctuations, the Hong Kong YSB employees had to keep a keen eye on gold and silver prices and maintain a delicate balancing act between buying and selling the precious metals. According to YSB archival records, its Hong Kong office held 500,000 dollars in silver assets when it opened in 1896, but this amount had risen to 2,390,000 dollars just three years later, a testament to the Hong Kong team's banking skills. The Hong Kong office was promoted to a branch in 1900 and, its mission successfully accomplished, it

```
━━━

行 銀 金 正 濱 横

Wang-pün-ching-kum Ngan-hong.
YOKOHAMA SPECIE BANK, LIMITED, Praya
Sakio Choh, manager
K. Hirota, sub-agent
T. Aizawa, accountant
T. Matsuzawa
J. Kanda
G. Iwamoto
T. Isobe
B. M. Castro
C. Henry Kim
(See Advertisement)

━━━
```

Figure 5.7: Hirota Kōkichi was a sub-agent of the Yokohama Specie Bank's Hong Kong branch. (Source: *Chronicle & Directory* for 1900.)

handed over the collection and dealing of silver to the Shanghai YSB branch in May 1906.[87]

Following his arrival in Hong Kong, Hirota initially worked as a clerk and was eventually promoted to deputy general manager.[88] His name appears twice on Hong Kong's list of jurors, in 1898 and 1900, and he must have spoken some English in order to communicate with his counterparts at other major banks in the territory dealing in foreign currencies, including at the Hongkong and Shanghai Banking Corporation. His 'abode' in the 1898 list was a house on Robinson Road, whereas by 1900 he had moved to a residence higher up the hill, on Peak Road, possibly as a result of his promotion.[89]

Hirota passed away on July 30, 1900, at the age of twenty-nine, and is buried in the Hong Kong Cemetery. The bank lost two more employees to illness within a couple of months of each other in 1906. NAKASONO Shūgo (中園修吾) died of the plague at the Government Civil Hospital on June 18, at the age of twenty-seven.[90] His grave stands in the same section as Hirota's. The two gravestones are similar in terms of shape and inscriptions, suggesting that the company arranged for their erection. Sub-manager SAKATA Teiichi (坂田定一) succumbed to dysentery in early December. A graduate of Tokyo University, where he studied law, Sakata joined YSB in Yokohama in 1898 and transferred to Hong Kong the following year. The forty-year-old left behind a wife and three children, among them an eight-year-old son, Fujio (富士男). Sakata Teiichi was a well-respected man within the Japanese community and over a hundred people attended his funeral in the Hong Kong Cemetery.[91] Fujio went on to study at Waseda University (早稲田) and become a village council member in 1925. His rise to a position of influence likely made it possible for Fujio to have his father's remains exhumed in September 1926, twenty years after his death, and returned to his hometown of Sakata in Yamato district, Fukuoka (福岡県山門郡坂田).[92]

A Developing International Business Elite

Mixing in the 'Right' Circles

Much like high-ranking British civil servants, who, in the absence of an aristocracy or traditional upper class, occupied the highest rung of Hong Kong's social ladder, so senior Japanese diplomats, as official representatives of the Meiji government, figured at the very top of the city's Japanese community. Many of these consuls and vice-consuls had travelled abroad, received an overseas education, and were able to communicate to varying degrees in a foreign language, usually English. They played a vital role both in collecting intelligence on Hong Kong, which they included in regular reports to the Foreign Ministry, and in relaying the Japanese government's official position on matters of state.[93]

From the opening of the Japanese Consulate in 1873, the names of the consuls appeared on the guest lists at many of the colony's most prestigious social gatherings, occasionally accompanied by their spouses. Indeed, the wife of Andō Tarō, Fumiko, was the only non-European name to feature among the ladies presented to the newly arrived Kitty Hennessy at a garden party on the lawns of Government House in May 1877.[94] In addition to attending various functions, the consul was responsible for welcoming important Japanese visitors to Hong Kong and for hosting the annual 'Emperor's Birthday', to which all the city's most distinguished figures were invited. Held in early November during the Meiji era, celebrations usually kicked off with the consul receiving prominent members of the Japanese community at his residence. A reception for the city's commercial and administrative elite followed.[95] The Mikado Ball of 1905 was reported to be one of the most glittering occasions Hong Kong had ever seen.

The signing of the first Anglo-Japanese Alliance in January 1902 signalled a new era of cooperation between the two nations, with Britain supplying the military and financial assistance that gave Japan a decided advantage in the Russo-Japanese War of 1904–1905. Though technically neutral during the conflict, the British were equally keen to rein in Russian expansionism in China. Japan emerged with notable advantages from the war, including recognition of its control over Korea, and this further enhanced its standing in colonial Hong Kong.[96] This new appreciation for Japan was very much in evidence at a lavish celebration organised by the upper echelons of the city's Japanese community to mark the Emperor Meiji's birthday on November 3, 1905.

The occasion was extensively covered by the local English-language press. In a preamble to the event, a *South China Morning Post* reporter commented that the 'two great wars', meaning the Sino-Japanese and Russo-Japanese wars, 'from both of which Japan emerged completely victorious, added lustre to her name, and rose from practical obscurity to a high place in the community of nations'. Japan's humbling of Russia had also silenced those in 'Continental quarters' who had ridiculed the Anglo-Japanese Alliance of 1902 and justified 'the confidence placed in her by the greatest Power in the world'.[97]

The hosts extended invitations to the colony's elite and 'only the most unavoidable of circumstances prevented a few – a very few – from accepting. The result was that there gathered in the City Hall one of the most brilliant assemblages ever seen in Hongkong, numbering close on five hundred.' Newspapers published the full list of guests in alphabetical order. Headed by the governor, Major Sir Matthew Nathan, it featured the crème de la crème of Hong Kong's military, administrative, diplomatic, and business establishments. The Parsee financier and broker Mr (later Sir) Hormusjee Naorojee Mody, who would subsequently contribute greatly to the founding of the University of Hong Kong, was mentioned, along with his partner in the 1890s Praya Reclamation Scheme, Sir Paul Chater. The names of just three Chinese invitees appeared in print: The Hon. Dr Ho Kai and Mr Wei Yuk, both members of the Legislative Council, and Mr Chan Hewan, the manager of the China Merchants' Steam Navigation Company.[98]

The ball's organising committee comprised the city's foremost Japanese residents, including the consul, NOMA Masaichi (野間政一), Mrs Noma, Captain TONAMI Kurakichi (外波内蔵吉; 1863–1937) of the Japanese navy, and the managers and senior executives of leading Japanese companies.[99] The only other Japanese names outside of this elite group on the extensive, multinational guest list were a medical doctor, MAJIMA Keinosuke (馬島珪之助), and the ball's artistic director, photographer ERA Hikotarō (恵良彦太郎), both of whom attended the event with their wives.[100]

The ball's organisers impressed their guests with an orientalist display that transformed City Hall into 'Japan in Hongkong'. Under Era's creative direction, the decor aimed to transport partygoers to a Japanese wonderland, with the representation of a rocky glade in Nikkō (日光), complete with waterfall and stork. The venue was festooned with cherry blossoms, yellow chrysanthemums, and 1,500 Japanese lanterns, which, in a nod to technology, were filled with electric lights rather than candles. A Japanese gardener constructed a display of three 'dwarf gardens' (盆栽), with

MENU.

—

Beef Tea.

Cold Fish à la Mayonnaise.

Paté de Foie Gras en Aspic.

Cold Chicken.

York Ham.

Roast Quail.   Roast Beef.

Roast Leg of Mutton.

Gooseberry Jelly.

Apricot Jelly.

Pear Jelly.

Chocolate Ice Cream.

Vanilla Ice Cream.

Assorted Cakes.

Fruits in Season.

Tea.   Coffee.

Cheese and Crackers.

Figure 5.8: Menu for the 'Mikado Ball' held on November 3, 1905, at City Hall. (Source: *Hongkong Telegraph*, November 4, 1905, 5.)

A Developing International Business Elite

miniature pines, firs, and cypress trees, in the supper room. Designers recreated the much-photographed Nikkō bridge on the staircase and celebrated the Anglo-Japanese relationship with the hanging of numerous Rising Sun flags and Union Jacks.[101] The whole effect was to be reproduced on an even grander scale at the 1910 Japan–British Exhibition in London. Held at the Great White City, Shepherds Bush, from May 14 to October 29, 1910, the exhibition attracted over 8,000,000 visitors and showcased a similar blend of orientalism and modernity.[102]

While the decor was very much Japanese, both the supper menu and the music were decidedly Western in style. The Royal West Kent Band performed a programme of waltzes and two-steps and heralded the start of supper with its rendition of 'The Roast Beef of Old England'. Indeed, one reporter was quick to note in his report on the function that 'Japan is not a dancing nation' and that Japanese ladies had been 'assiduously studying and practising the English dances' prior to the ball.[103]

The Hong Kong governor commented on the ball in a letter to his mother the next day. He appreciated the lengths the organisers had gone to in order to make the occasion a memorable one. His observations made it clear that the wives of the Japanese elite rarely attended public events, likely due to language issues and social mores that kept them at home. He further remarked on possibly the first formal meeting of the Japanese and Russian consuls since the signing of the Treaty of Portsmouth two months earlier.

> It was very well done, the decorations being carried out by gardeners specially sent down from Japan. It was the first occasion in which Japanese ladies had made a public appearance in Hong Kong. They were in their own costume and looked very neat. I danced the opening Lancers with Mrs. Noma the Consul's wife and also took her into supper and I even managed one turn of a valse [waltz] with the wife of the manager of the Japanese shipping line – a pretty little thing in a fawn coloured gown [Mrs Masa Mihara, wife of the NYK manager]. The Russian Consul and his wife put in their first appearance at a dance since the war and the greeting between them and the Japanese was very tactfully and prettily done. They are very nice people the Bologowskoys and have not had a very cheerful time in Hong Kong during the war.[104]

The grandeur of the event was very much in contrast to the more businesslike tiffin held to celebrate the launch of the Mitsubishi Mail Steamship Company's Yokohama–Hong Kong service twenty-six years earlier. On November 13, 1879, barely sixty guests, mainly colonial officials and merchants, attended the onboard ceremony, though over a hundred received invitations.[105] The Mikado Ball, on the other hand, was an unmissable highlight of the city's social calendar. It was an opportunity for Hong Kong's newly established Japanese commercial and diplomatic elite to come together and proclaim Japan's parity with other world powers. However, the rather sneering, condescending tone of the English-language press coverage confirms that despite their country's significant technological and societal progress, Japanese residents continued to inhabit an ambiguous space in the city and were generally not regarded as equals by their Euro-American counterparts.

In 1906, a couple of months after the ball, Noma was the first Japanese Consul admitted to the Hongkong Club.[106] Established in 1846, the club counted among its members the 'Who's Who' of Hong Kong's British merchant and administrative classes.[107]

Figure 5.9: Decorative menu for a dinner held in honour of the visiting Japanese fleet at the Hongkong Club on March 26, 1906. (Source: Oxford, Bodleian Libraries, MS. Nathan 353.)

A Developing International Business Elite

Club membership was an important marker of status. Several of Hong Kong's foreign commercial communities had their own clubs. The city's pre-eminent German firms, for example, all belonged to Club Germania.[108] The Nippon Club was officially established in 1905.[109] Its Ice House Street premises featured a billiard room, and dining and reading facilities. Furthermore, the club organised tennis matches and other social activities for its well-heeled members.[110]

Senior managers from all the city's leading Japanese companies, including Mitsui Bussan Kaisha, Mitsubishi/Nippon Yusen Kaisha, and YSB, either co-hosted or featured prominently at events such as the Mikado Ball. The names of Kusakabe & Co. employees did appear on the lists of invitees – Kusakabe was even, for a short while, a neighbour of Mitsui's Fukuhara at Lower Mosque Terrace.[111] Yet their more modest social backgrounds and the less extensive nature of their operations meant they found themselves somewhat on the fringes of Hong Kong's Japanese business elite.

In his memoirs, Ataka details various instances in which he was made to feel the relative poverty of his situation when compared with that of former classmates employed by larger concerns, such as Hirota. He writes that, at one point, 'eleven classmates from the Tokyo School of Commerce were working in Hong Kong [for leading Japanese companies]. They all made three times my salary. They rode on [sedan] chairs carried by two men, while their general managers travelled even more comfortably in chairs carried by four men. They drank soda water or *ramune* [a sweet, carbonated drink], sipped whisky, ate Western food and spent 20 yen on dining a month, whereas I only had 8 or 9 yen, never used sedan chairs and kept no soda water or *ramune* at home.' Though invited to attend a Japanese New Year reception at the consulate in January 1897, Ataka was the only guest to turn up in a plain black suit rather than the more elaborate, and expensive, frock coat, and was slightly ashamed of his improper attire.[112]

While his years in Hong Kong overlapped with those of Hirota, Ataka never mentions encountering him after their meeting in Shanghai and there is only a brief acknowledgement of Hirota's death in Ataka's memoirs.[113] It is as if the relative inequality of their professional positions precluded any further friendly contact between them.

Ataka was not alone in feeling excluded. Other long-term residents, such as small shop owners and traders, may have helped out with decorations at the Emperor's birthday celebrations, but they were certainly not admitted to these grand occasions as official guests. They occupied a position within Hong Kong's Japanese community that lay somewhere between the two poles of the diplomatic and commercial elite on the one hand, and the *karayuki-san* and brothel owners on the other.

6

Tradespeople and Professionals

KONISHI Tsuneshichi was an Osaka man who travelled back and forth between Hong Kong and Singapore selling kimono fabric. NAKAHARA Tomisaburō was a doctor . . . TAKANO Usaburō operated a sundry goods store. He took it over from TODOROKI Yoshijirō and the store is now called Arakawa. NISHIKAWA Unosuke operated an *udon* noodle shop. He didn't have any teeth and lived on Wellington Street . . . MORI Motojirō was a barber who moved to Saigon in Vietnam.[1]

[Oral history interview of Mrs KUSANO Kakuma (草野格馬), 1935]

This enumeration of selected Japanese tradespeople and professionals in Hong Kong in the early 1890s reveals not only the growing diversity of their occupations, but also the transient nature of these small-scale operations, with shops closing and reopening under different names. Sundry goods stores were among the first to arrive in the 1870s. These included Soon Po & Co. (駿浦號), which operated on Queen's Road between 1872 and 1877 selling lacquerware, curios, and miscellaneous items. Soon Po was the local branch of a much larger outfit in Yokohama which engaged in the lucrative sale of Japanese arts and crafts pieces to foreign buyers.[2]

Like any of the colony's other foreign inhabitants, the Japanese craved access to clothing, food, and services from home. The *karayuki-san* were key customers for the shopkeepers, who frequently located their premises in the same area as the Japanese brothels, initially in Central and later in Wan Chai.[3] Operators adapted to cater to the changing needs of their client base, supplementing the sale of sundries with that of kimonos, for example.[4] As Hong Kong's Japanese community expanded, so did the number of these businesses, gradually adding new areas of employment, such as photography and tattooing. These trades advertised in the English-language press and offered their services to both Japanese and non-Japanese clienteles.

While professionals such as doctors were welcome among the upper echelons of local Japanese society, many other small business owners were not. In this diasporic community of two halves, they sat somewhere on the social ladder between *karayuki-san* and brothel owners at the bottom and senior consulate and business figures at the top. Unlike major company representatives, these local retailers were, for the most part, long-term residents, some of whom remained in Hong Kong until their death.

Hairdressers

Japanese hairdressers and barbers were very much in demand in Meiji-era Hong Kong. Japanese stylists plied their trade in the city from the 1870s onwards and hairdressing remained one of the most common occupations for Japanese residents throughout the period. Hairdresser HIRASAWA Rokujirō (平澤録二郎) was the second Meiji-era Japanese buried in the Hong Kong Cemetery after YUKAWA Onsaku (湯川温作). However, unlike Yukawa, Hirasawa was working in the colony rather than just passing through. This made him the first Japanese resident since Rikimatsu in 1860 to be interred there.[5] Hirasawa passed away almost three months after Yukawa, on October 26, 1878, at the Government Civil Hospital, aged thirty-three.[6]

The Meiji government's modernisation efforts extended to hairstyling and clothing. Realising that attire played a key role in how the Japanese were perceived in the West, it issued an edict in 1871 that 'people were now free to cut their hair short, dress as they chose, and leave their swords at home except on formal occasions'. This last clause was clearly aimed at men from a *samurai* background, who traditionally wore their hair in a topknot, or *chonmage*. The other two applied more broadly, though change came more slowly for women.[7] Meiji officials were keen to avoid situations such as the one faced by a group of nineteen men from Satsuma who passed through Hong Kong on their way to Britain for study in April 1865. For the first four days of their eight-day stay in the city, they remained onboard their ship awaiting the delivery of European-style clothing and shoes so that they might escape the ridicule of the ship's foreign crew and feel comfortable enough to go ashore. The emperor had his hair cut short in 1873 and many followed his example in adopting more practical haircuts.[8] In Hong Kong, new and more traditional styles co-existed. In a photo taken during Hong Kong Governor John Pope Hennessy's 1879 stay in Japan, Consul ANDŌ Tarō (安藤太郎) and his wife, Fumiko (文子), sport Western-style fashion and hairdos.[9] The *karayuki-san*, in contrast, were more inclined to retain older styles of grooming, thereby differentiating themselves from the city's Chinese prostitutes.

These barbers came from a 'commoner' rather than *samurai* background, and hairdresser was regarded as a low-status occupation both within their own community and by the class-conscious British establishment.[10] They found ready employment in the colony's salons, including those patronised by Europeans. Hirasawa was interred under the name 'Jorio Kitchey' and given a Christian burial, officiated over by Anglican chaplain John Henderson.[11] His adoption of an anglicised name and conversion to the Christian faith hinted at his working at a European or American rather than Chinese or Japanese establishment.

In an 1882 advertisement promoting the services of his salon in the Hongkong Hotel, Philadelphia-born William Porter Moore announced that he had in his employ 'three competent Assistants who are always in attendance'.[12] One of Moore's assistants was twenty-six-year-old Japanese hairdresser HIMI Otokichi (比見音吉), or 'Otto Kitchu', as his name appeared in the *Chronicle & Directory*.[13]

Five Japanese hairdressers or barbers – four men and one woman – were working in Hong Kong in 1886. One of the men, thirty-three-year-old KOJIMA Jisaburō (小島治三郎), lodged at the Tōyōkan boarding house at 13 Aberdeen Street. A commoner from Tokyo, Kojima died of consumption on June 10 of that year and a grave was erected in his memory in the Hong Kong Cemetery.[14] The other three men all plied

HAIR DRESSING SALOON
HONGKONG HOTEL.

W. P. MOORE begs to inform the Gentlemen of Hongkong and Visitors that he
has reduced the price of Hair-Cutting to 50 cents.
Having now in his employ three competent Assistants who are always in attendance, he guar-
antees to execute this class of work, in all its
branches, with a perfection which cannot be ex-
celled in any part of the World.

Hair-Cutting.......................50 Cents.
Shampooing ....25 Cents.
Shaving ....25 Cents.
Trimming Beards ....25 Cents.

MONTHLY CUSTOMERS TAKEN AT REDUCED
RATES.
RAZORS MOST CAREFULLY RE-SET.

Moore, W. P., hairdresser, &c., Hotel
Buildings, Queen's Road Central
W. P. Moore, proprietor
C. H. Flores, book-keeper
Otto Kitchu, assistant
M. Reyes,   do.
Bonn,   do.

Figure 6.1: Left: An ad in the May 25, 1882, edition of the *Hongkong Telegraph*, promoting Moore's hairdressing services in the Hongkong Hotel. Right: Moore's entry in the 1882 *Chronicle & Directory* listing 'Otto Kitchu (Himi Otokichi)' as an assistant.

their trade at foreign-owned salons. Two styled hair at the Hongkong Hotel and the third, thirty-six-year-old MASUHARA Torakichi (増原虎吉), worked at a rival establishment, Henry Campbell's in the Bank Buildings on Queen's Road.[15]

Despite their jobs in the city's prestigious commercial district, these hairdressers lived in cheap accommodation and occasionally fell foul of the law. Masuhara was a troublesome employee and Campbell had him arrested in 1885 for failing to turn up for work. Four years later, the police held him in connection with the death of a Chinese man following a gambling row aboard a launch bound for Kowloon City (九龍城).[16] Barber Himi Otokichi had to testify in court when a stabbing incident involving two other Japanese men occurred at his lodgings in Bridges Street, on the edges of the Chinese tenement area of Tai Ping Shan (太平山).[17]

The number of hairdressers continued to grow in line with the Japanese resident population in Hong Kong and they counted the senior managers of Japanese companies among their customers.[18] In the late 1880s, MORITA Sakuichi (森田作市), after gaining experience at the Hongkong Hotel, opened his own barbershop, which doubled as a 'café'.[19] This was a common pattern, with Japanese barbers trained at the Paris Toilet Company – a hair salon and toiletries store – in Astor House, for instance, setting up Yayoye Toilet Company in Beaconsfield Arcade, just behind City Hall, in 1909.[20] By 1916, hairstylist was the fifth largest profession for men after company worker, shipping office worker, shopkeeper, and tailor, with thirty-four out of a total of 1,460 residents. Women were less numerous in the profession, with just fourteen working in this field.[21] However, in contrast to their male counterparts, several of them specialised in Japanese-style female hairdressing and serviced the many Japanese brothel businesses in the city.

Tattoo Artists

On March 1, 1889, the *Hongkong Telegraph* published an article announcing 'a new craze' in the city and that 'tattooing is fashionable'. The paper had sent a reporter to investigate and interview the self-proclaimed 'best tattoer [*sic*] from Japan', 'Hori Chiyo' (彫千代). Dressed in European attire, the tattooed 'Hori Chiyo' showed his visitor around his shop on Queen's Road East and introduced the tools of his trade. These included books filled with colourful drawings of all kinds and the prices for each tattoo, from 1 dollar for three butterflies to 100 dollars for a highly elaborate design. His instrument box contained 'a slab of black Chinese ink, some vermillion and dark red powders, and a drawer-full of pen-holders, on the ends of which were lashed tiny bunches of needles, from three to fifty'. A sign hanging on one of the walls declared that 'I do not business [if] fuddled', whereby he intended to reassure his clients that he did not operate when under the influence of drugs or alcohol. The article went on to describe the process of getting a tattoo:

> It was very simple. The patient just chose his design from the hundred or so drawings, the manipulator drew it on the part desired, and then, with a big bunch for the heavy black and a tiny one for the fine lines, the colors were punctured in. No blood is drawn and not much pain inflicted. A $20 dragon would take five hours, on account of the multitude of scales. Then the part was rubbed with vaseline, to allay the inflammation, and in a day or two the skin would come off. After that the marks would be indelible.[22]

The history of tattooing in Japan as a ritualistic and decorative practice can be traced back hundreds of years. Though it gained darker undertones during the Edo period (1603–1868), when the government used it as a means of marking criminals, this was also when it came into its own as an artistic form. Many of the tattoo images developed during this era were based on woodblocks – or *ukiyo-e* (浮世絵) – depicting scenes from famous novels of the time or of bustling, everyday life in the city of Tokyo. The Edo government was intent on maintaining *samurai* privileges and class distinctions through the regulation of dress and other aspects of external appearance. These intricate and colourful tattoos were a way for 'commoners' to rebel against these edicts. However, rather than ending with the advent of the Meiji era, official interference

Figure 6.2: A late nineteenth-century tattoo design template used in Nagasaki, where many of Hong Kong's tattoo artists were from. It showcases a mix of styles. Winged dragons, anchors, and pointing dogs did not feature in traditional Japanese tattoo art. (Source: Nagasaki Museum of History and Culture.)

in people's attire continued, but with a different intent. The new administration was concerned that Westerners might consider tattooing 'barbaric', and that this could undermine the 'civilised' impression it was so keen to convey. Therefore, it banned both the practice and the public display of tattoos in 1872.[23] Nevertheless, tattoo artists continued to operate in Japan, famously tattooing several members of the British royal family.[24]

Indeed, in the article, 'Hori Chiyo' claimed that he had tattooed a dragon on the arm of Britain's Prince George (the future George V) in Kyoto and that he had 'operated' on other prominent customers, including 'English ladies', in Yokohama. Business in Hong Kong was booming and he reckoned that he was earning about 500 dollars a month.[25] This was a considerable amount, a mere 14 dollars short of the monthly salary earned by the colonial surgeon, though probably an exaggeration.[26]

'Hori Chiyo' was the most famous tattooist outside Japan in the late nineteenth century. However, there is some dispute over his identity and the veracity of his claims regarding the British royal family. It is also possible that the man in the article had merely assumed the famous name as a means of promoting his business. This type of fraudulent behaviour was common and difficult to investigate.[27] Whoever 'Hori Chiyo' was, he likely spent only a short time in the city, looking to make as much money as possible before returning to Japan. Japanese tattooist NOMA Denjirō (野間傳次郎), meanwhile, who arrived with his family in 1894, made Hong Kong his home and resided in the colony for fifteen years. Judging from his first name, Noma was his parents' second son (jirō). With Japanese inheritance customs favouring the eldest male child, second and third sons (saburō) were just another mouth to feed and had greater freedom to leave Japan and make a living overseas.[28]

Like 'Hori Chiyo', Noma and his studio featured in an article in the *Hongkong Telegraph*, under the title 'A Queer School of Art: A Hongkong Tatooer's Atelier'. The writer describes his visit to 14 Queen's Road 'where Mr. D. Noma, a clever Japanese artist, with a staff of apprentices is kept fully engaged'. Despite his praise for Noma's handiwork, the author concludes his article with '[it] has been said that the veneer of civilization is a thin one after all and from the popularity of this primitive and barbaric art practice it would appear to be true in some degree at least', thereby confirming the Meiji government's own views on the disreputable nature of the profession and its enthusiasts.[29]

Noma advertised his services regularly in the English-language press. Like 'Hori Chiyo', he promoted his skills with the unproven claims that he had tattooed both Prince George in 1881 and the future czar Nicholas II in 1891 during their respective visits to Japan. 'The Public are informed that my Parlours are open from 9 A.M. all day. My 32 years' experience in TATTOOING is a guarantee of good work and prompt execution . . . Prices moderate and satisfaction guaranteed as attested by 3,700 Recommendations which I have received from all sources.'[30] As evidenced by the volume of endorsements, Noma had no difficulty securing customers among the thousands of seamen and soldiers of various nationalities who passed through the colony every year. Higher-class European and American residents or tourists might also have sought him out, though he was unlikely to find any takers among the city's Japanese diplomatic and business elite.

Noma's studio in Queen's Road was adorned with a sign that included his name and one of the drawings from his book of tattoo designs: a red-crowned crane with its

Figure 6.3: Noma Denjirō's shop sign is visible at the top of this photograph of Queen's Road taken by a Hungarian naval doctor in the first decade of the twentieth century. (Source: Dezső Bozóky, Hong Kong Queen's Road, Museum of Fine Arts Budapest-Hopp Ferenc Museum, 2024.)

wings spread, about to take flight. Unsurprisingly, considering the Japanese government's stance on the trade, the prominence of Noma's signage attracted some criticism from higher-class Japanese visitors. Nagasaki-based journalist INOKUCHI Ushiji (井口丑二; 1871–1930), who passed through the city in 1899, was particularly unimpressed, writing in his diary that the consulate should ban such displays.[31]

Noma was a visible member of Hong Kong's Japanese community. His shop sometimes doubled as an eatery for the many Japanese living in the city at that time who resided in boarding houses and did not have their own cooking facilities.[32] His artistic skills were also very much in demand. Though not invited to participate as a guest, he contributed to the decorations for the glittering Mikado Ball held in City Hall to mark the Emperor Meiji's fifty-third birthday on November 3, 1905, just two months after the end of the Russo-Japanese War.[33]

Noma Denjirō died of pneumonia and was laid to rest in the Hong Kong Cemetery. An English inscription on the back of the bilingual gravestone erected by his children, including daughter Hide, reads:

In memory of
Our Beloved Father
Denjiro Noma
Died
July 8 1909
Aged 50 years

A Japanese School for Hong Kong

Unlike the senior Japanese executives who came to Hong Kong in the late nineteenth century, long-term residents without company resources, like Noma, did not have the option of keeping their families in Japan in order for their children to attend school. In the absence of any Japanese institution in the city, they turned to local establishments, such as Hong Kong government subsidised schools, to educate their offspring.

From the earliest days of the colony, British administrators had sought to institute policies governing both English- and Chinese-language education. In 1847, the governor established an Education Committee and initiated a grants scheme to support selected schools.[34] For the next fifteen years, the opening and running of educational facilities was largely left to religious or missionary societies and other private organisations. Hong Kong's first secular, fully funded government school, today's Queen's College, opened in 1862. The school was initially intended as one for Chinese pupils only, but it officially began accepting boys of all nationalities in 1866.[35]

In 1870, pupils at Queen's College included five English, two Portuguese, fourteen Indian, and two Japanese boys.[36] Both Japanese students were boarders sent from Japan as part of the Meiji government's push to gain overseas experience, rather than the sons of residents of the city. Though the majority of these scholars travelled to Europe and the United States for their studies, a very small number did come to Hong Kong. One example, twenty-three-year-old IGAWA Totsurō (井川訥郎) from Shimane (島根), was despatched by his domain in 1871 and spent a year studying English at Queen's College.[37]

Later students were more likely to be the offspring of long-term residents. By 1890, the college had ten Japanese students and a representative of the Japanese Consulate regularly attended the annual prize-giving ceremonies.[38] YAMASAKI Munenao (山崎宗直; 1880–1954) and his younger brother attended Queen's College in the early 1900s, during the period of the Russo-Japanese War. The college reprinted part of an English-language composition Yamasaki wrote on the subject in its magazine, *The Yellow Dragon*. In it, he commented that the 'entry of Japan into the circle of the Great Powers, the revolutionary state of all Russia, the disturbance of balance of power in Europe and the awakening of China, these are the direct results of the war affecting the countries of the world in general'.[39] Admitted in September 1902, Yamasaki was clearly an outstanding student and received several prizes during his time at the institution, including the prestigious Davis Chinese Scholarship in 1906 to study at Oxford.[40] He used his language skills and cultural expertise to teach business English at various institutions after his return to Japan and worked at Tokyo University towards the end of his career.[41]

The Government Central School for Girls opened its doors in 1890 on Hollywood Road to provide an English education to Chinese and Eurasian girls of all classes, as well as 'European, Indian and other non-Chinese and non-Catholic girls, who at

Figure 6.4: Senior Belilios Scholar Yamasaki Munenao, seated second from right, photographed with fellow awardees at Queen's College in 1906. (Source: Queen's College History Museum.)

present have practically no school to go to'.[42] The wealthy merchant and philanthropist Emanuel Raphael Belilios (1837–1905) donated 25,000 dollars to erect a new building on the site of the old Queen's College, and the school was renamed Belilios Public School in his honour in 1893.[43] Japanese names appear in the annual list of prizes, with tattoo artist Noma's daughters winning awards for needlework in 1902.[44]

Priests of the Hongwanji centre in Wan Chai – an area which, by the turn of the century, had become the preferred location of Japanese brothels and associated small trades – offered ad hoc classes on topics such as Japanese history and the philosophy of Mencius to groups of children from as early as 1902. However, the growing number of children, like Noma's, residing in Hong Kong with their parents eventually led to calls to set up a more formal educational facility in the city.[45] Hong Kong's first Japanese primary school opened on August 1, 1909, with just ten students. Hongwanji priests continued to provide the teaching and handled administrative duties. As previously mentioned, the Japanese Benevolent Society (日本人慈善會), which had raised the funds needed to establish the school, took over its management in 1911.

As the number of students increased, it became clear that a proper framework and curriculum were required. In late 1915, the society appointed the school's first principal, and a Japanese Education Committee was formed to monitor the institution's operations. The committee consisted of members drawn from three organisations: the Japanese Benevolent Society, the Nippon Club, and a less formalised 'discussion group' that the consulate had set up following the Russo-Japanese War to enhance communication between various segments of Japanese society in the city. The three organisations committed to covering the school's operating costs, with funds supplemented by donations from Hong Kong's Japanese residents. By 1917, twenty-seven students attended classes at the school's premises at 1 Sharp Street, near Causeway Bay.[46] However, considering the area's association with the lowest echelons of the colony's Japanese community, most of the pupils were likely to be the children of tradespeople and shopkeepers. The offspring of Hong Kong's Japanese elite were often tutored at home. ASAI Umeko (浅井梅子; 1906–1985) was eight years old in 1914 when her father, ASAI Yoshiteru (浅井義啁), took up the position of Hong Kong general manager for the shipping company Osaka Shosen Kaisha (大阪商船會社). She opted for home tuition rather than travelling to the Japanese school from her home in Mid-Levels. In her recollections of her time in the colony, she writes: 'The [Japanese] elementary school in Hong Kong was far away and seemed rather crude. So I [stayed at home and] took lessons from my mother and followed the primary two curriculum.'[47]

Photographers

Photography as a trade was already well established in Hong Kong by the 1880s, with many European, American, and Chinese commercial studios opening from the mid-1840s onwards.[48] Residents from all walks of life wanted their picture taken, in groups or individually, as a record of their time in the city that could be sent to family, friends, and romantic interests. Photographers offered lasting mementos of important social occasions and sold postcards and albums of Hong Kong's main attractions and scenery to visitors.

UENO Hikoma (上野彦馬; 1838–1904) was already well known in Japan when he set up as a practitioner in Hong Kong in the mid-1880s.[49] The son of a wealthy merchant, Ueno studied chemistry at a Dutch-run medical training establishment in Nagasaki. There, European teachers, such as Johannes L. C. Pompe van Meerdervoort and Pierre Rossier, introduced him to photography practices. Ueno co-authored the first Japanese technical manual to describe a photographic process in 1862, the same year that he opened one of Nagasaki's earliest photography studios.[50] He continued to grow in prominence during the 1870s and was famous for his portraits of foreign visitors.

The French writer Pierre Loti called at Ueno's studio in Nagasaki during his stay in July 1885 and reproduced the experience in his semi-autobiographical work *Madame Chrysanthème*, published in 1887.[51] In the book, Loti visits 'Uyeno, the fashionable photographer in Nagasaki' for a portrait and describes his surroundings: 'The courtyard is irreproachably Japanese, with its lanterns and dwarf trees. But the studio where one sits might be in Paris or Pontoise [a city in the Paris suburbs associated with the impressionist painters Pissarro, Gauguin and Cézanne]; the self-same chair in "old oak," the same faded "poufs," plaster columns and pasteboard rocks.'[52]

Ueno did not spend much time in Hong Kong and probably left the running of his studio at 1 Queen's Road to various assistants, among them ERA Hikotarō (恵良彦太郎). After Ueno closed his operation in the city in August 1889, Era opened his own photography shop on Arsenal Street before moving to 14 Beaconsfield Arcade in 1900.[53]

Like tattooist Noma, Era's artistry was sought after by the upper echelons of Hong Kong's Japanese community and he was the chief designer for the much-admired decorations that festooned City Hall on the occasion of the November 1905 Mikado Ball.[54]

Era paid to erect the gravestone of one of his three assistants, nineteen-year-old NAGAMATSU Masamoto (永松正基), in Happy Valley. Nagamatsu, a native of Ōita (大分) in Kyushu, died of beriberi at the Government Civil Hospital on May 15, 1893.[55]

Figure 6.5: Era Hikotarō's photography studio was located on the top floor of 14 Beaconsfield Arcade, near City Hall. (Source: Frank Fischbeck Collection, The University of Hong Kong Libraries.)

UMEYA Shōkichi (梅屋庄吉; 1868–1934) is the most famous of all Japanese photographers to work in Hong Kong during the Meiji era as a consequence of his well-documented friendship with Sun Yat-sen (孫中山; 1866–1925).[56] Born in Nagasaki, Umeya displayed an entrepreneurial spirit from an early age, stowing away on a ship to Shanghai aged fourteen and living there for a year. In 1893, seeing the potential for Japanese businesses in other parts of Asia, he and his companion Tomiko left Japan for Singapore and set up a photography studio there. The outbreak of the Sino-Japanese War in 1894 caused them to depart for Hong Kong, which is where he met Sun.[57]

Umeya and Sun were first introduced at a party in late 1894 by James Cantlie, a co-founder of the Hong Kong College of Medicine from which Sun graduated in 1892. Subsequent to this encounter, Sun called on Umeya at his shop, 'M. Mumeya', in early January 1895 and won him over to the anti-Qing cause. Sun had several friends and financial backers among the Japanese besides Umeya, including the pan-Asianist philosopher MIYAZAKI Tōten (宮崎滔天; 1871–1922). Together, they helped Sun flee to Japan following the failure of the Guangzhou [Canton] uprising of October 1895. During his sixteen years in exile, Sun travelled around the world raising funds to promote his vision for China and continued to enjoy Umeya's support from Hong Kong and Japan.[58]

In addition to providing a meeting place for anti-Qing revolutionaries, Umeya was involved in other clandestine aspects of life in the city. His covert activities inevitably caused him to interact with the more criminal elements of Hong Kong society and he had connections within the Japanese boarding house and sex trafficking circles. Umeya makes an appearance in the memoirs of *zegen* – or pimp – MURAOKA Iheiji (村岡伊平治; 1867–1942 [assumed]). In his autobiography, Muraoka referred to Umeya as a 'big boss' and alleged that he tried to intervene in a dispute between two rival Japanese gangs in Hong Kong in 1906.[59]

A controversial figure within Hong Kong's Japanese community, Umeya was, nevertheless, the first tradesperson invited to join the Nippon Club.[60] However, his inclusion proved problematic following his studio's involvement in the notorious forged bank note case of 1912–1913.

At the end of December 1912, following a tip-off from Tokyo, the Hong Kong police arrested eight Japanese men, including two employees of Mumeya's, NISHIYAMA Kiyoto (西山清人) and SANO Fukuzō (佐野福蔵).[61] All eight men were charged with conspiracy to defraud the public and of forging 1,000,000 dollars' worth of Chinese currency notes. A police sting operation recovered some of the bank notes at the Mumeya photographic studio and near the Tokyo Hotel, where four of the defendants were staying. More were found in a basket at the bottom of the harbour. Two of the men, who had travelled from Tokyo to Hong Kong separately from the other six, had attempted to get rid of the notes by throwing them over the side of their ship, the *Awa Maru*. When crew members became suspicious, they claimed that the basket contained old cinematographic films that were useless in Hong Kong. The police promptly engaged a diver to recover the evidence.[62]

The sensational trial began on March 17, 1913. The first Japanese barrister admitted to the Hong Kong bar, MASUJIMA Rokuichirō (増島六一郎), who had trained at the Middle Temple in London, was one of the lawyers for the defence.[63] Hong Kong's first Japanese-language newspaper, *Honkon Nippō* (*Hong Kong Daily News*/香港日報), came under fire for its coverage of the events. Launched in September 1909 by Consul FUNATSU Tatsuichirō (船津辰一郎; 1873–1947), the paper enjoyed the support of the city's major Japanese businesses. Its contents included telegrams relating to political and commercial developments in Japan and Hong Kong, relevant Chinese news items, and society features.[64]

In two articles published soon after the arrests, the *Honkon Nippō* condemned the defendants as criminals deserving of severe punishment for jeopardising Sino-Japanese relations. The defence lawyers believed these comments affected their clients' right to a fair trial and the newspaper's editor, MATSUSHIMA Shūe (松島宗衛), was found to be in contempt of court.[65] The jury found seven of the men guilty. Nishiyama was sentenced to three years' imprisonment with hard labour and Sano to two.[66] Though Umeya himself was never directly implicated, Nishiyama's testimony made it clear that he was aware of the scheme.[67]

While undeniably connected to some of the city's seedier elements, Umeya was an astute businessman who followed the latest developments in the field of photography. By 1901, his studio had thirteen employees, including three women and at least one foreign staff member. This was more than the Yokohama Specie Bank and double the number employed by Hong Kong's other Japanese photographer, Era Hikotarō.[68] Umeya's studio at 8A Queen's Road Central offered various services, from portraits to

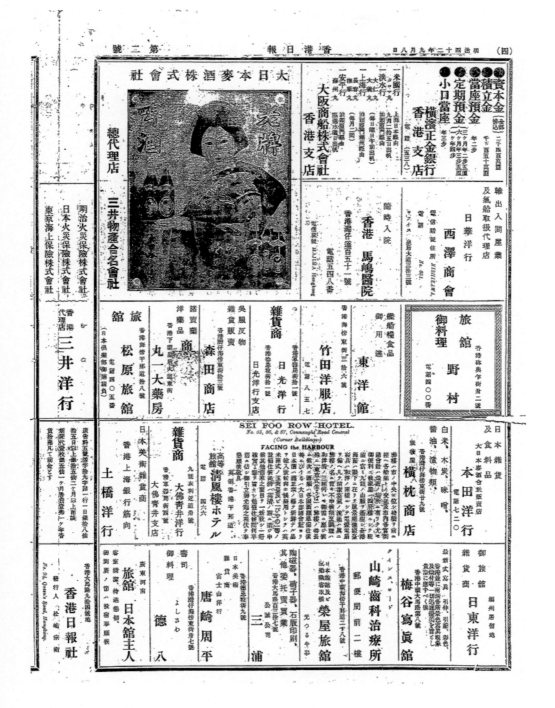

Figure 6.6: A page from the second edition of *Honkon Nippō*. Ads for the city's most prominent Japanese companies – Mitsui, Yokohama Specie Bank, and Osaka Shosen – feature at the top of the page. They are followed by notices for Majima's medical clinic, Japanese boarding houses and restaurants, and other service providers. (Source: JACAR, originally from the Diplomatic Archives of the Ministry of Foreign Affairs.)

postcards, assisted amateurs with developing and printing, and was regularly hired to photograph social events or provide illustrations for news items.[69] Indeed, when novelist NATSUME Sōseki (夏目漱石) passed through Hong Kong on his way to London in 1900, his party made a stop at Umeya's shop to purchase panoramic views of the city.[70]

Well-worded advertisements for 'Mumeya' featured prominently in English-language newspapers, alongside those for Mitsui Bussan Kaisha and Mitsubishi.[71] His quirky, full-page promotions in the *Chronicle & Directory* stood out from the other, staider offerings from banking, construction, trading, and shipping firms. One image of a Japanese woman, possibly one of his employees, pulling a face was particularly eye-catching.[72]

Umeya paid to erect two gravestones in the Hong Kong Cemetery, one in 1897, belonging to thirty-five-year-old marine officer MIZUMOTO Inosuke (水元猪之助), who passed away from diabetes at the Government Civil Hospital, and another in 1902, for twenty-five-year-old KOMINE Hashi (小嶺ハシ), possibly a *karayuki-san*.[73] Like Umeya, both Fukushima and Komine hailed from Kyushu.

Umeya was based in Japan from 1905 onwards, though his studio continued to operate under the name 'Mumeya and Sano'.[74]

Figure 6.7: Yokohama Specie Bank manager Hozumi Tarō photographed at Umeya's studio in Hong Kong on September 29, 1903. (Photo courtesy of Hirochika Matsuoka.)

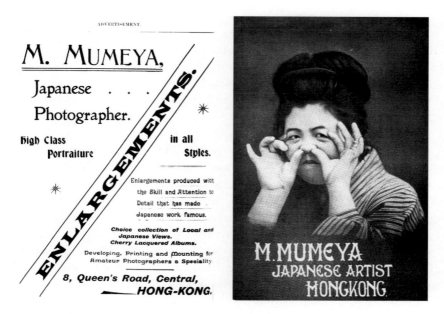

Figure 6.8: An advertisement for Umeya's photographic services in the *Chronicle & Directory* for 1903.

Dentists and Doctors

By the 1890s, Hong Kong's Japanese community counted well over two hundred men and women and was sufficiently large to support professions such as doctor and dentist. Japanese residents in the city would certainly have welcomed access to these services in their own language. Some of these practitioners, such as dentist SAKATA Ishinosuke (坂田石之助; 1863–1938), favoured American-style treatment methods and catered to non-Japanese customers. Certified to practise dentistry in 1891, Sakata studied modern dental techniques with one of the first Japanese dentists to adopt American methods. After practising in Yokohama for a couple of years, he worked in Vietnam before moving to Hong Kong.[75]

The colony presented both opportunities and challenges. Sakata began advertising the clinic he shared with Chinese dentist LAM Sam Shing at 55 Queen's Road Central in June 1894, at the height of Hong Kong's first major plague outbreak.[76] Just four months later, Sakata was involved in a bizarre case whereby a young American man had 30 dollars' worth of gold fillings done under false pretences. This was a sizeable sum, equivalent to six nights' board and lodging at the city's foremost hotel, and the fillings would have provided a safe way of smuggling the gold to wherever the wrongdoer was planning to go next.[77] Claiming to be a missionary from Guangzhou affiliated with the Basel Mission, the fraudster asked for the bill to be sent there. However, the mission denied any knowledge of him and the government had the twenty-three-year-old arrested, tried, and subsequently imprisoned.[78]

Sakata spent only two years in Hong Kong and left for Shanghai in spring 1896. Fluent in English and French, he remained there for thirty-two years serving the city's foreign communities.[79]

Nakahara and the Plague Epidemic of 1894

NAKAHARA Tomisaburō (中原富三郎) is the earliest known Japanese medical practitioner to have worked in Hong Kong. Though he was never listed in the Hong Kong government's register of 'persons qualified to practice medicine and surgery', his name and profession appeared on a December 1891 record of Japanese residents in Hong Kong.[80]

The plague was already endemic in China at the time of Hong Kong's 1894 outbreak. Guangzhou experienced a surge in cases in March of that year and the extremely contagious and deadly disease made its way across the border. The city reported its first cases in early May and numbers quickly exploded, with the overcrowded and unsanitary tenement district of Tai Ping Shan particularly affected.[81] The *Hygeia*, a purpose-built epidemic hospital ship moored in the harbour, was rapidly filled and the Kennedy Town police barracks put at the disposal of the government to receive the sick.[82] As the disease spread, the government converted a glassworks factory and later a slaughter house into temporary medical facilities to treat predominantly Chinese patients.[83] Misinformation was rife and the colony's Chinese inhabitants refused to be sent to the *Hygeia*, claiming that its Western doctors were subjecting uninfected Chinese to terrible medical procedures.[84] Indeed, many Chinese residents suspicious of the British administration's drastic anti-plague measures fled the city in the hope of avoiding infection. By the time the epidemic subsided in October 1894, at least 2,485 people had died, including six Japanese, thirty-seven-year-old Nakahara among them.[85]

Nakahara contracted the plague as a consequence of his efforts to support the work of Japanese bacteriologist KITASATO Shibasaburō (北里柴三郎; 1853–1931) and his colleagues.[86] A trained physician who had studied at the University of Berlin from 1885 to 1891, Kitasato was director of the Institute of Infectious Diseases in Tokyo at the time. The Japanese government dispatched Kitasato to Hong Kong with the aim of identifying the plague bacillus. He arrived on June 12, 1884, and was welcomed by James Lowson (1866–1935), the acting superintendent of the Government Civil Hospital and medical officer in charge of the epidemic treatment facilities.[87]

Lowson provided Kitasato and the team accompanying him, including doctors AOYAMA Tanemichi (青山胤通; 1859–1917) and ISHIGAMI Tōru (石神亨; 1857–1919), with facilities at the Kennedy Town hospital, as well as samples for analysis. Aoyama concentrated on interviewing patients about their symptoms and providing organs from deceased plague victims for Kitasato to examine under the microscope.[88] Communicating with Chinese patients was a struggle. Aoyama recorded his medical notes in German but spoke no English and had to rely on interpretation from Chinese to English to Japanese.[89]

The room in which Aoyama and his assistants carried out the autopsies was little more than a storage room and very cramped. A coffin lid stood in for the operating table and there was a shortage of proper equipment, such as gloves.[90] This was where Nakahara worked, providing support with menial tasks, such as washing organs. The room's small window had to be guarded to stop anyone from looking in and discovering what they were doing. The idea of dissecting a corpse was shocking to many, especially to Chinese who believed bodies should be kept intact after death, and Aoyama's activities had to be kept secret to avoid causing a major disturbance.[91]

Tradespeople and Professionals

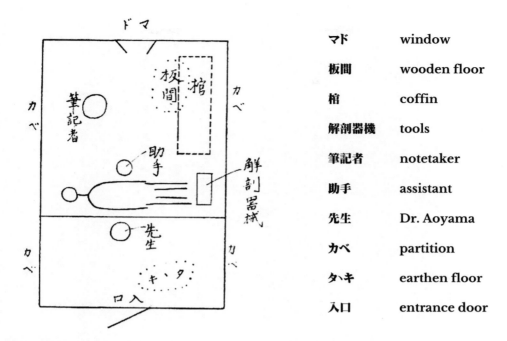

マド	window
板間	wooden floor
棺	coffin
解剖器機	tools
筆記者	notetaker
助手	assistant
先生	Dr. Aoyama
カベ	partition
タキ	earthen floor
入口	entrance door

Figure 6.9: A sketch of the room in the Kennedy Town plague hospital used by Dr Aoyama for body dissections. (Source: 木下 [Kinoshita], 1927, 60.)

Kitasato announced that he had identified the bacillus on June 15 and subsequently published discussions of his results in the *China Mail*, *Hongkong Telegraph*, and *The Lancet*.[92] Concurrently, Swiss-French physician Alexandre Yersin (1863–1943) of the Pasteur Institute arrived in Hong Kong on June 15, 1894, with the same goal of investigating the source of the disease. Yersin identified the bacillus a few days later, with his findings challenging the precision of Kitasato's work. Though there was no disputing the value of both bacteriologists' contributions, debate continued within the international medical community over how to attribute the discovery.[93]

Like Nakahara, Aoyama and Ishigami contracted the plague at the end of June 1894. Aoyama started to feel unwell on June 28, shortly before an important dinner he and Kitasato were hosting to thank government officials and others who had supported their efforts. One of the team's junior doctors wrote in his memoirs that he believed that the three men had been infected during the final autopsy conducted in Kennedy Town.[94] This was confirmed by Lowson's own diary entry for June 28: 'Dine with Kitasato & Aoyama at Hong Kong Hotel. After getting home, called up an hour later & went back to Hotel to find Aoyama & Ishigami with high temperatures and glands – Aoyama axillary & Ishigami femoral. Aoyama got it from mortuary case.'[95]

Nakahara, Aoyama, and Ishigami were transferred to and treated aboard the hospital hulk *Hygeia*.

Aoyama and Ishigami recovered and eventually returned to Japan, but Nakahara died on July 3, 1894.[96]

Forty-five-year-old HARUNO Ino (春野以之) was another Japanese victim of the disease.[97] She passed away on June 29, 1894, at the Kennedy Town hospital. Unlike

Figure 6.10: The hospital hulk *Hygeia*, named for the Greek goddess of health, moored off Kennedy Town in 1905. (Source: Louise Helen Petersen Collection.)

Nakahara, whose grave whereabouts are unknown, Ino's marble tombstone still stands in the Hong Kong Cemetery. Kimono dealer TAKANO Usaburō (高野卯三郎) erected a plaque featuring a delicate butterfly and thistle design in her memory.[98] The translation of Ino's Japanese name – spring field – implies a connection to the sex industry, with 'spring' a euphemism for prostitution. Furthermore, the thistle was an unusual addition, more Scottish than Japanese. This suggests Ino was the concubine of a Scottish man who paid for the headstone but had Takano make the arrangements.

The plague remained an issue for Hong Kong for the next twenty-five years, flaring up periodically and causing over 1,000 deaths annually in the late 1890s, early 1900s, 1912, 1914, and 1922.[99] Victims included Japanese residents NAKASONO Shūgo (中園修吾) of the Yokohama Specie Bank, and MORI Kichi (森キチ), who succumbed at her Ship Street brothel.

Majima's 'Japanese Hospital'

Dr MAJIMA Keinosuke (馬島珪之助; 1868–1919) and his wife arrived in the colony from Yokohama aboard the German ship *Bayern* on September 26, 1904.[100] A specialist in infectious diseases, Majima trained under Dr Kitasato and qualified as a physician at the Imperial University's Medical College in Tokyo on March 30, 1898. He was managing a hospital in Taiwan when the Dōjinkai (同仁会) assigned him to Hong Kong to investigate the city's sanitary measures.[101]

The Dōjinkai – translated as the Association for Universal Benevolence – was founded in 1902 by a group of doctors and prominent businesspeople with the stated

Figure 6.11: A thistle and butterfly feature on the marble gravestone of Haruno Ino. Ino died during Hong Kong's first major plague outbreak in the summer of 1894. (Photo credit: Yoshiko Nakano.)

aim of promoting Japanese medical philanthropy in China. Much like the semi-governmental Tōa Dōbunkai (東亜同文會 East Asia Common Culture Association) with which it was affiliated and shared members, the Dōjinkai was keen to promote China-Japan cooperation as a means of countering the influence of Western powers in East Asia. However, alongside its humanitarian mission, the Dōjinkai undoubtedly played a role in advancing Japanese imperialism, particularly after 1918 when the government began to support it financially. It is unclear why the Dōjinkai sent Majima to Hong Kong.[102] The clinic he set up was a small one that treated mainly Japanese patients, though he must have reported to Tokyo on medical developments and epidemic control measures in the colony.[103]

Unlike Nakahara's, Majima's name appeared in the Hong Kong Register of Medical and Surgical Practitioners from 1905 onwards, meaning that he was qualified to practise in the city. Two years later he moved his practice to 'Killadoon' at 151 Wanchai Road.[104] The area, to the west of Central, offered more affordable housing options and had a mix of Chinese, European, and Eurasian residents. At the time of its construction in the early 1900s, Killadoon was the largest European-style house on Wanchai Road.[105] Majima likely occupied just two or three rooms, one for his living quarters and a couple for his clinic.

Majima tended to Japanese patients from all walks of life at his private 'Japanese Hospital' (馬島病院). Consul Funatsu Tatsuichirō relied on his expertise when suffering from typhoid fever.[106] He treated SAKATA Teiichi (坂田定一), a sub-manager at the Yokohama Specie Bank, for dysentery, tattoo artist Noma Denjirō for pneumonia, and boarding house owner MATSUBARA Jisaburō (松原治三郎) for injuries sustained in the 1918 Happy Valley Racecourse fire; all three eventually died at his clinic.[107] He also paid to erect at least three graves in the Hong Kong Cemetery, including that of brothel manager Mori Kichi, who died of the plague.[108]

Majima and his wife received invitations to all the prestigious Japanese social events in Hong Kong, but, through his profession, he also interacted with the lower echelons of the city's Japanese community. He was involved with the Japanese Benevolent Society, which provided financial assistance to the sick and destitute. Boarding house, brothel, and 'café' managers, as well as small traders such as kimono and porcelain dealers, made up the bulk of its membership, with much of the society's funding coming from the sale of sweepstakes tickets at the annual Happy Valley horse races.[109] Majima supported the organisation's efforts to erect a Japanese crematorium in So Kon Po in 1911–1912 and was a signatory on the lease for the plot allocated by the Hong Kong government for this purpose.[110]

Majima fell ill in the autumn of 1919 and left Hong Kong with his wife.[111] He passed away a few weeks after their arrival in Tokyo.[112] The hospital bearing his name continued to operate at 151 Wanchai Road until 1925.[113]

Bridging the Gap

Majima was not alone in his attempts to bring Hong Kong's divided Japanese community together. Prior to the early years of the twentieth century, upper- and lower-class Japanese had largely stuck to their own social spheres, organised separate activities to celebrate the Emperor's birthday, and set up distinct associations. However, tensions between the two groups escalated in 1908 when the then consul, Funatsu Tatsuichirō, interfered with the tradespeople's plans to invite senior officers from a visiting Japanese fleet for dinner. Funatsu advised the officers not to join any occasions organised by these lower-status individuals. The latter were particularly upset when they found out about Funatsu's intervention, as they typically supplied food and other care items to navy ships passing through Hong Kong and this felt like a deliberate slight.

A small delegation comprised of two sundry goods shopkeepers, a boarding house operator, a reporter, and a tailor descended on the consulate to demand an explanation. Funatsu claimed at first that he was new and that this was merely a misunderstanding, but this explanation was ridiculed. To resolve the situation, he suggested setting up an informal association that could meet on a regular basis and foster greater communication between the two sides. The Japanese Discussion Group (日本人懇話會) was established that same year with around twenty members, mostly small business owners and professionals. The group succeeded in improving relations, at least for the duration of Funatsu's time in Hong Kong. After a rather inauspicious start, the consul came to be very much appreciated for his efforts to bring people from different backgrounds together.[114] As the Japanese community expanded following the end of the Meiji era in 1912 and the Nippon Club required new sources of funding to stay afloat, it finally began opening up to tradespeople.[115]

7
Conclusion

> In the afternoon, we visited the famous cemeteries belonging to people from various countries. . . . Westerners call the place [Happy Valley]. The cemeteries are neatly separated according to religious affiliation: Protestants, Roman Catholics, Parsees, Jews, Muslims, etc. all have their own sections. The Protestant ground is the best laid out with a fountain at its centre. Trees create natural arches with their prolific branches and foliage. Flowers bloom all year round. The Chinese cemetery, though, is located elsewhere . . . Generally speaking, Westerners take better care of their graves than the Japanese. This attention to their dead is an admirable social and cultural quality.[1]
>
> > [Section from the journal of Hongwanji priest Asakura Meisen (朝倉明宣), who accompanied Ōtani Kōzui on an 1899 stopover in Hong Kong.]

This late nineteenth-century Japanese visitor's account fails to mention whether he and his party located their compatriots' tombstones within the 'Protestant ground'. His comments suggest, however, that, even then, the Meiji-era (1868–1912) Japanese graves in the Hong Kong Cemetery were overlooked.

Yet the examination of these burial sites and their occupants provides valuable insight into the make-up of this significant pre–First World War community, about which little has been written in English. It sheds light not only on its internal workings, but also on how its members lived and were perceived within the colony's highly segregated society as a whole.

The advent of the Meiji era marked a major turning point in Japan's relationship to the rest of the world. The country began to measure itself against the foreign nations determined to infiltrate its borders. Whereas clan and domain affiliations prevailed during the Tokugawa period, Meiji political leaders were keen to develop a modern sense of what it meant to be Japanese, with the emperor serving as a unifying symbol. The lifting of the travel ban in 1866 and the realisation that the country needed to adapt and learn from the European and American powers accessing its resources made it possible for thousands of Japanese to venture abroad. Hong Kong was both a necessary transit point for those on their way to Europe and a destination for individuals and, later, commercial concerns looking to make a living or turn a profit. Some stayed for just a few years, while others made the colony their home until their death.

From just a handful in the 1870s, the number of Japanese residing in the city totalled over a thousand by the second decade of the twentieth century. In 1912, the Japanese formed the fourth largest group of non-Chinese residents in Hong Kong, after the British, Portuguese, and Indians. By 1921, they were the third largest and had their own column in the Hong Kong government census. Indeed, in his report to the Legislative Council, the census officer writes:

> Japanese have increased from 958 to 1,585 [since the 1911 census], and are now to be found in nearly every kind of trade, in the professions, crafts and domestic service. Numbers of them have now brought their families to the Colony, and the number of married women and children is largely increased. Ten years ago the number of married women was very small, but there are now 293 married women. Japanese have largely displaced Europeans in the last ten years in the middle levels between Kennedy and May Roads, while most of the artisans and small shopkeepers are to be found along the Praya in Wanchai between Arsenal Street and Morrison Hill.[2]

A Divided Community

Hong Kong's Japanese community in the late nineteenth and early twentieth centuries was one of two halves, as evidenced by the occupations of those interred in the cemetery. The male deceased had found employment in service professions such as hairdresser, photographer, tattoo artist, and boarding house operator, as well as clerical or managerial roles in major commercial concerns. Most of the women buried in Happy Valley during the Meiji era, meanwhile, had worked in just one industry, the sex industry. The monument to prostitute, or *karayuki-san*, KIYA Saki (木谷佐喜) was the first of more than ninety belonging to women connected to the brothel business added between 1884 and 1912. This represents almost a quarter of the approximately 380 identifiable Japanese graves erected during that period.[3]

As the region's pre-eminent transportation hub, Hong Kong played a central role in the transnational traffic of Japanese sex workers to other parts of the British Empire until Singapore became the preferred transit point in the late 1880s. Prostitutes like Saki, from impoverished rural areas near the newly opened treaty port of Nagasaki, travelled clandestinely aboard ships transporting coal to Hong Kong, where they were sold to brothels in the colony or transferred to destinations across South East Asia and as far afield as Australia. Some, if not all, of Hong Kong's Japanese male boarding house owners were significantly involved in this traffic, providing accommodation and other necessities to the women on arrival in the city and liaising between brothels and procurers in Japan. This was their most lucrative source of revenue, with the offering of beds and meals to independent Japanese travellers like HONDA Seiroku (本多静六), NATSUME Sōseki (夏目漱石), and INOUE Teijirō (井上貞治郎) more of a sideline. Boarding house owners were key members of the Japanese Benevolent Society, which was established in 1890 mainly for the purpose of raising funds for the burial of the destitute. The society paid for a minimum of forty-eight graves between 1892 and 1910, chiefly from the proceeds of its booth at the annual Derby Day horse races in Happy Valley.[4]

Small store owners selling sundry goods and items such as kimonos initially derived much of their income from the Japanese brothels. However, they gradually

Conclusion

acquired customers from beyond their own community. Indeed, a large percentage of Hong Kong's Japanese nineteenth-century residents, including the *karayuki-san*, relied on a foreign clientele to make money. Japanese brothels catered predominantly to European, American, Indian, and Malay men, while Japanese hairdressers plied their trade at Hong Kong's foremost hotel for European guests. Professionals such as tattoo artists and photographers, who set up their businesses in the 1890s, advertised extensively in the English-language press and depended to a great extent on non-Japanese customers to make a living.

The Meiji era's most prominent multinational companies are also represented in the Hong Kong Cemetery. As Japan pressed on with reforms aimed at modernising its institutions and engaged further with the outside world, the Meiji government desired a more formal presence in the colony. Hong Kong's Japanese Consulate opened in April 1873, and large commercial concerns soon followed, among them the semi-governmental agency of Kōgyō Shōkai, which specialised in dried seafood products from Hokkaido, and the trading firm of Kusakabe & Co. Mitsui Bussan Kaisha was the first major Japanese company to establish an office in the city in 1878. In October 1879, the Mitsubishi Mail Steamship Company launched Japan's first commercial shipping line between Yokohama and Hong Kong. Both Mitsui and Mitsubishi played a central role in supplying what would become Japan's most lucrative export to Hong Kong in the late nineteenth century: coal. The colony was a major market for coal, and Mitsubishi's Takashima and Mitsui's Miike mines provided the fuel needed to power the Pacific's expanding commercial and military fleets.

Together with the Yokohama Specie Bank (YSB), which came slightly later, in 1896, Mitsui Bussan and Mitsubishi were at the forefront of Japan's push to project a modern vision of the country in the British colony of Hong Kong. The early managers of smaller concerns, such as Kusakabe & Co., came from Osaka or Nagasaki and did not have a university education. Mitsui, Nippon Yusen Kaisha (NYK) – the successor to the Mitsubishi Mail Shipping Company – and YSB, meanwhile, recruited their senior staff from Kobe and Yokohama and turned to graduates from prestigious universities to manage their offices. Some had spent time learning the ropes in Shanghai before coming to Hong Kong, while others had experience travelling or studying overseas. These were worldly, adaptable individuals who had the skills necessary to operate in a multicultural environment like Hong Kong's. Several spoke a good standard of English or else improved their language abilities during their stay. For many, the colony proved a stepping stone to even greater things. Mitsui's SHUGYŌ Hiromichi (執行弘道) and FUKUHARA Eitarō (福原榮太郎) moved on to international postings, one to New York and the other to London. Shugyō and NYK's MIHARA Andrew Shigekichi (三原繁吉) both became leading figures in the curation or collection of Japanese woodblocks – *ukiyo-e* (浮世絵) – and socialised in New York's artistic circles.[5]

However, the number of graves belonging to *karayuki-san* in the cemetery indicates that Hong Kong's early Japanese community was a fragmented one. The extent of the Japanese sex industry's operations in the city, with Japanese prostitutes and concubines second in number only to the Chinese, undermined the efforts of senior consular officials and company representatives to promote the desired image of Japan as a commercial and cultural equal to the region's colonial powers.

These internal divisions influenced who was and was not invited to prestigious Japanese occasions, such as the Meiji Emperor's birthday celebrations. They played out spatially as well, with brothels concentrated in the lower, less respectable reaches of Central and Wan Chai, while Japanese company executives lived higher up the hill in the more affluent vicinity of the consulate in Caine Road and MacDonnell Road. Despite several attempts by consular officials to limit the number of Japanese brothels, they remained a thorn in the side of the city's Japanese elite throughout the Meiji era and beyond. The 1921 Hong Kong government census recorded 139 Japanese prostitutes in the territory, the only 'non-Chinese population' with an entry in this category of employment.[6]

Occupying an Ambiguous Space

The Japanese graves are located on the steeper fringes of the Hong Kong Cemetery. The burial ground's more accessible areas were generally reserved for the Christian dead. This configuration is indicative of how the fragmented make-up of Hong Kong's Japanese community further complicated its already ambiguous situation. Neither Chinese nor European, Japanese residents occupied a shifting position in the colony's social structure and the British administration struggled with where to place them within it.

Early Meiji travellers passing through the colony, including the Iwakura Embassy in 1873, contrasted Hong Kong's impressive, Western-style harbourfront buildings with the squalid streets of the predominantly Chinese areas of the city. They blamed opium addiction and a weak Qing government unable to resist foreign encroachment for China's decline and sought to distance themselves from the country's plight. Eventually, the Meiji government's modernisation of its army and navy along French and British lines allowed it to pursue its own territorial ambitions in China and Korea more effectively. Ongoing tensions between China and Japan following the Sino-Japanese War of 1894–1895 found expression in Hong Kong as well. Matters came to a head in 1908 when Chinese merchants, upset at Japan's negotiating tactics during the *Tatsu Maru II* affair in neighbouring Guangzhou, initiated a months-long Japanese boycott.

The Meiji era's second major conflict, the Russo-Japanese War of 1904–1905, along with the first Anglo-Japanese Alliance signed two years prior to its start, had a particularly significant impact on British attitudes towards Hong Kong's Japanese community. Japan emerged from the war with an enhanced status in the eyes of the world's imperialist powers and this boosted the prominence of its elite in the colony. Whereas only slightly over half of those invited to the Mitsubishi Mail Steamship Company's tiffin in 1879 showed up, the Mikado Ball held in November 1905, a couple of months after the end of the war, was an unmissable highlight of the colony's social calendar that year. English-language newspapers praised Japan's increased standing on the global stage, yet the tone remained condescending – while the country had made great strides forward, it could, of course, never hope to match the greatness of the British Empire.

Senior consular officials and company representatives appeared on the guest lists of prestigious European social occasions – the Hongkong Club even admitted its first Japanese member in 1906. Despite this, the colonial government did not consider the Japanese on a par with the city's American and European communities. Examples of differences in treatment include the issuance of liquor licences. The government

Conclusion 121

had distinct regulations for Chinese- and non-Chinese-run establishments and faced a conundrum when handling applications from Japanese restaurants and inns. After discussing whether to create a new licence exclusively for Japanese venues, the licensing board opted for an alternative, discriminatory arrangement.

As suspicion of Japan's predatory ambitions in East Asia grew, its relationship with Britain began to sour and the activities of its residents in Hong Kong came under increased scrutiny. An application by Mitsui Bussan Kaisha in late 1910 to lease a large tract of Crown land for a coaling depot was opposed by the commander of the British troops in south China and Hong Kong. He argued that the new development would attract a sizeable workforce of Japanese men, who had all completed compulsory military service and might easily be confused with the Chinese now that the latter had discarded their 'pigtail'. The facility might be used to accumulate explosives, facilitate spying activities, and, therefore, prove a future threat to the colony's security. In a letter to Governor Lugard explaining his position, Major-General Charles Anderson writes:

> It is not impossible that at some time within the next 75 years Japan may be hostile to [Great Britain] and under such circumstances the presence in our midst . . . of such a rallying point for the assemblage of all the Japanese in the place as would be offered by the premises of this Steamship Company [meaning Mitsui Bussan Kaisha] would I consider be a source of deep anxiety and danger to the defence. It would also be a menace to the safety of our dockyards, water supplies, cables, electric installations and all the other arteries of the life and defence of the Colony.[7]

The members of Hong Kong's diverse Japanese community had to navigate this colonial space, contending with external, often racially motivated restrictions, as well as their own internal divisions. The distinctiveness of their situation persisted in the arrangements for their dead. While other, much smaller groupings with a shared faith or place of origin secured a dedicated burial ground, the Meiji-era Japanese never had their own cemetery. Instead, an informal arrangement between their consul and the Hong Kong government permitted the erection of their graves around the edges of a cemetery largely reserved for American and European Protestants. This explains the unusual, hybrid style of most of their monuments, their designs a mix of Japanese and European elements with multilingual inscriptions.

Finding Common Ground

In 1909, following complaints from other mourners, the Sanitary Board voted to ban the use of incense sticks in the Hong Kong Cemetery. The board was clearly taking aim at the cemetery's non-Christian users, the vast majority of whom were unbaptised Japanese. This decision set off a sequence of events that resulted in a rare coming together of the city's Japanese residents to request a dedicated place to dispose of their dead. However, they were asking for a crematorium, not a cemetery.

Cremation had gradually become the preferred mode of disposing of human remains for Buddhists during the Meiji era. For the Japanese diasporic community in Hong Kong, it meant that families could afford to return the ashes of their loved ones to Japan for burial, should they so wish. Though spearheaded by the Japanese Benevolent Society and Nishi Hongwanji, the scheme had the support of the consulate and large commercial concerns, including Nippon Yusen Kaisha.

Several factors underpinned this previously avoided alliance of the upper and lower ranks of the city's Japanese residents on a matter of communal interest. Japan's increase in international standing following the Sino-Japanese and Russo-Japanese wars inspired a greater sense of national pride and of belonging to the same country that occasionally overrode regional affiliations and social status considerations. Within two months of Japan formally declaring war on Russia in February 1904, Consul Noma coordinated donations from the city's Japanese residents, first to the navy and then the army. A list of donors published in April 1904 indicated that over half of the city's Japanese community contributed to the war effort. The 456 names included not only prominent figures among the Japanese elite but also *karayuki-san* and other members of the Japanese Benevolent Society. The range of donors, as well as the speed and organised nature of the collection, was unmatched by the Japanese diasporic communities in Shanghai and Singapore.[8]

Furthermore, by the first decade of the twentieth century, the number and diversity of occupations of the Japanese in Hong Kong had grown, meaning that the sex industry, while still visible, accounted for a smaller percentage of overall employment figures. Major incidents, such as the Japanese boycott, for example, had a unifying effect, with different businesses working to repair relations with their Chinese counterparts. Ultimately, Japanese employed in service occupations such as boarding house owner, tailor, and storekeeper wanted their voices to be heard by the senior diplomats and company representatives who used their skills and purchased their products. Their demands led to the setting up of a discussion group in 1908 to enhance communication with the consulate and ensure that their contributions to the community were properly recognised.

Japan's enhanced standing after 1905 and the Sanitary Board's desire to limit Japanese usage of the Hong Kong Cemetery doubtless ensured the Hong Kong government's approval of the application to construct a Japanese crematorium, the first of its kind in the colony. The land allocated for the purpose in So Kon Po, south of Causeway Bay and close to today's Hong Kong Stadium, was surrounded by grasslands and had to be levelled to accommodate the furnace and other buildings.

The crematorium opened in 1912 for use by all Japanese in the colony. Nevertheless, this did not mean a complete halt to their interments in the Hong Kong Cemetery. In 1909, the government set aside a small, remote section of the cemetery for non-Christians and asked the Anglican bishop to consecrate the rest. Japanese burials did continue. However, they were far fewer in number. Many of the ninety or so graves added since 1912 belong to stillborn babies or very young children, though some older residents did have monuments erected in their memory. With most opting for cremation and the carriage of ashes back to Japan, the Japanese graves in Happy Valley no longer afforded the same level of insights into the make-up of this diverse community and its ambiguous position within Hong Kong society.

After 1945

Japanese forces invaded Hong Kong in December 1941 and occupied the territory for the next three years and eight months. Upon Britain's resumption of authority in August 1945, any Japanese citizens remaining in the territory were ordered to leave. This left no relative or caretaker to tend to the Meiji graves.

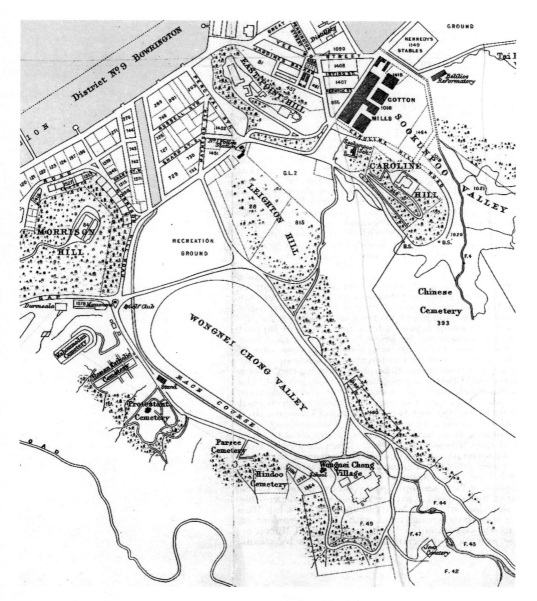

Figure 7.1: A section of a 1900 map showing the various Happy Valley cemeteries – 'Mahommedan', 'Roman Catholic', 'Protestant', 'Parsee', 'Hindoo', and 'Jews'. The Japanese crematorium, which opened in 1912, was located in So Kon Po valley, closer to the Chinese Cemetery (upper right-hand corner of this image). (Source: Bibliothèque nationale de France.)

There is no evidence of intentional damage to the graves due to anti-Japanese sentiment immediately before or after the Second World War. The absence of a dedicated 'Japanese Cemetery' and the graves' remote location within a cemetery managed by the colonial administration meant that they escaped attention. Rather, the colonial government focused its efforts on the dismantling of the 'Tower of Triumph (忠霊塔)'. Japanese occupying forces had begun erecting the imposing edifice on Mount Cameron to mark their conquest of Hong Kong and honour their dead. The half-finished structure was eventually blown up in a controlled explosion on February 26, 1947, at a cost of 36,000 dollars.[9]

The Japanese Consulate reopened its doors in 1952 and the Bank of Tokyo established its Hong Kong Branch in 1953. The bank was formed after the Second World War and succeeded the Yokohama Specie Bank in its foreign exchange functions. By 1955, the numbers of Japanese in the city had grown sufficiently to warrant their own association. The non-profit Hongkong Japanese Club started operating that year with just over a hundred corporate and individual members. The general manager of the Bank of Tokyo, a precursor of what is today the Mitsubishi UFJ Financial Group, Inc. (MUFG), served as its first president.[10]

Figure 7.2: This image of Miura Seiichi's funeral in early 1920 depicts the Memorial to Ten Thousand Souls in its original location to the left of the Japanese crematorium in So Kon Po. Miura was the agent for several Japanese brands – Jintan, Morinaga, and Lion – that had embraced modern manufacturing methods. (Photo courtesy of Ko Tim Keung.)

Conclusion

The Japanese graves in the Hong Kong Cemetery were left largely untended for almost forty years after the war. However, in 1982, at the suggestion of the Japanese Consulate, the Hong Kong government contacted the Hongkong Japanese Club with a request to move the Memorial to Ten Thousand Souls from its original emplacement next to the now-demolished Japanese crematorium in So Kon Po. The Benevolent Society had erected the imposing memorial in 1919 in memory of the victims of the previous year's Happy Valley Racecourse fire. The club assisted by relocating the monument to the non-Christian, predominantly Japanese area of the Hong Kong Cemetery, and it now stands as the focal point of that section. This marked the beginning of the club's involvement with the cemetery's Japanese graves. In 1992, it secured the support of the Japanese Foreign Ministry to carry out extensive restoration work and now regularly checks on the state of the remaining monuments.

The club eventually established a Preservation Committee (墓地管理委員会) and has, since 2000, conducted an annual ceremony to remember these early members of the Japanese community. In August 2002, a respected Kabuki actor, ICHIMURA Manjirō (市村萬次郎), travelled to Hong Kong for two performances at the Hong Kong Cultural Centre. He and his wife suggested positioning trees in locations important to the Japanese community, including the cemetery. Of the original fourteen cherry blossom trees of the Kawazu-zakura variety that were planted on February 14, 2004, six continue to flower, dotted along the paths to where the majority of the Japanese graves are situated.[11]

Despite these efforts, the cemetery's graves remain vulnerable to the elements and accidental damage. In 2022, the headstone of Japanese concubine TANAKA Seiko (田中清子) was felled by a falling tree. Seiko's grave resembles others from that era with its bilingual inscriptions. The back of her white marble headstone has her name in Chinese characters, whereas the front bears the English words 'In loving memory of O-Sai-San Tanaka, died at Hong Kong 20th January 1895, aged 22 years, erected by a sorrowing friend', no doubt chosen by her foreign lover. He was likely responsible for the verse on the base as well:

OUR DEAREST ONE ON EARTH HAS GONE
THE VOICE WE LOVED IS STILL
A VACANT PLACE IS IN HER HOME
WHICH NEVER CAN BE FILLED

Figures 7.3 and 7.4: Left: the front of O-Sai-San (Tanaka Seiko)'s headstone 'erected by a sorrowing friend'. Right: the headstone lies shattered on the ground after being hit by a falling tree branch in 2022. (Photo credits: Miyuki Kume and Georgina Challen.)

As the years pass, inscriptions get harder and harder to make out. While there have been at least three attempts to create a listing of some or all of the Japanese graves, it will soon be impossible to verify any errors or omissions.[12] With few first-person accounts for many of the graves' occupants surviving, the names and personal information carved into these granite and marble surfaces are often the only remaining clues to their lives in Hong Kong. Within the next few decades, this valuable entry point into gaining a greater understanding of the city's Meiji-era Japanese community will have disappeared altogether.

Brief Timeline

Year	Japan	Hong Kong	Japanese Graves
1840s		Hong Kong Island formally ceded to Britain in **1842**.	Opening of the Hong Kong Cemetery in **1845**.
1850s	Arrival of Commodore Matthew Perry in **1853**. Series of treaties between **1854** and **1858** leads to formal opening of five ports.		
1860s	Rescinding of the ban on overseas travel in **1866**. **Meiji Restoration in 1868.**	Cession of the Kowloon Peninsula to Britain in **1860**.	**Rikimatsu** – shipwrecked seaman (**23 Sep 1860**)
1870s	Iwakura Embassy visits the United States and Europe from **1871** to **1873**. Mitsubishi Mail Steamship Company established in **1875**. Mitsui Bussan Kaisha established in **1876**.	Opening of the Japanese Consulate in **1873**. Mitsui Bussan Kaisha opens Hong Kong Office in **1878**. Mitsubishi launches Yokohama–Hong Kong service in **1879**.	**Yukawa Onsaku** – overseas student (**5 Aug 1878**)
1880s	Yokohama Specie Bank starts operations in **1880**. Establishment of Nippon Yusen Kaisha in **1885**.		**Honda Masajirō** – Mitsubishi Hong Kong General Manager (**2 Nov 1880**) **Kiya Saki** – *karayuki-san* (**8 Jun 1884**)
1890s	Sino-Japanese War of **1894–1895**.	*Fushiki Maru* tragedy in **1890**. First major plague epidemic in **1894**. Opening of the Yokohama Specie Bank office in **1896**. Ninety-nine-year lease of the New Territories to Britain in **1898**.	**Fukuhara Kayo** – daughter of Mitsui's Hong Kong general manager (**28 May 1892**) **Nakahara Tomisaburō** – doctor (**3 Jul 1894**) **Hirose Matsujirō** – Kusakabe & Co. errand boy (**May/Jun 1898**)

Year	Japan	Hong Kong	Japanese Graves
1900s	Signing of the first Anglo-Japanese Alliance in **1902**.	Mikado Ball Held on 3 Nov **1905**.	**Yamamoto Hisa** – brothel manager (**7 Dec 1902**)
	Russo-Japanese War of **1904–1905**.	*Tatsu Maru II* incident and Japanese boycott in **1908**.	**Terumine Hirokichi** – captain of the *Tatsu Maru II* (**28 Mar 1908**)
			Noma Denjirō – tattoo artist (**8 Jul 1909**)
1910s	End of Meiji era and beginning of Taishō era in **1912**.	Opening of the Japanese Crematorium in So Kon Po in **1912**.	**Uetsuki Kakuzō** – manager of the Tokyo Hotel (**26 Feb 1918**)
		Happy Valley Racecourse fire in **1918**.	**Matsubara Jisaburō** – manager of the Matsubara Ryokan (**7 Mar 1918**)

Annex: List of Japanese-Related Graves

Note: We have followed Patricia Lim's system for the grave emplacements. 'Section' is followed by 'Row' and then 'Location'.

Edo Period

1) RICKOMARTZ Lucy and RICKOMARTZ Maria Lucy

Lucy (baptised 'Maria Lucy') died November 23, 1851, aged 10 months, F. Maria Lucy (baptised 'Lucy Maria') died May 22, 1860, aged 2 years and 6 months, F (grave #2153 [Lucy], Section 9/11/2)

Lucy and Maria Lucy were the daughters of shipwrecked Japanese seaman Rikimatsu and his wife Henrietta Ambrook.

2) RICKOMARTZ Adonia (力松)

Died September 23, 1860, aged 39, M (grave #2240, location unknown)

Rickomartz was the adopted surname of shipwrecked Japanese seaman Rikimatsu. Unable to return to Japan, he was taken under the wing of German Lutheran missionary and sinologue Karl Gutzlaff and converted to Christianity. He married an American woman, Henrietta Ambrook, in 1849 and settled in Hong Kong. Two of his daughters are buried in the Hong Kong Cemetery.

Meiji Era

3) YUKAWA Onsaku (湯川温作)

Died August 5, 1878, aged 22, M (grave #4372, Section 27/2/14)

This is the oldest identifiable Meiji-era Japanese grave in the Hong Kong Cemetery. Born in the Chōshū domain (now part of Yamaguchi prefecture) in 1856, Yukawa was awarded a scholarship to travel to France for military training in 1872. He was on his way back to Japan via Hong Kong when he succumbed to consumption aboard his ship, the S.S. *Djemnah*.

4) HIRASAWA Rokujirō (平澤録二郎)

Died October 28, 1878, aged 33, M (grave #4386, ossuary niche 451)

Hirasawa was a barber. Though there is no grave marker for Hirasawa, his date and place of death, as well as his profession, match those for 'Jorio Kitchey' in the Hong Kong Cemetery burial register.

5) SHIMIZU Masanosuke (清水政之助)

Died May 10, 1879, aged 22, of diarrhoea, M (grave #4421, Section 27/3/15) (May 10 is the date on his grave. His death certificate lists his date of death as May 23, 1879.)

Shimizu was from Wakayama Prefecture and served aboard the Japanese naval corvette *Nissin*. His name is included on a memorial for seven sailors in the Hong Kong Cemetery erected by the Japan Seafarers Relief Association (Section 31/4/3).

6) Infant son of HATSU (ハツ)

Died July 23, 1879, aged 1 hour, of debility, M (grave #4430, location unknown)

Hatsu was a maid travelling back to Japan in the entourage of UENO Kagenori (上野景範), the Japanese Minister to Britain. She must have lost her child either just before arriving in Hong Kong or during her ship's stopover in the city.

7) Stillborn child of Mrs TERADA Ichirō (寺田一郎)

Died March 18, 1880 (grave #4466, location unknown)

Mrs Terada was the wife of Japanese consular official TERADA Ichirō, who arrived in Hong Kong in March 1878.

8) HONDA Masajirō (本田政次郎)

Died November 2, 1880, aged 35, of consumption, M (Section 31/4/5)

Honda was a commoner from Nagasaki. He was appointed Hong Kong general manager by the Mitsubishi Mail Steamship Company when the company launched its first service to the city from Yokohama in October 1879. Honda's remains were returned to his family in Japan after his death. His gravestone in the Hong Kong Cemetery was erected in the 1910s at the initiative of the Japan Seafarers Relief Association. (Honda's first name in Japanese also appears as 政治郎 and 政二郎, and his last name as 本多, in some of the Mitsubishi archival records.)

9) YAMAGUCHI (山口某)

Died February 20, 1881, aged 21, of chronic pneumonia at the Government Civil Hospital, M (grave #4510, Section 24/16/4)

Yamaguchi was a seaman.

10) MURAKAMI Hideshi (邨上秀士)

Died June 8, 1881, aged 21, of remittent fever, M (grave #4523, Section 31/4/4)

Murakami was born in Ōita and came from a *samurai* background. He joined the Mitsubishi Mail Steamship Company in January 1880 and was working in Hong Kong when he died. His time in the city overlapped with that of Mitsubishi's first Hong Kong general manager, HONDA Masajirō.

11) 'KAUSTIONI Oto'

Died September 9, 1881, aged 32, of diarrhoea at the Government Civil Hospital, M (grave #4545, location unknown)

Kaustioni was a fireman aboard the German-owned S.S. *Brutus*.

Annex: List of Japanese-Related Graves

12) KONDŌ Kizō (近藤貴蔵)

Died December 27, 1881, aged 27, of tuberculosis, M (grave #4566, Section 31/2/3)

Kondō was born in Kumamoto. After graduating from Japan's Imperial College of Engineering (later absorbed into the precursor of the University of Tokyo) in October 1879, he spent a year at the Royal School of Mines in London (now part of Imperial College London). He was on his way back to Japan aboard the *Venetia* when he passed away in Hong Kong.

13) KIYA Saki (木谷佐喜)

Died June 8, 1884, aged 30, F (grave #4713, Section 31/4/24)

Originally from Nagasaki City, Saki (Osaki) was a *karayuki-san* living at 27 Graham Street. She committed suicide by drowning herself in Victoria Harbour after receiving sad news from home. She is the first Japanese woman buried in the Hong Kong Cemetery. Her grave was erected by sixty-two female friends.

14) YOKOTE Umejirō (横手梅次郎)

Died October 31, 1885, aged 36, of chronic diarrhoea at the Government Civil Hospital, M (grave #4819, Section 31/5/25)

Yokote was from Nagasaki and claimed to come from a *samurai* background. He first served in the Japanese Navy before joining the crews of various commercial shipping companies operating routes to Chinese treaty ports, including the Mitsubishi Mail Steamship Company. He fell ill in Hong Kong and appealed to the consulate for financial aid to cover his medical costs. He died a destitute and the consulate paid to erect his grave.

15) YOKOSE Toyotarō (横瀬豊太郎)

Died May 8, 1886, aged 3 years and 9 months, M (grave #4854, Section 26/13/9)

Yokose was the son of YOKOSE Yōkichi (横瀬要吉), the operator of the Tōyōkan boarding house at 13 Aberdeen Street. The Yokose family was from Nagasaki.

16) KOJIMA Jisaburō (小島治三郎)

Died June 10, 1886, aged 33, of consumption, M (grave #4859, Section 33)

Kojima was from Nihonbashi, Tokyo. He worked as a barber and was lodging at the Tōyōkan boarding house at 13 Aberdeen Street when he died.

17) TOMINAGA Matsu (富永松)

Died April 13, 1888, aged 23, F (grave #5059, Section 33/1/20)

Originally from Minami-Takaki district in Shimabara, Matsu was a *karayuki-san* living at 27 Graham Street. She also went by the name of Ohesa/O-hisa. She died in a fire. Her grave was erected by MIYANO Yoshijirō (宮野芳治良/芳次郎), a 'café' manager at 6 Peel Street.

18) SAWANO Kakutarō (澤野格太郎)

Died October 8, 1891, aged 20, from typhoid fever at the Government Civil Hospital, M (grave #5376, Section 29/1/3)

Sawano was from Noto, Ishikawa prefecture. While a student based at the Japanese Consulate in Guangzhou, he travelled regularly to Hong Kong. He served as a guide for HONDA Seiroku (本多静六) when he was passing through the colony on his way to study forestry in Germany in April 1890.

19) FUKUHARA Kayo (福原香世)

Died May 28, 1892, aged 5 months, of convulsions, F (grave #5434, Section 28/6/2)

Kayo was the daughter of Mitsui Bussan Kaisha general manager FUKUHARA Eitarō (福原榮太郎) and his wife Ei.

20) YAMAMOTO Sode (山本ソデ)

Died January 26, 1892, aged 28, of phthisis, F (grave #5411, Section 30/3/9)

Sode was the sister or friend of YAMAMOTO Hisa, who paid for and is buried in the same grave.

21) NAGAMATSU Masamoto (永松正基)

Died May 15, 1893, aged 19, of beriberi at the Government Civil Hospital, M (grave #5509, Section 30/2/10)

Nagamatsu was from Ōita City in Kyushu. He worked as an assistant at the photographic studio of ERA Hikotarō (恵良彦太郎), who paid for his grave.

22) HARUNO Ino (春野以之)

Died June 29, 1894, aged 45, of the plague in Kennedy Town Hospital, F (Section 34B/2/15)

Her marble gravestone is adorned with thistle and butterfly engravings. It was erected by kimono dealer TAKANO Usaburō (高野卯三郎).

23) NAKAHARA Tomisaburō (中原富三郎)

Died July 3, 1894, aged 37, of the plague aboard the hospital ship *Hygeia*, M (grave location unknown)

Nakahara was a medical practitioner in Hong Kong. He assisted, in a minor capacity, the team sent by the Japanese government to identify the plague bacillus during the city's first major outbreak in 1894.

24) KANDA Nobuko (神田信子)

Died October 29, 1894, aged 34, F (grave #5653, Section 34/1/25)

Nobuko (or Shin) was a commoner from Ishikawa and managed a brothel at 46 Stanley Street in 1886. Her gravestone was erected in December 1901, seven years after her death, by five 'friends', including fellow brothel manager Yamamoto Hisa, concubine Hayashizaki Kiku, and kimono dealer Takano Usaburō.

25) TANAKA Seiko (田中清子)

Died January 20, 1895, aged 22, F (grave #5675, Section 34B/4/5)

Seiko (O Sai-san) was likely the concubine of a Western man, who erected her bilingual marble gravestone.

Annex: List of Japanese-Related Graves

26) ŌTAKA Saichi (大高佐市)

Died April 24, 1896, aged 39, of emphysema at the Government Civil Hospital, M (grave #5791, Section 34B/4/2)

Originally from Nagasaki, Ōtaka was the manager of the Ōtaka Ryokan located at 21 Praya Central. Two of his children are buried in the Hong Kong Cemetery: a daughter, ŌTAKA Takako (多嘉子), who died May 1, 1896, aged 2 (grave #5795, Section 41/3/7), and a son, ŌTAKA Shirō (四郎, meaning 'fourth son'), who died February 29, 1897, aged 1 (grave #5903, Section 41/4/3).

27) MIZUMOTO Inosuke (水元猪之助)

Died October 9, 1897, aged 32, of diabetes at the Government Civil Hospital, M (grave #5947, Section 34B/3/6)

Mizumoto was a marine officer from Minami-Naka district, Myazaki prefecture, who was also known by the name of FUKUSHIMA Yūzaburō (福島祐三郎). His grave was partly paid for by photographer and businessman UMEYA Shōkichi (梅屋庄吉).

28) HIROSE Matsujirō (廣瀬松次郎)

Died in May/June 1898, aged 17, of the plague, M (grave #6831, Section 35/2/4)

Hirose came from Minakami (today's Tanba) in Hyōgo prefecture. He was an errand boy at the trading company of Kusakabe & Co. An inscription on the gravestone he shares with HORII Yasaburō mentions that it was erected in their memory by ATAKA Yakichi (安宅彌吉) and KUSAKABE Heijirō (日下部平次郎).

29) Infant sons of MIHARA Andrew Shigekichi and Masa

(graves #6142 & #7117, Section 28/1/1)

A. S. Mihara (三原繁吉) was the Hong Kong manager for Nippon Yusen Kaisha from 1897 to 1907. The joint grave is badly damaged and the dates of birth and death of the two infants are impossible to make out, though from the numbers inscribed on the grave's pedestal, one may have been born on June 25, 1899, and died two days later, on June 27, 1899, and the other may have been stillborn on August 25, 1906.

30) HIROTA Kōkichi (廣田耕吉)

Died July 30, 1900, aged 29, M (grave #6277, Section 6/3/12)

Hirota was from Daishōji, Ishikawa prefecture, and worked as a deputy general manager at the Yokohama Specie Bank in Hong Kong. He came from the same domain and studied at the same vocational school as ATAKA Yakichi.

31) KOMINE Hashi (小嶺ハシ)

Died June 9, 1902, aged 25, F (grave #6574, Section 35/3/14)

Hashi was from Shimabara, Kyushu. Her grave was paid for by photographer and businessman UMEYA Shōkichi.

32) YAMAMOTO Hisa (山本ヒサ)

Died December 7, 1902, aged 47, of acute peritonitis, F (grave #6641, Section 30/3/9)

Hisa was from Hyōgo. She was recorded as a *shamisen* player and teacher living at 19 Hollywood Road in 1886. She became a major trafficker and was running her own brothel with 12 *karayuki-san* at 7 Gage Street in 1901. Her afterlife name is 'big sister of tourism'. Hisa is buried in the same marble grave as her friend or sister, YAMAMOTO Sode.

33) HORII Yasaburō (堀井彌三郎)

Died June 20, 1904, aged 25, of typhoid fever at the Peak Hospital, M (grave #6831, Section 35/2/4)

Horii came from Ishiyama, Shiga prefecture, and was an employee of the trading company Kusakabe & Co. An inscription on the gravestone he shares with HIROSE Matsujirō mentions that it was erected in their memory by ATAKA Yakichi (安宅彌吉) and KUSAKABE Heijirō (日下部平次郎).

34) NAKASONO Shūgo (中園修吾)

Died June 18, 1906, aged 27, of the plague at the Government Civil Hospital, M (grave #7088, Section 6/3/22)

Nakasono was from Tsukiji in Tokyo. He was an employee with the Yokohama Specie Bank in Hong Kong at the time of his death.

35) SAKATA Teiichi (坂田定一)

Died December 4, 1906, aged 40, of dysentery, M (grave #7157)

Sakata's family was from Fukuoka in Kyushu. He was a deputy general manager at the Yokohama Specie Bank in Hong Kong. He passed away at the clinic of medical doctor MAJIMA Keinosuke (馬島珪之助). His remains were exhumed in 1926 and returned to Japan.

36) UMETSU Koku (梅津コク)

Died in August 1907, aged 47, F (grave #7245, Section 35/2/17)

Koku was from Minami-Takaki district in Shimabara. She was the sister of UMETSU Sami, who paid for her grave.

37) TERUMINE Hirokichi (照峰廣吉)

Died March 28, 1908, aged 33, of acute pneumonia, M (grave #7323, Section 34B/1/7)

Terumine was from Akō in Hyōgo prefecture. He was the captain of the ill-fated *Tatsu Maru II*, which, in February 1908, was boarded by Qing officials in the waters off Macau under suspicion of purveying arms to anti-Qing revolutionaries in southern China. Terumine fell ill in Guangzhou, where the ship was held, and died before he could return home. His body was transferred to Hong Kong for burial.

38) MORI Kichi (森キチ)

Died June 6, 1908, aged 48, of the plague and heart failure, F (grave #7357, Section 35/3/1)

Kichi was from Minami-Takaki district in Shimabara. She was a brothel manager in Ship Street, Wan Chai. Medical doctor MAJIMA Keinosuke (馬島珪之助) and the Japanese Benevolent Society paid for her grave.

Annex: List of Japanese-Related Graves

39) NOMA Denjirō (野間傳次郎)

Died July 8, 1909, aged 50, of pneumonia, M (grave #7537, Section 34C/5/6)

Noma was from Urakami, Nagasaki City. He was a tattoo artist, who arrived in Hong Kong with his family in 1894 and plied his trade in the city for fifteen years. He passed away at the clinic of medical doctor MAJIMA Keinosuke.

40) UMETSU Sami (梅津サミ)

Died April 10, 1910, aged 42, of apoplexy and paralysis of the heart, F (grave #7634, Section 34C/3/4)

Sami was from Minami Takaki district in Shimabara. Her grave has an inscription in English that lists her profession as 'nurse', though she was probably a nanny. She paid for the grave of her sister, UMETSU Koku.

Taishō Era

41) UETSUKI Kakuzō (植月覚三)

Died February 26, 1918, aged 45, M (grave #8269, Section 35/2/27)

Uetsuki came from today's Tsuyama in Okayama prefecture. He was the operator of the Tokyo Hotel and Sei Foo Row Annex, an adjacent hotel and upmarket restaurant, located on Connaught Road. He perished in the Happy Valley Racecourse fire. Several of his family members are buried in the Hong Kong Cemetery: Yoneko (米子, died October 1, 1911, aged 30, of hyperemesis gravidarum [severe sickness in pregnancy] and paralysis of the heart, F); Tomiko (冨子, died July 20, 1912, age unknown, F); Masao (昌夫, died September 9, 1912, aged 1 month and 1 day, M); and Chizuko (千鶴子, died February 12, 1914, aged 7, F). Uetsuki married more than once. His widow, also Yoneko (米子), was a former geisha from Tsuyama, Okayama, and took over his operation after Uetsuki's death.

42) MATSUBARA Jisaburō (松原治三郎)

Died March 7, 1918, aged 54, of injuries sustained in the Happy Valley Racecourse fire of February 26, 1918, M (grave #8285, Section 31/4/1)

Matsubara came from Ishikawa prefecture. He was the operator of the Matsubara Japanese Hotel located at 18 Connaught Road. He passed away at the clinic of medical doctor MAJIMA Keinosuke.

43) MIURA Seiichi (三浦清一)

Died December 31, 1919, aged 47, of uraemia and paralysis of the heart, M (Section 26/13/10)

Miura was a merchant from Inaba, Gifu prefecture. He traded in a wide range of products, including Japanese porcelain, clocks, and sundry goods, and was an agent for the Japanese brands Jintan, Morinaga, and Lion in Hong Kong. Miura's infant son, MIURA Seiji (三浦清治), who died on October 15, 1906, aged 1 month, is also buried in the cemetery (grave #7135, Section 26/13/12).

Notes

Chapter 1

1. Authors' own translation. Rikimatsu was serving as interpreter on the H.M.S. *Sybille* at the time of his encounter with Japanese official RIKIISHI Katsunosuke (力石勝之助). The ship was anchored at Hakodate from April 28 to May 2, 1855, and their private conversation was recorded in a diary kept by the Hakodate Magistrate's Office. 東京大学史料編纂所 編 Historiographical Institute, University of Tokyo, ed., 「三月十二日より十六日に至る英船箱館沖碇泊中日記」 [Diary of the British Ship's Stay in Hakodate, March 12 to 16], in 『大日本古文書——幕末外国関係文書之10』 [*Historical Documents of Great Japan: International Relations in Late Tokugawa*, Vol. 10] (Tokyo: Tokyo University Press, 1918), 70–71; and 春名徹 Haruna Akira, 『世界を見てしまった男たち』 [*Men Who Travelled the World*] (Tokyo: Bungei Shunju, 1981), 290–91. The *Friend of China* published Rikimatsu's account of the stay on August 8, 1855.

2. Katherine Plummer, *The Shogun's Reluctant Ambassadors: Japanese Sea Drifters in the North Pacific*, 3rd ed. (Portland: Oregon Historical Society Press, 1991), 110–18; and Stephen W. Kohl, 'Strangers in a Strange Land: Japanese Castaways and the Opening of Japan', *Pacific Northwest Quarterly* 73, no. 1 (1982): 22. Only Rikimatsu's first name is known. He did not have a family name, as was common for farmers and labourers from a rural background at that time.

3. Andrew Cobbing, *The Japanese Discovery of Victorian Britain: Early Travel Encounters in the Far West* (Richmond, Surrey: Japan Library, 1998), 3.

4. One of Rikimatsu's companions aboard the *Morrison*, Kyūkichi, was an employee of the British trade office in Macau, which was ordered to relocate to Hong Kong and form its first colonial government in February 1842. Ernest John Eitel, *Europe in China: The History of Hong Kong from the Beginning to the Year 1882* (London: Luzac & Company; Hong Kong: Kelly & Walsh, 1895), 181–82.

5. Registers of Marriage 1838–1876, Hong Kong Sheng Kung Hui Archives, PRO HKMS40–1–13; and Susanna Hoe, *The Private Life of Old Hong Kong: Western Women in the British Colony, 1841–1941* (Hong Kong: Oxford University Press, 1991), 91–92. Henrietta died in Shanghai on July 2, 1860, aged twenty-seven. For more on their surviving daughters, see Patricia Pok-kwan Chiu, 'A Position of Usefulness: Gendering History of Girls' Education in Colonial Hong Kong (1850s–1890s)', *History of Education* 37, no. 6 (2008): 797–99. Bessie passed away from consumption in Australia in March 1883. 'Incidents in the Life of a Missionary Candidate', *Female Missionary Intelligencer* 4, New Series (1884): 42–47.

6. Rikimatsu erected a grave for two of his daughters in the Hong Kong Cemetery: Maria Lucy (just 'Lucy' on the grave), who died aged ten months on November 23, 1851, and Lucy

Maria ('Maria Lucy' on the grave), who died aged two years and six months on May 22, 1860.

7. The total of at least 7,000 is from Patricia Lim's *Forgotten Souls: A Social History of the Hong Kong Cemetery* (Hong Kong: Hong Kong University Press, 2011), 3.

8. The Anglican records contain the deceased's name, date of burial, and, if available, their age, profession, and provenance or abode. See also 奥田乙治郎 Okuda Otojirō, 『明治初年に於ける香港日本人』 [*Japanese Residents in Hong Kong during the Early Meiji Era*] (Taipei: Taiwan Sōtokufu Nettai Sangyō Chōsa-kai, 1937), 202–7.

9. The Uenos' infant son also passed away in Athens during the voyage. For more on Ueno, see Andrew Cobbing, 'Ueno Kagenori, 1845–1888: A Most Influential Diplomat [London, 1874–1879]', in *Japanese Envoys in Britain, 1862–1964*, ed. Ian Nish (Boston: Brill, 2007), 35–45.

10. Hirasawa Rokujirō/Jorio Kitchey's remains were removed to the Hong Kong Cemetery Ossuary, niche 451, in the 1960s or 1970s.

11. Andrew Gordon, *A Modern History of Japan: From Tokugawa Times to the Present*, 4th ed. (New York: Oxford University Press, 2020), 19–20.

12. For more on this, see Andrew Cobbing, *Kyushu: Gateway to Japan: A Concise History* (Leiden: Brill, 2008), 216.

13. Kanagawa, a settlement on the main east–west highway, was initially selected as a treaty port, but the Japanese objected and built a new town at the nearby fishing village of Yokohama. Shimoda was briefly an open port prior to 1859. James Hoare, ed., *Culture, Power & Politics in Treaty Port Japan, 1854–1899: Key Papers, Press and Contemporary Writings*, Vol. 1, *Historical Perspectives* (Amsterdam: Amsterdam University Press, 2018), xvii, xx. Hyōgo was used to refer to present-day Kobe, and Edo or Yedo for Tokyo.

14. China opened five ports, including Shanghai, to foreign trade and residence as a result of the Treaty of Nanking [Nanjing], which ended the First Opium War of 1839–1842. A further eleven were added in 1858. Catherine L. Phipps, *Empires on the Waterfront: Japan's Ports and Power, 1858–1899* (Cambridge, MA: Harvard University Asia Center, 2015), 5–9.

15. Gordon, *A Modern History of Japan*, 51.

16. The Tariff Convention, signed on July 25, 1866, clarified the Japanese government proclamation of May 23, 1866, that permitted all Japanese subjects to travel to any foreign country for the purposes of trade or study. United States, *Compilation of Treaties in Force: Prepared under Act of July 7, 1898*. Washington: Government Printing Office. https://heinonline-org.eproxy.lib.hku.hk/HOL/P?h=hein.ustreaties/ctforpu0001&i=1.

17. Catherine L. Phipps, *Empires on the Waterfront*, 67.

18. Forces loyal to the last *shōgun* continued their fight against the Meiji regime for the next fifteen months in a brutal civil war, the Boshin War. The new government faced several other challenges, particularly from discontented *samurai*, the largest of which was the Satsuma rebellion of 1877. For an historical overview, see Gordon, *A Modern History of Japan*, 58–59, 85–86. The Satsuma domain became part of today's Kagoshima prefecture, Chōshū of Yamaguchi prefecture, Tosa of Kōchi prefecture, and Hizen province was divided into Saga and Nagasaki prefectures.

19. Between 1868 and 1912, the Meiji government hired at least 2,000 foreign engineers, teachers, and other specialists. See Chushichi Tsuzuki, *The Pursuit of Power in Modern Japan, 1825–1995* (Oxford: Oxford University Press, 2000), 70–72. The Tokugawa government organised several expeditions overseas prior to its downfall. The first was in 1860. Cobbing, *The Japanese Discovery of Victorian Britain*, 19.

20. Itō Hirobumi travelled to Europe as one of the famous 'Chōshū Five', along with INOUE Kaoru (井上馨; 1836–1915). The group of students from the Chōshū domain made their way to London clandestinely in 1863 with the assistance of Jardine Matheson & Co. Cobbing, *The Japanese Discovery of Victorian Britain*, 24.

21. Andō's first name is given as Tadatsune (忠経) rather than Tarō in the official records of the mission.

22. 安藤太郎 Andō Tarō, 「美家古廼波奈誌」 [Stories from the Battle in Miyako], in 『舊幕府』 [*The Former Government*] 3 (Tokyo: Kyūbakufu-zasshi-sha, 1897), 1–11.

23. For more on the Embassy's itinerary, see Ian Nish, ed., *The Iwakura Mission in America and Europe: A New Assessment* (Richmond, Surrey: Japan Library, 1998). The unequal treaties would not be fully superseded until 1899. Britain was the first to give up extraterritoriality in 1894. Hoare, *Culture, Power & Politics*, xxiii.

24. 'The Results of the Japanese Embassy', *China Mail*, October 25, 1873, 4.

25. Kunitake Kume, *The Iwakura Embassy, 1871–1873: A True Account of the Ambassador Extraordinary and Plenipotentiary's Journal of Observation Through the United States of America and Europe*, Vol. 5, ed. Graham Healey and Chushichi Tsuzuki, trans. Graham Healey, Eugene Soviak, and Chushichi Tsuzuki (Chiba: The Japan Documents, 2002), 340–45.

26. John M. Carroll, *A Concise History of Hong Kong* (Hong Kong: Hong Kong University Press, 2007), 9–28. The New Territories were leased to Britain in 1898 for ninety-nine years. The Qing (1644–1911) was China's last imperial dynasty.

27. Carroll, *A Concise History of Hong Kong*, 18–35. For more on the importance of opium in colonial Hong Kong's development, see Christopher Munn, 'The Hong Kong Opium Revenue, 1845–1885', in *Opium Regimes: China, Britain, and Japan, 1839–1952*, ed. Timothy Brook and Bob Tadashi Wakabayashi (Berkeley: University of California Press, 2000), 105–26. For more on Hong Kong and Chinese migration to California, see Elizabeth Sinn, *Pacific Crossing: California Gold, Chinese Migration, and the Making of Hong Kong* (Hong Kong: Hong Kong University Press, 2012).

28. Cobbing, *The Japanese Discovery of Victorian Britain*, 35, 54.

29. 林陸朗 Hayashi Rokurō, 『長崎唐通事——大通事林道栄とその周辺　増補版』 [*Chinese-Language Interpreters in Nagasaki: Head Interpreter Hayashi Dōei and His Associates*, Revised edition] (Nagasaki: Nagasaki Bunken-sha, 2010), 291.

30. Letter from Ueno Kagenori to the office of Sir Harry S. Parkes, British Envoy Extraordinary and Minister Plenipotentiary, dated March 13, 1873. The National Archives of the UK (TNA): CO 129/166, 374; and letter from Sir Harry Parkes to the Earl Granville, Secretary of State for Foreign Affairs, dated August 11, 1873. TNA: CO 129/166, 449–50. Hayashi belonged to a family of Chinese interpreters but had received tuition in English as well and was considered proficient in the language. 林, 『長崎唐通事』, 246–81.

31. *Hongkong Daily Press*, April 21, 1873, 2.

32. *China Mail*, April 16, 1873, 3.

33. 林, 『長崎唐通事』, 292–315; and 「林副領事自殺ノ届」 [Report of Vice-Consul Hayashi's Suicide], 公文録・明治六年・第九十九巻 [Official Records, 1873, Vol. 99] dated September 1873, Japan Center for Asian Historical Records (JACAR), originally from the National Archives of Japan, https://www.digital.archives.go.jp/img/3032272.

34. One of the best-known guides on Western-style clothing and manners at the time was authored by the influential founder of Keio University, FUKUZAWA Yukichi (福澤諭吉; 1835–1901), https://dcollections.lib.keio.ac.jp/en/fukuzawa. For more on Fukuzawa, see Olive Checkland, *Japan and Britain after 1859: Creating Cultural Bridges* (New York: Routledge, 2003), 3–13.

35. Cobbing, *The Japanese Discovery of Victorian Britain*, 53.

36. As translated in Matthew Fraleigh, *'New Chronicles of Yanagibashi' and 'Diary of a Journey to the West': Narushima Ryuhoku Reports from Home and Abroad* (Ithaca, NY: Cornell University Press, 2010), 156.

37. For more on Japanese attitudes to China in the 1860s, see Joshua A. Fogel, *The Literature of Travel in the Japanese Rediscovery of China, 1862–1945* (Stanford: Stanford University Press, 1996), 46–57.

Notes 139

38. Examples of comments on the unsanitary conditions of the Chinese quarters of the city can be found in the diaries of MORI Ōgai (森鴎外; 1862–1922) and HONDA Seiroku (本多静六; 1866–1952). For more on Mori and Honda, see Chapter 3.

39. Claude MacDonald (1852–1915), British Minister to China and, subsequently, Japan, is believed to be the originator of this phrase in 1900. Comparisons between Japan as 'the Island Empire of the East' and Britain as 'the Island Empire of the West' were prevalent during the first decade of the twentieth century, particularly following the signing of the first Anglo-Japanese Alliance in January 1902, though relations had begun to sour by the time of the 1910 Japan–British Exhibition in London. Ayako Hotta-Lister, *The Japan–British Exhibition of 1910: Gateway to the Island Empire of the East* (Richmond, Surrey: Japan Library, 1999), 1–2, 9–37.

40. The 1876 Census published in the *Hong Kong Government Gazette* of February 24, 1877, counted five Shintō followers, presumably Japanese (Table 4). The 1881 Census published in the *Hong Kong Government Gazette* of June 11, 1881, counted three Shintō followers (Table 4).

41. 奥田, 『明治初年に於ける香港日本人』, 109–13. For more on *karayuki-san* in Hong Kong, see Chapter 2.

42. Kimura worked for the trading company of Kōgyō Shōkai (廣業商會), which specialised in the export of seafood products from Hokkaido, during the early 1880s. For more on Kōgyō Shōkai, see Chapter 5. Kimura's descriptions of Hong Kong are from an oral history interview in 1935. He was, by then, one of the city's oldest Japanese residents. 奥田, 『明治初年に於ける香港日本人』, Appendix 6.

43. Sheila E. Hamilton, *Watching Over Hong: Private Policing 1841–1941* (Hong Kong: Hong Kong University Press, 2008), 17. Ordinance 14 of 1870 (repealing earlier ordinances). A further notification was issued in 1871 requiring both passes and lighted lamps. The ordinance was finally repealed in 1897.

44. 奥田, 『明治初年に於ける香港日本人』, 190–200. The Japanese source put the number of short- and long-term residents at 147. However, one resident, OKAYAMA Heisuke (岡山兵助), was listed twice. The 146 total did not include three consular staff. A pencilled 'June 7' on the original file suggests that the survey was taken either on or around that date. The *kashizashiki* system came about as a result of an 1872 Meiji government decree, which freed women held in bondage by brothels to pay for their parents' debts. Brothel owners found a way around this by setting up 'rental rooms' and paying a licence fee for employing prostitutes outside the bondage system. See Brian Burke-Gaffney, *Nagasaki: The British Experience, 1854–1945* (Folkestone: Global Oriental, 2009), 64–65.

45. This average is based on the ages given for ninety-five of the ninety-six female residents, including five girls aged thirteen, nine, eight, six, and three.

46. For more on Nagasaki's role in the traffic of *karayuki-san*, see Chapter 2.

47. This average is based on the ages given for thirty-nine of the fifty male residents, including three boys aged fourteen, seven, and four.

48. Gracia Liu-Farrer, 'Creating a Transnational Community: Chinese Newcomers in Japan', in *Japan's Minorities: The Illusion of Homogeneity*, 2nd ed., ed. Michael Weiner (London: Routledge, 2009), 116–38, at 117.

49. Minami served as Japanese Consul in Hong Kong from 1885 to 1888.

50. Letter from John William Jones to the Secretary of State to the Colonies, Henry Thurstan Holland, 1st Viscount Knutsford (1825–1914), dated January 3, 1890. TNA: CO 129/248, 814–16.

51. 奥田, 『明治初年に於ける香港日本人』, 191.

52. Seiichiro Yonekura and Shimizu Hiroshi, 'Entrepreneurship in Pre-World War II Japan: The Role and Logic of the Zaibatsu', in *The Invention of Enterprise: Entrepreneurship from*

Ancient Mesopotamia to Modern Times, ed. David S. Landes, Joel Mokyr, and William J. Baumol (Princeton: Princeton University Press, 2012), 506.

53. One hundred and twenty-two residents are listed as 'commoners' and nineteen have a 'nil' response.

54. Two of the four Mitsui employees featured on the Hong Kong government's 1886 Jury list of 'Common Jurors', with their abode recorded as 9 Remedios Terrace. *Hong Kong Government Gazette*, February 27, 1886. The Japanese Consulate address was given as 7 Caine Road in the *Chronicle & Directory* for 1885, 253.

55. For more on the Sino-Japanese War, see Tsuzuki, *The Pursuit of Power in Modern Japan*, 121–38.

56. 奥田、『明治初年に於ける香港日本人』, 313–16.

57. The ministry included thirty-eight Taiwanese (twenty-nine men and nine women) and twenty-three Koreans (twenty-one men and two women) in its 1916 count of Japanese residents in Hong Kong and their occupations. 外務省通商局 編、『香港事情』, 348–49.

58. Roger Daniels, 'The Japanese Diaspora in the New World', in *Japanese Diasporas: Unsung Pasts, Conflicting Presents, and Uncertain Futures*, ed. Nobuko Adachi (Abingdon: Routledge, 2006), 25–34.

59. The Japanese government suspended contract labour emigration to Hawaii for sixteen years after the first group in 1868. Daniels, 'The Japanese Diaspora', 31. For more on Japanese pearl divers on Thursday Island, see Chapter 3.

60. Yun Hui Tsu, ed., *Japan and Singapore: A Multidisciplinary Approach* (Singapore: McGraw-Hill Education [Asia], 2006), 28.

61. For more on the Hongkong Club, see Vaudine England, *Kindred Spirits: A History of the Hong Kong Club* (Hong Kong: The Hong Kong Club, 2016), 60. For more on Hong Kong's class structure prior to the Second World War, see Henry Lethbridge, *Hong Kong: Stability and Change: A Collection of Essays* (Hong Kong: Oxford University Press, 1978), 163–88. See also Carroll, *A Concise History of Hong Kong*, 35–46.

62. For more on the Osaka Military Academy, see Masaya Nakatsu, 'Les Missions Militaires Françaises au Japon entre 1867 et 1889', Doctoral thesis for the Université Sorbonne Paris Cité (2018), 295–97. Yukawa and six companions sailed from Yokohama on November 12, 1872, aboard the Messageries Maritimes steamship *Phase*. After a change of vessel in Hong Kong, they headed for Marseille, landing there on December 16, 1872. *China Mail*, November 18, 1872, 2; and 奥村功 Okumura Isao, 「明治初期のあるフランス留学生――湯川温作」 [A Student in France during the Early Meiji Period], in 『幕末・明治期の国民国家形成と文化変容』 [*The Formation of the Nation-State and Transformation of Culture in the Late Tokugawa and Meiji Periods*], ed. 西川長夫・松宮秀治 Nishikawa Nagao and Matsumiya Hideharu (Tokyo: Shinyō-sha, 1995), 581–82.

63. The Iwakura Embassy had travelled from Dover to Paris that same day, though there is no indication that Yukawa met with any of the members of the Embassy during their stay in the capital. Richard Sims, 'France', in Nish, *The Iwakura Mission in America and Europe*, 69–73.

64. Michiko Maejima, 'Édifier et Équiper les Bases de l'Armée Japonaise: Transferts de Technologie, France-Japon 1868–1930', Doctoral thesis for the Conservatoire National des Arts et Métiers (2014), Annexe 2. Yukawa's name appears as 'Yonkavva' in the École Polytechnique's record of his registration.

65. Philippe Burty was a collector of Japanese prints and is sometimes credited with coining the term 'Japonisme', though there is still some debate over who was the first to use it. See Elwood Hartman, 'Japonisme and Nineteenth-Century French Literature', *Comparative Literature Studies* 18, no. 2 (June 1981): 141–66.

66. Bibliothèque nationale de France. Fonds Victor Hugo. III – Carnets. 1er Janvier–31 décembre 1876. Page 15r. https://gallica.bnf.fr/ark:/12148/btv1b530382945/f31.item.

Authors' own translation. An entry in Hugo's diary dated December 23, 1875, mentioned hosting a Mister 'You' for dinner, possibly the same 'You Ka Va'. Bibliothèque nationale de France. Fonds Victor Hugo. Agenda. 1er juillet–31 décembre 1875, https://gallica.bnf.fr/ark:/12148/btv1b10085737w/f152.item.

67. *Hongkong Daily Press*, August 5, 1878. Kosaka was among the first group of Military Academy students sent to France. Hiro was a member of the second group, along with Yukawa. See Maejima, 'Édifier et Équiper les Bases de l'Armée Japonaise', Annexe 2.

68. 奥田、『明治初年に於ける香港日本人』, 65–66.

69. Yukawa's cause of death is given as consumption on his death certificate. Hong Kong Births and Deaths General Register Office.

70. There is some debate over the actual date of its opening. See Tim-Keung Ko, 'A Review of Development of Cemeteries in Hong Kong: 1841–1950', *Journal of the Royal Asiatic Society Hong Kong Branch* 41 (2001): 241–80.

71. See Ken Nicolson, *The Happy Valley: A History and Tour of the Hong Kong Cemetery* (Hong Kong: Hong Kong University Press, 2010), 2–3.

72. Burial records list at least six Chinese interments in 1856 and 1857, including four converts to Christianity whose funeral services were conducted by the sinologist and missionary James Legge (1815–1897). Another entry in 1857 was for a 'Malay' seaman, whose burial took place 'without the knowledge of either clergyman or sexton'. Burial Registers 1853–1930, Hong Kong Sheng Kung Hui Archives, PRO HKMS44–1.

73. Ko, 'A Review of Development of Cemeteries in Hong Kong', 247–54.

74. Andō arrived as vice-consul and was promoted to full consul in 1877.

75. Kate Lowe and Eugene McLaughlin, 'Sir John Pope Hennessy and the "Native Race Craze": Colonial Government in Hong Kong, 1877–1882', *The Journal of Imperial and Commonwealth History* 20, no. 1 (January 1992): 223–47. See also John M. Carroll, *Edge of Empires: Chinese Elites and British Colonials in Hong Kong* (Hong Kong: Hong Kong University Press, 2005), 49–53. Founded in 1869 to provide dedicated medical services for the city's Chinese residents, the Tung Wah Hospital's committee soon exceeded this mandate to become a major voice for the Chinese community on other issues as well. See Elizabeth Sinn, *Power and Charity: The Early History of the Tung Wah Hospital, Hong Kong* (Hong Kong: Oxford University Press, 1989). (Republished in 2003 as *Power and Charity: A Chinese Merchant Elite in Colonial Hong Kong* by Hong Kong University Press.)

76. James Pope-Hennessy, *Verandah: Some Episodes in the Crown Colonies, 1867–1889* (London: George Allen and Unwin, 1964), 95–100.

77. For more on Pope Hennessy's visit to Japan and tenure as governor in Hong Kong, see P. Kevin MacKeown, *A Stormy Petrel: The Life and Times of John Pope Hennessy* (Hong Kong: City University of Hong Kong Press, 2020), 189–267; and 江森泰吉 編 Emori Taikichi, ed., 『大隈伯百話』 [*One Hundred Tales of Earl Okuma*] (Tokyo: Jitsugyo no Nihon Sha, 1909).

78. We have not uncovered correspondence or other documentation confirming any arrangement between the Japanese Consulate and the colonial administration regarding Yukawa's burial in the Hong Kong Cemetery. However, the fact that there were no burials of unbaptised Japanese prior to Yukawa and that the consulate was clearly involved suggests that this was the case. Unlike the 'Malay' seaman, whose burial on January 18, 1857, took place 'without the knowledge of either clergyman or sexton', Yukawa's was authorised. Burial Registers 1853–1930, Hong Kong Sheng Kung Hui Archives, PRO HKMS44–1.

79. The original emplacement of the Meiji-era gravestones is unknown. Over the years, typhoons, landslides, and relocations have impacted the Hong Kong Cemetery's layout. In 1975, the government relocated thousands of remains to allow for the construction of the Aberdeen Tunnel that connects the northern and southern sides of Hong Kong Island. *Hong Kong Government Gazette* 48, November 1975: 3609–95.

80. Yun Hui Tsu, 'Post-Mortem Identity and Burial Obligation: On Blood Relations, Place Relations, and Associational Relations in the Japanese Community in Singapore', in *The Culture of Association and Associations in Contemporary Japanese Society*, ed. Hirochika Nakamaki (Osaka: National Museum of Ethnology, 2002), 93–114.

81. 目賀多信順 編 Megata Nobuyori, ed., 「陸軍埋葬地ニ葬ルノ法則」 [Burial Rules at Army Burial Grounds], in 『官省布告類纂』明治8年巻1 [*Government Rules and Announcements: 1875*], Vol. 1 (Tokyo: Megata Nobuyori, 1875), 82–83; and 横山篤夫 Yokoyama Atsuo, 「戦没者の遺骨と陸軍墓地──夫が戦没した妻たちの六〇年後の意識から」 [The Remains of the War Dead and Military Cemeteries: From the Viewpoint of War Widows 60 Years On], 『国立歴史民俗博物館研究報告』 [*Bulletin of the National Museum of Japanese History*] 147 (December 2008): 98. Yukawa's rank of second lieutenant listed in the Chinese character inscription was awarded posthumously.

82. Fees for monuments varied depending on the size of the structure. Government Notification no. 15 published in the *Hong Kong Government Gazette* 29, no. 3, January 20, 1883. A steerage class fare from Hong Kong to Kobe on a Mitsubishi Mail Steamship Company ship cost 15 dollars in 1883. *Chronicle & Directory* 1883, 590.

83. Tomb of Onsaku Yukawa, Japanese Officer, deceased in Hong Kong on August 5, 1878, at the age of twenty-two, while returning to his homeland from France. Authors' own translation. For correspondence on the issue of which department should bear responsibility for Yukawa's burial costs, see 「外務大書記官 香港において死亡の湯川少尉埋葬諸費立替分返済要請」 [Letter from a Senior Secretary in the Foreign Ministry to a Senior Officer in the Army: A Request to Reimburse the Burial Expenses for Lieutenant Yukawa Who Died in Hong Kong] dated December 5, 1878, JACAR, originally from the National Institute for Defense Studies, https://www.jacar.archives.go.jp/das/image/C09120521700.

84. Andrew Bernstein, *Modern Passings: Death Rites, Politics, and Social Change in Imperial Japan* (Honolulu: University of Hawai'i Press, 2006), 1–2, 39.

85. A more traditional Japanese funeral monument erected for boarding house owner MATSUBARA Jisaburō (松原治三郎) in March 1918 was probably designed in and shipped from Japan.

86. The Sanitary Bureau estimated that the average annual number of Japanese deaths in Hong Kong for the years 1904 to 1909 was 21.8. 'Sanitary Board', *China Mail*, July 7, 1909, 5.

87. The Legislative Council approved and published the bye-law in the *Hong Kong Government Gazette*, December 4, 1908. The Sanitary Board was established in 1883 to 'supervise and control the practical Sanitation of the Colony'. *Hong Kong Government Gazette* 29, no. 18, April 21, 1883. Two appointed Chinese members, Ho Kom Tong and Lau Chu Pak, actively participated in the Sanitary Board's meetings in the first half of 1909. *Hong Kong Blue Book* 1909.

88. 'A Buddhist Cemetery', *China Mail*, July 7, 1909, 4.

89. 'Joss-Sticks in Chinese Cemeteries: Rites and Ceremonies', *China Mail*, April 14, 1909, 5; and 'A Buddhist Cemetery', *China Mail*, July 7, 1909, 4.

90. 'Joss-Sticks in Chinese Cemeteries: Rites and Ceremonies', *China Mail*, April 14, 1909, 5. Hong Kong's better-off Chinese residents had no permanent cemetery of their own until 1913. Ko, 'A Review of Development of Cemeteries in Hong Kong', 247–54.

91. Letter from FUNATSU Tatsuichirō to the Acting Colonial Secretary A. M. Thomson dated June 29, 1909. 「香港ニ於テ日本人専属墓地新設ノ件」 [Regarding a Plan to Establish a New Cemetery for the Exclusive Use of the Japanese in Hong Kong], March 1909, JACAR, originally from the Diplomatic Archives of the Ministry of Foreign Affairs, https://www.jacar.archives.go.jp/das/image/B12082599000; and *Laws of Hong Kong: A Selection of Constitutional Documents, Conventions and Treaties*, Appendix IV (Hong Kong: Government Printer; Revised edition, 1964).

Notes

143

92. 'The Proposed Cemetery for Buddhists', *China Mail*, July 6, 1909, 5; 'Sanitary Board', *China Mail*, July 7, 1909, 5; and letter from Governor Frederick Lugard to the Secretary of State for the Colonies dated November 17, 1909. TNA: CO 129/358, 424–26.

93. Ordinance No. 38 of 109 – An Ordinance to set apart certain Crown Land to be used as a burial ground for persons professing the Christian Religion (*Hong Kong Government Gazette*, November 12, 1909). The bye-law relating to the burning of joss sticks was amended to apply to the consecrated portion of the cemetery only (*Hong Kong Government Gazette*, December 3, 1909). For more on the dedication ceremony, see 'Protestant Cemetery: Impressive Dedication Ceremony', *China Mail*, March 30, 1910, 4. There was ultimately no attempt to relocate the Japanese graves that fell within consecrated ground. TNA: CO 129/358, 424–26.

Chapter 2

1. *China Mail*, June 10, 1884, 3.

2. *China Mail*, June 13, 1884, 2.

3. 'O' is a prefix frequently used in Japanese. If a *karayuki-san* is mentioned more than once in the text, only her given name is used after the first mention. *Karayuki-san* were generally addressed by their given or nicknames.

4. While the Meiji government had abolished social divisions when it came to power, class distinctions persisted. See Seiichiro Yonekura and Hiroshi Shimizu, 'Entrepreneurship in Pre-World War II Japan: The Role and Logic of the Zaibatsu', in *The Invention of Enterprise: Entrepreneurship from Ancient Mesopotamia to Modern Times*, ed. David S. Landes, Joel Mokyr, and William J. Baumol (Princeton: Princeton University Press, 2012), 506.

5. 奥田乙治郎 Okuda Otojirō, 『明治初年に於ける香港日本人』 [*Japanese Residents in Hong Kong during the Early Meiji Era*] (Taipei: Taiwan Sōtokufu Nettai Sangyō Chōsa-kai), 1937, 190–200.

6. *China Mail*, June 9, 1884, 2.

7. Quoting an 1895 report by the Japanese Consul in Singapore, economic historian Hiroshi Shimizu advises that 'in Singapore there were 450 to 460 Japanese residents, of whom some 400 were prostitutes or those related to them'. Hiroshi Shimizu, 'Rise and Fall of the Karayuki-san in the Netherlands Indies from the Late Nineteenth Century to the 1930s', *Review of Indonesian and Malaysian Affairs* 26, no. 2 (Summer 1992): 19.

8. Mikiso Hane, *Peasants, Rebels, and Outcastes: The Underside of Modern Japan* (New York: Pantheon, 1982), 218.

9. Andrew Gordon, *A Modern History of Japan: From Tokugawa Times to the Present*, 4th ed. (New York: Oxford University Press, 2020), 95. See also Sachiko Sone, 'The Karayuki-san of Asia 1868–1938: The Role of Prostitutes Overseas in Japanese Economic and Social Development', *Review of Indonesian and Malaysian Affairs* 26, no. 2 (Summer 1992): 44–62.

10. 長崎県南高来郡役所 Minami-Takaki County Office, Nagasaki Prefecture, 『長崎県南高来郡町村要覧 上』 [*Annals of the Minami-Takaki Counties, Towns and Villages, Nagasaki Prefecture, Vol. 1*] (1893), 13.

11. 長崎県南高来郡役所, 『要覧 上』, 6.

12. Infanticide may have persisted up to the legalisation of abortion in Japan in 1949. *Mabiki* likens infants to rice seedlings, some of which need to be uprooted to allow others the space and light to thrive. Gordon, *A Modern History of Japan*, 29; and Fabian Drixler, *Mabiki: Infanticide and Population Growth in Eastern Japan, 1660–1950* (Berkeley: University of California Press, 2013), 1–2.

13. 森崎和江 Morisaki Kazue, 『からゆきさん』 [*Karayuki-san*] (Tokyo: Asahi Shimbun-sha, [1976] 2022), 228–29.

14. Though used orally, the term *karayuki-san* did not appear in the *Asahi* newspaper until the 1930s, in connection with the release of the 1937 film *Karayuki-san*, directed by KIMURA Sotoji (木村荘十二). The term *shūgyōfu* or 'woman in ugly business' was far more commonly used in writing to describe girls and women engaging in sex work overseas. For more on the evolution of the term, see Bill Mihalopoulos, 'The Making of Prostitutes: The Karayuki-san', *Bulletin of Concerned Asian Scholars* 25, no. 1 (1993): 41–56.

15. *Hong Kong Blue Book* for the year 1884.

16. Elizabeth Sinn, 'Women at Work: Chinese Brothel Keepers in Nineteenth-Century Hong Kong', *Journal of Women's History* 19, no. 3 (2007): 88.

17. Kazuhiro Oharazeki, *Japanese Prostitutes in the North American West, 1887–1920* (Seattle: University of Washington Press, 2016), 25.

18. 奥田、『明治初年に於ける香港日本人』, 111.

19. 師岡国 編 Morooka Kuni, ed., 『板垣君欧米漫遊日記』 [*Itagaki's Diary of a Journey to Europe and the U.S.*] (Tokyo: Matsui Chūbei, 1883), 8. Authors' own translation; and 陳湛頤 Chan Cham-yi, 〈香港早年的日本娼妓〉 [Japanese Prostitutes in the Early Years of Hong Kong], in 《日本與亞洲華人社會　歷史文化篇》 [*Chinese Societies in Japan and East Asia: History and Culture*], ed. 原武道 Hara Takemichi et al. (Hong Kong: Commercial Press, 1999), 137.

20. Catherine L. Phipps, *Empires on the Waterfront: Japan's Ports and Power, 1858–1899* (Cambridge, MA: Harvard University Asia Center, 2015), 32.

21. For more on this, see Phipps, *Empires on the Waterfront*, 96–99.

22. Phipps, *Empires on the Waterfront*, 89.

23. William D. Wray. *Mitsubishi and N.Y.K., 1870–1914: Business Strategy in the Japanese Shipping Industry* (Cambridge, MA: Harvard University Press, 1984), 157.

24. See Brian Burke-Gaffney, *Nagasaki: The British Experience, 1854–1945* (Folkestone: Global Oriental, 2009), 106–7.

25. Bill Mihalopoulos, 'Women, Overseas Sex Work and Globalization in Meiji Japan', *The Asia-Pacific Journal* 10.35, no. 1 (August 2012): 6–7.

26. Mihalopoulos, 'Women', 7.

27. 'Blue Funnel's "Butterflies"', *Swire News* 25, no. 3 (1998): 28.

28. Sone, 'The Karayuki-san of Asia 1868–1938', 44.

29. *China Mail*, April 10, 1888, 3, summarising an article from the *Nagasaki Express*.

30. David Sissons, 'Karayuki-san: Japanese Prostitutes in Australia, 1887–1916 (1)', *Historical Studies* 17, no. 68 (1977): 339. (Reprinted in *Bridging Australia and Japan*, Vol. 1, *The Writings of David Sissons, Historian and Political Scientist*, ed. Arthur Stockwin and Keiko Tamura (Canberra: Australian National University Press, 2016.)

31. *China Mail*, March 27, 1890, 3.

32. 「伏木丸一件」 [Fushiki Maru Incident], 東京朝日新聞 [*Tokyo Asahi Shimbun*], May 9, 1890, Morning Edition, 2. Kiku was Identified as Watana Teta in the *China Mail* article of March 28, 1890. All four women were from Nagasaki prefecture: Kiku and Setsu from the city itself, Hama from Nishi Sonogi, and Suma from Minami Takaki.

33. Identified as Soara Shiki in the *China Mail* article of March 28, 1890.

34. *China Mail*, March 28, 1890, 3.

35. *China Mail*, March 27, 1890, 3.

36. 本多静六 Honda Seiroku, 『明治二十三年　洋行日誌』巻一 [*Travel Diary, 1890*], Vol. 1 (Shōbu-machi, Saitama: Honda Seiroku Hakase o Kinensuru-kai, 1998), 9. Authors' own translation.

37. *Asahi*, May 9, 1890, 2.

38. *China Mail*, April 23, 1890, 3, summarising an article from the *Nagasaki Express*.

39. *China Mail*, April 23, 1890, 3. The *China Mail* reported another tragic example of the dangers inherent in this clandestine mode of travel in January 1902. Divers working to refloat the wreck of the Norwegian steamer *Skramstad*, which had collided with another vessel in the

Notes 145

harbour two months earlier, came across a 'ghastly find': the corpse of a Japanese girl. Her ankles had become trapped during the collision and she had been unable to swim to safety. 'The limbs were intact and white as alabaster, except where broken at the ankles; but the scalp and face were completely eaten away. The body was still covered by an ordinary kimono.' 'A Ghastly Find on the "Skramstad"', *China Mail*, January 14, 1902, 4.

40. By 1897, consuls general were sending biannual reports on the numbers and activities of the *karayuki-san* in their area to the Japanese Minister of Foreign Affairs. See Sone, 'The Karayuki-san of Asia 1868–1938', 47.

41. Letter from Japanese Consul in Shanghai Andō Tarō to Foreign Minister YOSHIDA Kiyonari (吉田清成; 1845–1891), dispatch 112 dated September 26, 1884; and 賣淫婦女ノ海外渡航ニ關スル法律ノ制定ヲ要スル理由 [Reasons Why It Is Necessary to Establish Laws with Regard to Prostitutes Going Abroad] in 1917, 「本邦人不正業取締関係法規雑纂 第1・2巻」 [Miscellaneous Matters Pertaining to Laws and Regulations on Illegitimate Japanese Businesses, Vols. 1 and 2], from the Diplomatic Archives of the Ministry of Foreign Affairs, 4.2.2.34.

42. Instruction from INOUE Kaoru (井上馨) to the governors of Nagasaki, Fukuoka, Yamaguchi, Hyōgo, Osaka, and Kanagawa prefectures dated July 6, 1885, 「本邦人不正業取締関係法規雑纂 第1巻」 [Miscellaneous Matters Pertaining to Laws and Regulations on Illegitimate Japanese Businesses, Vol. 1], from the Diplomatic Archives of the Ministry of Foreign Affairs, 4.2.2.34.

43. James Francis Warren, Ah Ku *and* Karayuki-san*: Prostitution in Singapore 1870–1940* (Singapore: Oxford University Press, 1993), 29. Historian Bill Mihalopoulos argues that *karayuki-san* could return to their communities and face little or no stigma. Mihalopoulos, 'Women', 19.

44. 'Japanese Girls Kidnapped. How Hongkong Is Supplied', *China Mail*, August 30, 1906, 5.

45. For more on the racial dimensions of the colonial government's regulation of prostitution, see Philip Howell, 'Race, Space and the Regulation of Prostitution in Colonial Hong Kong', *Urban History* 31, no. 2 (2004): 229–48.

46. Ann Laura Stoler, *Carnal Knowledge and Imperial Power* (Berkeley: University of California Press, 2002), 45.

47. *Hong Kong Government Gazette*, vol. 3, no. 126, November 28, 1857.

48. Arthur Starling et al., eds., *Plague, SARS and the Story of Medicine in Hong Kong* (Hong Kong: Hong Kong University Press, 2006), 89.

49. *Hong Kong Government Gazette*, vol. 13, no. 30, July 27, 1867.

50. R. J. Miners, 'State Regulation of Prostitution in Hong Kong, 1857 to 1941', *Journal of the Hong Kong Branch of the Royal Asiatic Society* 24 (1984): 143–61.

51. *Report of the Commissioners Appointed to Inquire into the Working of the Contagious Disease Ordinance, 1867, in Hong Kong* (published in 1879), 6. The Report concluded that the earlier ordinances had little effect in curbing the number of unlicensed brothels or the spread of venereal diseases, but in reality little changed. This classification of establishments along racial lines endured up to the 1930s. See Sinn, 'Women at Work', 91.

52. John M. Carroll, 'A National Custom: Debating Female Servitude in Late Nineteenth-Century Hong Kong', *Modern Asian Studies* 43, no. 6 (2009): 1463–93.

53. Appendix to the Report, 4.

54. Sinn, 'Women at Work', 91.

55. Philippa Levine, *Prostitution, Race, and Politics: Policing Venereal Disease in the British Empire* (New York: Routledge, 2003), 206.

56. Letter from the Colonial Surgeon to the Colonial Secretary dated April 26, 1893. The National Archives of the UK (TNA): CO 129/259, 141–43.

57. Appendix to the Report, 13.

58. Appendix to the Report, 30.

59. Chinese brothel keepers were always women. For more on this issue, see Sinn, 'Women at Work', 92.

60. *Hong Kong Blue Book* for the year 1879.

61. Appendix to the Report, 31.

62. Letter from Japanese Consul in Hong Kong MINAMI Teisuke (南貞助; 1847–1915) to Acting Colonial Secretary Frederick Stewart dated October 20, 1885; and letter from Acting Colonial Secretary Frederick Stewart to Japanese Consul in Hong Kong Minami Teisuke dated November 5, 1885, 「本邦人不正業取締関係法規雑纂 第1巻」 [Miscellaneous Matters Pertaining to Laws and Regulations on Illegitimate Japanese Businesses, Vol. 1], from the Diplomatic Archives of the Ministry of Foreign Affairs, 4.2.2.34.

63. Benjamin Wai-ming Ng, 'Making of a Japanese Community in Prewar Period (1841–1941)', in *Foreign Communities in Hong Kong, 1840s–1950s*, ed. Cindy Yik-yi Chu (New York: Palgrave Macmillan, 2005), 121.

64. 奥田, 『明治初年に於ける香港日本人』, Appendix 6.

65. 奥田, 『明治初年に於ける香港日本人』, 313–16; and Howell, 'Race, Space', 245. For more on the development of Wan Chai, see Carl T. Smith, 'Wanchai: In Search of an Identity', in *Hong Kong: A Reader in Social History*, ed. David Faure (Hong Kong: Oxford University Press, 2003), 157–207.

66. 河東碧梧桐 Kawahigashi Hekigotō, 『支那に遊びて』 [*Touring China*] (Tokyo: Ōsaka-yagō Shoten, 1919), 100–105. Authors' own translation; and 陳湛頤 Chan Cham-yi, 《日本人訪港見聞錄：1898–1941》 [*Japanese Visitors to Hong Kong: 1898–1941*] (Hong Kong: Joint Publishing, 2005), 174–85.

67. See Osbert Chadwick, *Mr. Chadwick's Reports on the Sanitary Condition of Hong Kong; with Appendices and Plans* (Hong Kong, 1882).

68. Saki's death certificate lists her as attached to brothel no. 38, which is listed on page 267 of the 1878 Report as a licensed brothel for foreigners located at 13 Graham Street. The *China Mail* article of June 10, 1884, however, has Saki living as 'an inmate of an immoral house, No. 27, Graham Street'.

69. *China Mail*, April 13, 1888, 3.

70. *China Mail*, April 13, 1888, 3.

71. The term 'resident' was applied to Alice Ho Kai (née Walkden), for example, the English wife of one of the most prominent members of the Chinese community, who was buried in the Hong Kong Cemetery just two days before Saki. Burial Registers 1853–1930, Hong Kong Sheng Kung Hui Archives, PRO HKMS44–1.

72. Tominaga Matsu's name does not appear in the 1886 list of Japanese residents in Hong Kong, which means that she either arrived after the date of the census or that there was no record of her presence available.

73. 河東, 『支那に遊びて』, 108–9. Authors' own translation.

74. Ōhashi's real name was Matatarō (又太郎). 大橋乙羽 Ōhashi Otowa, 『歐山米水』 [*European Mountains, American Waters*] (Tokyo: Hakubun-kan, 1900), 17–24. Authors' own translation.

75. 河東, 『支那に遊びて』, 87–88.

76. Appendix to the Report, 10.

77. Stoler, *Carnal Knowledge*, 48.

78. Ernest John Eitel, Inspector of Schools, 'Girls' School', Report dated July 5, 1889, and presented to the Legislative Council on November 20, 1889.

79. For more on Michinaga Ei, see Brian Burke-Gaffney, 'The Tattoos of Michinaga Ei and Nicholas II', *Crossroads: A Journal of Nagasaki History and Culture* 1 (1993); and Burke-Gaffney, *Nagasaki: The British Experience*, 138.

80. 奥田, 『明治初年に於ける香港日本人』, 190–200.

Notes

81. Burke-Gaffney, *Nagasaki: The British Experience*, 62.

82. Minami Teisuke, who was Japanese Consul in Hong Kong from 1885 to 1888, married Englishwoman Eliza Pittman (1849–1902) in London in 1872. They travelled to Japan in 1873 and registered their marital status with the Japanese government under the recently promulgated decree recognising such unions. Theirs is regarded as Japan's first official 'international marriage'. They divorced in 1883 and Eliza returned to England. Minami remarried and his second wife, IZAWA Sen (伊澤せん), accompanied him to Hong Kong. Noboru Koyama, 'Three Meiji Marriages between Japanese Men and English Women', in *Britain and Japan: Biographical Portraits*, Vol. 4, ed. Hugh Cortazzi (Leiden: Brill, 2002), 383–96.

83. Burke-Gaffney, *Nagasaki: The British Experience*, 118.

84. Kiku and Komatsu's family name is given as Hayasaki (早崎) and Kiku is written as 'Okiku' in Mallory's will. Last Will and Testament of Lawrence Mallory dated December 15, 1903, Probate No. 148 of 1904. PRO HKRS144-4-1704. The furniture was put up for public auction on August 24, 1905. 'Auctions', *South China Morning Post*, August 24, 1905, 3.

85. Kiku eventually moved to Singapore. 奥田,『明治初年に於ける香港日本人』, Appendix 11.

86. Letter from Hong Kong senior consular official TAKAGI Sumisaburō (高木澄三郎) to Deputy Foreign Minister KOBAYASHI Jutarō (小林寿太郎).「海外ニ於ケル本邦醜業婦周旋人ノ義ニ関シ在香港帝国領事館ヨリ具申之件」 [Report on the Procurers of Japanese Prostitutes Abroad by the Consulate of the Japanese Empire in Hong Kong], dispatch 9 dated January 23, 1898; and letter from the governor of Hyōgo prefecture ŌMORI Shōichi (大森鍾一) to the Foreign Ministry's Head of the International Commerce Section UCHIDA Kōsai (内田康哉), dispatch 337 dated March 7, 1898,「本邦人不正業取締関係雑件　第一巻」 [Miscellaneous Matters Pertaining to the Control of Illegitimate Japanese Businesses, Vol. 1], 4.2.2.27.

87. Letter from Japanese Consul in Hong Kong UENO Suesaburō (上野季三郎) to Foreign Minister AOKI Shūzō (青木周蔵), dispatch 16 dated September 7, 1900; and letter from the Foreign Ministry's Head of International Commerce Section Uchida Kōsai, dispatch 899 dated October 6, 1900,「本邦人不正業取締関係雑件　第一巻」 [Miscellaneous Matters Pertaining to the Control of Illegitimate Japanese Businesses, Vol. 1], 4.2.2.27.

88. Kanda Nobuko (or Shin) appeared on the 1886 record, where she was listed as a *kashizashiki* manager at 46 Stanley Street. 奥田,『明治初年に於ける香港日本人』, 190–200.

89. Hisa's sister or friend YAMAMOTO Sode (山本ソデ) is buried in the same grave. Sode was just twenty-eight when she died in 1892 and has a more standard, six-character afterlife name, 春香知報信女, which translates to 'fragrant spring and one who is well informed'. 'Spring' might be an allusion to 'selling spring', a Japanese euphemism for prostitution.

90. D. Stratton, 'History of Nursing in Government Hospitals', *The Hong Kong Nursing Journal* 14 (May 1973): 34–37.

91. 'Japanese Women Abroad', *The Japan Weekly Mail*, May 30, 1896, 609.

92. Tomoko Yamazaki, *Sandakan Brothel No. 8: An Episode in the History of Lower-Class Japanese Women*, trans. Karen Colligan-Taylor (Armonk, NY: M.E. Sharpe, 1999). Original in Japanese: 山崎朋子 Yamazaki Tomoko,『サンダカン八番娼館——底辺女性史序章』 [*Sandakan Brothel No. 8: Journey into the History of Lower-Class Japanese Women*] (Tokyo: Chikuma Shobō, 1972); 森崎,『からゆきさん』.

93. Warren, *Ah Ku and* Karayuki-san; Sissons, 'Karayuki-san: Japanese Prostitutes in Australia, 1887–1916 (1&2)', 323–41, 474–88; and Oharazeki, *Japanese Prostitutes*.

94. Shimizu, 'Rise and Fall of the Karayuki-san', 36–38.

95. Carol Gluck, *Japan's Modern Myths: Ideology in the Late Meiji Period* (Princeton: Princeton University Press, 1985), 49, 77, 88–90, 93, 102–3, 177–78, 204.

Chapter 3

1. 森鴎外 Mori Ōgai, 「航西日記」 [Diary of a Voyage to the West], in 『新日本古典文学大系——明治編 5 海外見聞集』 [*New Collection of Japanese Classics: Meiji*, Vol. 5, *International Travels*], ed. 中野三敏, 十川信介, 延広真治, 日野龍夫 Nakano Mitsutoshi, Togawa Shinsuke, Nobuhiro Shinji, and Hino Tatsuo (Tokyo: Iwanami Shoten, 2009), 416. Authors' own translation.

2. Mori Ōgai is the pen name of Mori Rintarō (森林太郎).

3. For more on Mori's life, see Donald Keene, 'The Diaries of Mori Ōgai', in *Modern Japanese Diaries: The Japanese at Home and Abroad as Revealed through Their Diaries* (New York: Henry Holt and Company, 1995), 189–212.

4. 森, 「航西日記」, 416. Authors' own translation.

5. For more on Sōseki, see Keene, *Modern Japanese Diaries*, 213–24.

6. 山田迪生 Yamada Michio, 「漱石の欧州航路体験」 [Soseki's Experiences on His Way to Europe], 『海事史研究』 *Journal of the Japan Society for Nautical Research* 74 (2017): 44.

7. 夏目漱石 Natsume Sōseki, 『漱石全集——第15巻日記及断片』 [*The Sōseki Collection*, Vol. 15, *Diaries and Fragments*] (Tokyo: Sōseki Zenshū Kankō-kai, 1936), 10–11.

8. The *yado-ya* (宿屋) is another type of boarding house, not too far removed from the *ryokan*.

9. 奥田乙治郎 Okuda Otojirō, 『明治初年に於ける香港日本人』 [*Japanese Residents in Hong Kong during the Early Meiji Era*] (Taipei: Taiwan Sōtokufu Nettai Sangyō Chōsa-kai, 1937), 254–59.

10. 奥田, 『明治初年に於ける香港日本人』, 202. Tōyōkan translates as 'Oriental House'. The Yokoses were long-time residents in Hong Kong. Their young son, YOKOSE Toyotarō, who died on May 8, 1886, at the age of three years and nine months, is buried in the Hong Kong Cemetery.

11. 村岡伊平治 Muraoka Iheiji, 『村岡伊平治自伝』 [*Autobiography of Muraoka Iheiji*] (Tokyo: Kodansha, 1987), 152.

12. For more on challenges to the veracity of Muraoka's autobiography, see Motoe Terami-Wada, 'Karayuki-san of Manila: 1890–1920', *Philippine Studies* 34 (1986): 287–316.

13. 村岡, 『村岡伊平治自伝』, 16. Authors' own translation. Muraoka identified the Tōyōkan owner as Nishiyama rather than Yokose. Nishiyama was possibly either managing or employed at Tōyōkan.

14. 村岡, 『村岡伊平治自伝』, 17–21. Tōyōkan was still operating as a *ryokan* with Yokose Yōkichi as its manager in 1901, though it functioned mainly as a food supply business by then. 奥田, 『明治初年に於ける香港日本人』, 311–14; 前田寶治郎 Maeda Hōjirō, 『香港概観』 [*Hong Kong Overview*] (Tokyo: Maeda Hōjirō, 1915), 134; and 林金五郎 Hayashi Kingorō, 『南洋——前編』 [*The South Seas*, Part 1] (Tokyo: Kiryūya Shōkai Shuppan-bu, 1917), 95.

15. 奥田, 『明治初年に於ける香港日本人』, 273–74.

16. Sawano Kakutarō passed away from typhoid fever in Hong Kong on October 8, 1891, and was laid to rest in the Hong Kong Cemetery.

17. 本多静六 Honda Seiroku, 『明治二十三年 洋行日誌』 巻一 [*Travel Diary, 1890*], Vol. 1 (Shōbu-machi, Saitama: Honda Seiroku Hakase o Kinensuru-kai, 1998), 9. Authors' own translation. Honda's assertion that there were no other Japanese hotels in Hong Kong in 1890 is clearly a mistake.

18. 本多, 『洋行日誌』, 10. The Peak Tram started operating in 1888.

19. Heng Fa Lou, which means 'apricot flower', first opened in 1846 and operated until the 1930s. Po Hung Cheng, *Early Hong Kong Eateries* (Hong Kong: University Museum and Art Gallery, University of Hong Kong, 2003), 25. It was located at 325 Queen's Road Central in the 1885 *Chronicle & Directory*, 306.

20. 本多, 『洋行日誌』, 10–11. Authors' own translation.

Notes

149

21. Honda came to be known as the 'father of the public park'. Oleg Benesch and Ran Zwigenberg, *Japan's Castles: Citadels of Modernity in War and Peace* (Cambridge: Cambridge University Press, 2019), 75.

22. The inscription on his grave is very faint. He could have been aged thirty-five when he died, though his death certificate records his age as forty.

23. Two of Ōtaka's children are also buried in the Hong Kong Cemetery.

24. 奥田,『明治初年に於ける香港日本人』, Appendix 25.

25. Christina Ealing-Godbold, 'Pearling Luggers of the Torres Strait', *State Library of Queensland*, November 19, 2014, https://www.slq.qld.gov.au/blog/pearling-luggers-torres-strait.

26. David Sissons, 'The Japanese in the Australian Pearling Industry', *Queensland Heritage* 3, no. 10 (1979): 9. (Reprinted in *Bridging Australia and Japan*, Vol. 1, *The Writings of David Sissons, Historian and Political Scientist*, ed. Arthur Stockwin and Keiko Tamura, Canberra: Australian National University Press, 2016.) The practice of crimping involved unscrupulous individuals of various nationalities enlisting sailors through swindling or coercion.

27. 井上貞次郎 Inoue Teijirō, 「私の履歴書――香港へ渡る」 [My Personal Story: On to Hong Kong], 『日本経済新聞』 *The Nikkei*, July 10, 1959. Authors' own translation. Inoue shared his life story with a reporter from the *Nikkei* newspaper, who then wrote up his account and published it in a series of articles.

28. 井上, 「私の履歴書――内地へ帰る」 [My Personal Story: Returning to Japan], 『日本経済新聞』 *The Nikkei*, July 11, 1959. Authors' own translation.

29. Douglas R. Reynolds, 'Training Young China Hands: Tōa Dōbun Shoin and Its Precursors, 1886–1945', in *The Japanese Informal Empire in China, 1895–1937*, ed. Peter Duus, Ramon H. Myers, and Mark R. Peattie (Princeton: Princeton University Press, 2014), 210–71. For more on the Tōa Dōbun Shoin and its connections to the Japanese intelligence services, see Richard J. Samuels, *Special Duty: A History of the Japanese Intelligence Community* (Ithaca, NY: Cornell University Press, 2019), 35–38.

30. 塩山正純 Shioyama Masazumi, 「『大旅行誌』の思い出に記された香港――昭和期の記述より」 [Hong Kong in the *Journal of the Grand Tour* during the Shōwa Period], 『愛知大学国際コミュニケーション学会 文明 21』 *Civilization 21*, Association for International Communication, Aichi University 40 (March 2018): 42–43.

31. Matsubara died without a will and an administration bond was drawn up on April 18, 1918, naming Yasu as his lawful widow (Hong Kong Public Records Office HKRS143-2-1690).

32. 奥田,『明治初年に於ける香港日本人』, 315.

33. 槇山榮次 Makiyama Eiji,『百年前の留学記』 [*Study Abroad Diary from a Century Ago*] (Tokyo: Shinpū-sha, 2005), 25–26.

34. 槇山,『百年前の留学記』, 26–27, 29–30.

35. *South China Morning Post*, November 7, 1912, 3; and 「上等兵免職の件」 [Dismissal of a Lance Corporal], in 「貳大日記8月」 [*The Daily Record*, II], August 1898, Japan Center for Asian Historical Records (JACAR) and National Institute for Defense Studies, https://www.jacar.archives.go.jp/das/image/C06083028400.

36. See the Hong Kong government's 'Report of the Commission on Alcoholic Liquors', August 12, 1898, and Ordinance no. 9 of 1911, 'An Ordinance to consolidate and amend the law relating to Intoxicating Liquors', *Hong Kong Government Gazette*, March 31, 1911, 92–124.

37. *Hongkong Daily Press*, April 14, 1908, 2.

38. *South China Morning Post*, November 9, 1911, 8.

39. 三宅克己 Miyake Kokki,『欧洲絵行脚』 [*Art Journey around Europe*] (Gahō-sha, 1910), 23. Authors' own translation.

40. 三宅,『欧洲絵行脚』, 25–27.

41. *South China Morning Post*, November 6, 1913, 7.

42. 外務省通商局 編 International Trade Bureau, Foreign Ministry, ed.,『香港事情』 [*Hong Kong Current Affairs*] (Tokyo: Keisei-sha, 1917), 136–41.

43. 小山健三 Koyama Kenzō, 『作州からみた明治百年』上巻 [*Sakushū City in the One Hundred Years since the Meiji Restoration*, Vol. 1] (Tsuyama: Tsuyama Asahi Shimbun-sha, 1970), 250–51. Like Matsubara, Uetsuki died without a will and an administration bond was drawn up on May 28, 1918, naming Yoneko as his lawful widow (Hong Kong Public Records Office HKRS143-2-1689).

44. 'Japanese Women Abroad', *Japan Weekly Mail*, May 30, 1896, 609.

45. James Francis Warren, *Ah Ku and Karayuki-san: Prostitution in Singapore 1870–1940* (Singapore: Oxford University Press, 1993), 203.

46. Terami-Wada, 'Karayuki-san of Manila', 298.

47. Ōtaka's first name is transcribed as 'Yoishi' in the 1897 statement. This is likely a mistake in the romanisation of 'Yoichi'.

48. Queensland State Archives, Item ID ITM861850. See also Martin Dusinberre, 'Japan, Global History, and the Great Silence', *History Workshop Journal* 83, no. 1 (Spring 2017): 138–39.

49. Matsubara Jisaburō appears on an 1891 list of Hong Kong residents, though alternative *kanji* are used for his first name. 奥田, 『明治初年に於ける香港日本人』, 311.

50. Again, there is a difference in how 'Yoichi' is transcribed. He is written as 'Yōichi' in Muraoka's autobiography, with different characters used for his Japanese name: 奥市 (Yoichi) and 用一 (Yōichi). However, given the rarity of this combination of first name and surname, we believe that Ōtaka Yoichi and Ōtaka Yōichi are the same man.

51. 村岡, 『村岡伊平治自伝』, 264–65.

52. The four defendants were eventually found guilty of manslaughter and sentenced to ten years' hard labour. For details of the case, see *South China Morning Post*, April 6, 1907, 2; April 15, 1907, 8; May 9, 1907, 2; May 10, 1907, 2; June 19, 1907, 2; June 20, 1907, 2; and June 21, 1907, 3.

53. 大原関 一浩 Ōharazeki Kazuhiro, 「20世紀転換期オーストラリアにおける日本人売買春——合衆国の事例との比較から」 [Japanese Prostitution in Turn-of-the-Century Australia: In Comparison with the Cases in the United States], in 『西南学院大学 国際文化論集』 *Seinan Journal of Cultures* 36, no. 1 (2021): 144.

54. 外務省通商局 編, 『香港事情』, 353–55.

55. 外務省通商局 編, 『香港事情』, 353.

56. There was only one major annual racing meeting of four days' duration at this time, usually held in late February or early March.

57. Roy Eric Xavier, 'Death at the Races: The Portuguese Presence during the Happy Valley Fire of 1918', *Journal of the Royal Asiatic Society Hong Kong Branch* 53 (2013): 89–92.

58. 'The Race Course Holocaust: Death Roll Almost 600', *South China Morning Post*, February 28, 1918, 6.

59. 外務省通商局 編, 『香港事情』, 353.

60. See Richard M. Jaffe, 'Buddhist Material Culture, "Indianism," and the Construction of Pan-Asian Buddhism in Prewar Japan', *Material Religion* 2, no. 3 (2006): 266–92; and Brij Tankha, 'Exploring Asia, Reforming Japan: Ōtani Kōzui and Itō Chūta', in *Japan on the Silk Road: Encounters and Perspectives of Politics and Culture in Eurasia*, ed. Selçuk Esenbel (Leiden: Brill, 2018), 155–80.

61. Kosui Ōtani, 'The Japanese Pilgrimage to the Buddhist Holy Land: A Personal Narrative of the Hongwanji Expedition of 1902–03', *The Century Illustrated Monthly Magazine* 72 (October 1906): 866–78.

62. TAKADA is sometimes transcribed as TAKATA. 本願寺史料研究所 編 Hongwanji Historical Institute, ed., 『本願寺史 第三巻』 [*The History of Hongwanji*, Vol. 3] (Kyoto: Hongwanji Shuppan-sha, 2019), 451.

63. 奥田, 『明治初年に於ける香港日本人』, Appendix 19.; 林, 『南洋』, 86–89. For more on the school, see Chapter 6.

64. 『婦人雑誌』 [*The Lady's Magazine*] 15, no. 6 (1900): 29.

Notes

65. Ōtani Kōzui was in Hong Kong from January 26 to February 2, 1899. 陳湛頤 Chan Cham-yi, 《日本人訪港見聞錄：1898–1941》 [*Japanese Visitors to Hong Kong: 1898–1941*] (Hong Kong: Joint Publishing, 2005), 210.

66. Benjamin Wai-ming Ng, 'Making of a Japanese Community in Prewar Period (1841–1941)', in *Foreign Communities in Hong Kong, 1840s–1950s*, ed. Cindy Yik-yi Chu (New York: Palgrave Macmillan, 2005), 111–32, at 114–15.

67. Arnold Wright, ed., *Twentieth Century Impressions of Hong Kong, Shanghai, and Other Treaty Ports of China: Their History, People, Commerce, Industries, and Resources* (London: Lloyd's Greater Britain Publishing Company, Ltd, 1908), 172. By 1911, the club had moved to 6 Wyndham Street, Central. Map of Hongkong Central 1911, published in connection with 'Massey's Commercial Map & Directory'. The map is reprinted in Hal Empson, *Mapping Hong Kong: A Historical Atlas* (Hong Kong: Government Information Services, 1992).

68. A 1917 Handbook on the South Seas lists all 149 club members. Matsubara is not among them. 『香港日報』 [*Honkon Nippō*], Vol. 1, September 1, 1909: 4, in 「新聞雑誌操縦関係雑纂／香港日報」 [Miscellaneous Matters Related to Newspapers and Magazines: *Honkon Nippō*], JACAR, originally from the Diplomatic Archives of the Ministry of Foreign Affairs, https://www.jacar.archives.go.jp/das/image/B03040612400; 奥田，『明治初年に於ける香港日本人』，22; and 林，『南洋』，72–78.

69. 外務省通商局 編，『香港事情』，357–58.

70. 左右田昌幸 Sauda Masayuki,「花山火葬場について」 [On the Kazan Crematorium] 『本願寺史料研究所報』 *Hongwanji Shiryō Kenkyūjo Hō* 29 (July 2006): 10–12.

71. Andrew Bernstein, 'Fire and Earth: The Forging of Modern Cremation in Meiji Japan', *Japanese Journal of Religious Studies* 27, no. 3/4 (2000): 328.

72. Letter from the Governor, Frederick Lugard, to the Secretary of State for the Colonies dated March 22, 1911, enclosing correspondence with the Japanese Consul FUNATSU Tatsuichirō (船津辰一郎) on the construction of a crematorium. The National Archives of the UK (TNA): CO 129/376, 123–34.

73. Hong Kong Government Administrative Reports for the Year 1911. Report of the Director of Public Works, Appendix P, 6. The site granted was Inland Lot 1879.

74. A copy of the lease for Inland Lot 1879 is available at the Hong Kong Public Records Office HKRS265-11A-1973-1. The five signatories on the lease were MATSUBARA Jisaburō, boarding house operator; MAJIMA Keinosuke, medical doctor; TAKEDA Naozō, Western-style tailor; TSUMURA Garyo, Hongwanji priest; and KUSUMOTO Taketoshi, manager of Nippon Yusen Kaisha. For more on Majima, see Chapter 6.

75. 'Japanese Crematorium', *Hongkong Telegraph*, November 5, 1912, 1.

76. Hong Kong Government Administrative Reports for the Year 1913. Report of the Head of the Sanitary Department, Annexe A, L3–4. Ordinance No. 5 of 1914, providing for the regulation of the burning of human remains and to enable crematoria to be established, was passed by the Legislative Council and printed in the *Hong Kong Government Gazette* of February 27, 1914.

77. 外務省通商局 編,『香港事情』, 357–58.

78. The Hong Kong government retook custody of the crematorium after the Second World War. The crematorium's buildings were demolished in the late 1950s. Hong Kong Public Records Office HKRS156-1-316.

79. 'Japanese Buddhists in Hongkong', *Overland China Mail*, December 17, 1910, 21.

80. Hong Kong Public Records Office HKRS58-1-60-73.

81. Hong Kong Government Administrative Reports for the Year 1912. Report of the Director of Public Works, Appendix P, 7, and Hong Kong Public Records Office HKRS58-1-60-73. The site granted was Inland Lot 1920.

82. Jaffe, 'Buddhist Material Culture', 280.

83. 'Racecourse Conflagration: Official Statement', *South China Morning Post*, March 1, 1918, 6.

84. 'The Happy Valley Catastrophe: Eighth Day's Proceedings', *South China Morning Post*, March 19, 1918, 10.

85. Xavier, 'Death at the Races', 91.

86. 'The Race Course Holocaust: Death Roll Almost 600', *South China Morning Post*, February 28, 1918, 6.

87. Fukuda may be the Japanese businessman mentioned in Doreen Jorge Cotton's account of her grandfather, Aureliano Jorge, who died while attempting to rescue a Japanese business-man. 'A Man on Fire', January 31, 2011, https://doreenjorgecotton.com/?cat=4. Cotton's version of events is included in Xavier, 'Death at the Races', 99–100.

88. 'The Race Course Holocaust: Death Roll Almost 600', *South China Morning Post*, February 28, 1918, 6.

89. The proceedings concluded on April 12, 1918. 'The Happy Valley Disaster: The Jury's Finding', *South China Morning Post*, April 13, 1918, 3.

90. Hong Kong Legislative Council Minutes, May 23, 1918, https://www.legco.gov.hk/1918/h180523.pdf.

91. 'Racecourse Conflagration: Official Statement', *South China Morning Post*, March 1, 1918, 6.

92. Another memorial to the hundreds of Chinese who perished in the fire erected by the Tung Wah Hospital sits over the hill in So Kon Po, near the Hong Kong Stadium. Tung Wah Group of Hospitals, 'The Race Course Fire Memorial', https://www.tungwah.org.hk/en/heritage/historical-architecture/the-race-course-fire-memorial/.

93. 外務省通商局 編, 『香港事情』, 359.

94. *South China Morning Post*, October 27, 1919, 4.

95. *South China Morning Post*, October 28, 1916, 3.

Chapter 4

1. Toast made by Thomas Hayllar, Q.C., representing Hong Kong's Attorney General, at the tiffin held to launch the Mitsubishi Mail Steamship Company's new Yokohama to Hong Kong route, as reported in the *China Mail* of November 13, 1879, 3.

2. Honda's first name in Japanese also appears as 政治郎 and 政二郎, and his last name as 本多 in some of the Mitsubishi archival records.

3. *China Mail*, November 13, 1879, 3.

4. 岩崎家傳記刊行會 編 Iwasaki Family Biography Project Team, ed., 『岩崎彌太郎傳』下 [*Biography of Iwasaki Yatarō*, Vol. 2] (Tokyo: Tokyo University Press, 1980), 171–75; and William D. Wray, *Mitsubishi and the N.Y.K., 1870–1914: Business Strategy in the Japanese Shipping Industry* (Cambridge, MA: Harvard University Press, 1984), 1, 97.

5. See Chapter 1 for more on the establishment of Japan's treaty ports. Amoy was used to refer to Xiamen, Tientsin for Tianjin, and Canton for Guangzhou.

6. Wray, *Mitsubishi and the N.Y.K., 1870–1914*, 4, 15, 32.

7. 岩崎家傳記刊行會 編, 『岩崎彌太郎傳』下, 630; and Wray, *Mitsubishi and the N.Y.K., 1870–1914*, 22–23.

8. Wray, *Mitsubishi and the N.Y.K., 1870–1914*, 24–25, 29.

9. 岩崎家傳記刊行會 編, 『岩崎彌太郎傳』下, 203–8. An 1875 Japanese government directive granted all thirteen steamships to Mitsubishi without charge on several conditions, includ-ing that the company change its name from Mitsubishi Steamship Company (三菱蒸気船會社; Mitsubishi Jōkisen Kaisha) to Mitsubishi Mail Steamship Company (郵便汽船三菱; Yūbin Kisen Mitsubishi) and not engage in any business other than shipping, with the exception of coal mining, since coal was needed to power its fleet. Wray, *Mitsubishi and the N.Y.K., 1870–1914*, 43, 51–52, 60, 78–79.

10. Wray, *Mitsubishi and the N.Y.K., 1870–1914*, 84–88, 94–97.

Notes 153

11. The *Takasago Maru*, formerly *Delta*, and *Niigata Maru*, formerly *Behar*, were purchased from P&O for 100,000 dollars each in 1874. Hans Lengerer, 'Pre-History of the Sino-Japanese War 1894–1895: The Taiwan Expedition: Impulse to the IJN's First Expansion and Basis for the Formation of a Merchant Marine', *Warship International* 56, no. 2 (2019): 122. Wilson rose to the rank of superintending captain before his retirement from Mitsubishi's successor, Nippon Yusen Kaisha, in 1889. He settled in Nagasaki and opened the Cliff House Hotel. At the time of his death in 1914, he had spent forty-six years in Japan. Brian Burke-Gaffney, *Nagasaki: The British Experience, 1854–1945* (Folkestone: Global Oriental, 2009), 88–95, 124–25, 153–54, 196–97.

12. 'A Japanese Ship in the Thames', *Edinburgh Evening News*, August 4, 1877, 3.

13. The college was nationalised in 1882 and eventually became the Tokyo University of Mercantile Marine in 1953. In 2003, it merged with the Tokyo University of Fisheries to form the Tokyo University of Marine Science and Technology (東京海洋大学). Tokyo University of Marine Science and Technology, 'History', https://www.kaiyodai.ac.jp/en/overview/summary/#gsc.tab=0; and 三菱グループ．「三菱人物伝——岩崎彌太郎物語，Vol. 15 商船学校・商業学校」 [Stories of Prominent Mitsubishi People: Iwasaki Yatarō, Vol. 15. Nautical College; Commerce College], https://www.mitsubishi.com/ja/profile/history/series/yataro/15/.

14. *Shipping and Mercantile Gazette*, January 29, 1877, 2. See also Burke-Gaffney, *Nagasaki: The British Experience*, 97–99; and Lewis Bush, *The Life and Times of the Illustrious Captain Brown: A Chronicle of the Sea and of Japan's Emergence as a World Power* (Tokyo: The Voyagers' Press, and Rutland and Tokyo: The Charles E. Tuttle Company, 1969), 70–71.

15. 'A Japanese Ship in the Thames', 3.

16. Despite difficulties finding a suitable interpreter, the sailor was found guilty and sentenced to four weeks in prison. *Paisley and Renfrewshire Gazette*, May 25, 1878, 6.

17. The Mitsubishi Archives put the cost of the refit at 69,000 pounds. 三菱社誌刊行会 編 Mitsubishi Corporate History Project, ed., 『三菱社誌』 [*Mitsubishi Corporate History*], Vol. 4 (Tokyo: Tokyo University Press, 1979), 70.

18. *London and China Telegraph*, December 9, 1878, 1039.

19. Andō came to Hong Kong in 1874 as vice-consul before being promoted to full consul in 1877 and remained in that post until 1882. *China Mail*, November 7, 1877, 2.

20. John Pope Hennessy assumed the governorship of Hong Kong in April 1877 and remained for five years, departing in March 1882. Pope Hennessy, his wife Kitty, and their son Bertie set off for Japan on May 31, 1879, and returned to Hong Kong via Shanghai on September 6, 1879.

21. Born in England in 1832, Henry John Howard Tripp arrived in Hong Kong in 1861. After working for P&O, he joined Mitsubishi and was their agent in Hong Kong until leaving for Shanghai in 1898. He died there in April 1912. *Who's Who in the Far East 1906–07*; Hong Kong: *China Mail*, 1906, 316; and *China Mail*, April 8, 1912, 4.

22. *China Mail*, November 13, 1879, 3.

23. *London and China Telegraph*, January 27, 1868, 39; and *China Mail*, September 1, 1893, 3.

24. John Curtis Perry, 'Great Britain and the Emergence of Japan as a Naval Power', *Monumenta Nipponica* 21, no. 3/4 (1966): 312. At the time of the tiffin, Archibald Lucius Douglas (1842–1913) was the commander of the *Egeria*, part of the British Navy's China Station squadron. *Chronicle & Directory*, 1879.

25. *China Mail*, November 13, 1879, 3.

26. *Chronicle & Directory*, 1879. For more on John S. Mosby, see James A. Ramage, *Gray Ghost: The Life of Col. John Singleton Mosby* (Lexington: University Press of Kentucky, 1999). For more on Ryrie's appointment, see Henry Ching, *Pow Mah: A Historical Sketch of Horse and Pony Racing in Hong Kong and of the Royal Hong Kong Jockey Club* (Hong Kong: South China Morning Post, 1965), 12.

154   Notes

27. *China Mail*, November 13, 1879, 3.
28. 三菱社誌刊行会 編, 『三菱社誌』, Vol. 7, 454.
29. 三菱社誌刊行会 編, 『三菱社誌』, Vol. 7, 455–58.
30. Letter from Iwasaki Yatarō to John Pope Hennessy dated January 1, 1880, Oxford, Bodleian Libraries, Papers of Sir John Pope-Hennessy, MSS.Brit.Emp.s.409, Box 4/4.
31. 'The Mitsu Bishi Company', *China Mail*, November 28, 1879, 2.
32. *China Mail*, April 9, 1881, 3.
33. *Chronicle & Directory*, 1880, 496–97.
34. Freight income: 2,131,137 yen; Passenger income: 683,053 yen; Total income: 3,287,826 yen. Wray, *Mitsubishi and the N.Y.K., 1870–1914*, 93–94.
35. *China Mail*, December 24, 1879, 3.
36. 横浜支社E. B. Jonesよりの英文往翰写 [Outgoing Correspondence from E. B. Jones, Yokohama Branch], 1879, The Mitsubishi Archives, MA-01305.
37. Letter from William Bramsen to Captain Wilson Walker dated November 29, 1879, 「Niigata Maru 宛英文書簡控」 [Outgoing Correspondence to the *Niigata Maru*], The Mitsubishi Archives, MA-01249.
38. Letter from William Bramsen to Captain Wilson Walker dated April 12, 1880, The Mitsubishi Archives, MA-01249.
39. For more on the development of the insurance industry in Japan, see Peter Borscheid and Niels Viggo Haueter, eds, *World Insurance: The Evolution of a Global Risk Network* (Oxford: Oxford University Press, 2012), 415–28, 496–501.
40. The Tokio Marine Insurance Company was set up with 600,000 yen in capital; both Mitsubishi and Mitsui & Co were agents for the company in its formative years. Japan Business History Institute, eds, *The Tokio Marine & Fire Insurance: The First Century, 1879–1979* (Tokyo: The Tokio Marine and Fire Insurance Co., 1980).
41. 三菱社誌刊行会 編, 『三菱社誌』, Vol. 7, 440.
42. Letter from Frederick Krebs to Captain Wynn of the *Niigata Maru* dated August 6, 1881, The Mitsubishi Archives, MA-01249. Wynn took over from Walker as captain of the *Niigata Maru* in April 1881. *China Mail*, April 9, 1881, 3.
43. The situation had improved slightly by 1882, with five Japanese names in the list of forty-two commanders and four in the list of thirty-five chief engineers. Mitsubishi's (by then Nippon Yusen Kaisha) last foreign captain, Briton Francis Cope, retired in 1920. Burke-Gaffney, *Nagasaki: The British Experience*, 201–2.
44. Letters sent on behalf of the Directors of the Company to Captain Wilson Walker dated April 12, 1880; May 10, 1880; May 11, 1880; and December 20, 1880, The Mitsubishi Archives, MA-01249.
45. 三菱社誌刊行会 編, 『三菱社誌』, Vol. 7, 500.
46. Letter sent on behalf of the Directors of the Company to Captain Wilson Walker dated August 2, 1880, The Mitsubishi Archives, MA-01249.
47. Letter from William Bramsen to Captain Wilson Walker dated June 10, 1879; and letter from Frederick Krebs on behalf of the Directors of the Company to Captain Wynn of the *Niigata Maru* dated April 13, 1881, The Mitsubishi Archives, MA-01249.
48. *Chronicle & Directory*, 1876, 282. The Procurement Department is translated as Stationery Department in company materials and Honda probably looked after office supplies.
49. *Chronicle & Directory*, 1876; and 三菱社誌刊行会 編, 『三菱社誌』, Vol. 8, 539–41.
50. *China Mail*, September 27, 1879, 4.
51. By 1880, the Mitsubishi office had moved to 50A Queen's Road Central. *China Mail*, March 1, 1880, 2.
52. 三菱社誌刊行会 編, 『三菱社誌』, Vol. 8, 541.
53. 本田政次郎 Honda Masajirō, 「香港概況」 [Hong Kong Overview], 各船来翰 [Incoming Correspondence from Overseas] 1879, The Mitsubishi Archives, MA-07271. Authors'

Notes 155

own translation. Kōgyō Shōkai's offices were at 8 Queen's Road Central in the *Chronicle & Directory*, 1879. As mentioned in Chapter 1, a survey conducted by the Japanese Consulate counted eighty-six Japanese living in the city in April 1880. Honda is clearly not including the *karayuki-san* working in Hong Kong at that time. 奥田乙治郎 Okuda Otojirō, 『明治初年に於ける香港日本人』 [*Japanese Residents in Hong Kong during the Early Meiji Era*] (Taipei: Taiwan Sōtokufu Nettai Sangyō Chōsa-kai, 1937), 109–13.

54. The City Hall mentioned in Honda's report was completed in 1869. It was built on the site now occupied by the HSBC Hong Kong headquarters and old Bank of China Building. The merchant John Dent presented the fountain to the colony in 1864. Most of the old City Hall was demolished in 1933. 'Old Hongkong (by "Colonial.").' *South China Morning Post*, June 19, 1933, 15.

55. Bird returned briefly to the city on January 6, 1879, before leaving again on January 11, 1879, for Singapore, via Saigon [Ho Chi Minh City].

56. Isabella L. Bird, *The Golden Chersonese and the Way Thither* (Kuala Lumpur: Oxford University Press, 1967), 39. First edition published by John Murray, Albemarle Street, London, in 1883.

57. This error was most likely due to confusion over information she reviewed much later, when readying her travel writings for publication. There is no mention of Mitsubishi in the letter she sent to her sister Henrietta describing the same scene (see Kay Chubbuck, ed., *Letters to Henrietta* (London: John Murray, 2002), 207). Isabella L. Bird, *Unbeaten Tracks in Japan: An Account of Travels in the Interior, Including Visits to the Aborigines of Yezo and the Shrines of Nikkô and Isé*. In *Collected Travel Writings of Isabella Bird*, Volume 5 (Bristol: Ganesha Publishing and Tokyo: Edition Synapse, 1997), 320. First edition published by John Murray, Albemarle Street, London, in 1880.

58. 本田、「香港概況」, The Mitsubishi Archives, MA-07271.

59. See John McMaster, 'The Takashima Mine: British Capital and Japanese Industrialization', *The Business History Review* 37, no. 3 (1963): 217–39.

60. Letters from Iwasaki Yatarō to H. J. H. Tripp and Jardine Matheson & Co. dated January 23, 1882; and letter from H. J. H. Tripp to the Directors of the Mitsubishi Mail Steam Ship Company dated April 2, 1882, 「来翰 長崎支社 明治14年」 [Incoming Correspondence to the Nagasaki Branch, 1881], The Mitsubishi Archives, MA-04428.

61. 香港支那横浜来翰刺 明治14–16 年」 [Incoming Correspondence from Hong Kong, China, and Yokohama, 1881–1883], The Mitsubishi Archives, MA-07977. Coal prices are quoted from the *Overland China Mail*'s 'Commercial Summary' printed in its issue of April 27, 1883.

62. The Mitsubishi Archives, MA-07977. For more on Miike coal, see Shinya Sugiyama, *Japan's Industrialization in the World Economy, 1859–1899* (London: The Athlone Press, 1988), 170–212.

63. 三菱社誌刊行会 編, 『三菱社誌』, Vol. 7, 458–59.

64. 「海外旅券願」 [Passport Application], February, 18, 1880, The Mitsubishi Archives, MA-00905-002; and *China Mail*, March 1, 1880, 2.

65. Honda's grave marker in the Hong Kong Cemetery gives his month of death as December. However, his death certificate and an entry in the November 4, 1880, issue of the *Hongkong Daily Press* confirms that this should be November. The discrepancy may be due to the fact that Honda's obelisk was only erected at the initiative of the Japanese Seafarers Relief Association in the early 1910s, over thirty years after his death. Whoever prepared the engraving may have confused the characters for November (十一) and December (十二). *Hongkong Daily Press*, November 4, 1880, 2.

66. The *Sumida Maru* was another Mitsubishi steamer that served the Hong Kong route in the early 1880s.

67. 久保扶桑 (在神戸) 宛 神田愛次郎 (在香港) 書翰 [Letter from Kanda Aijirō to Kubo Fusō, the Deputy General Manager of Mitsubishi's Kobe Branch], dated October 29, 1880, 「各

船来翰 神戸支社 明治13年」 [Incoming Correspondence to the Kobe Branch, 1880], The Mitsubishi Archives, MA-107.

68. 武田尚子 Takeda Naoko, 『ミルクと日本人——近代社会の「元気の源」』 [*Milk and the Japanese: A 'Source of Energy' in Modern Society*] (Tokyo: Chūo Kōron Shinsha, 2017), 41–65.

69. 神田愛次郎 Kanda Aijirō, 「本田政次郎病氣容躰上申書」 [Report on Honda Masajirō's Illness], dated October 29, 1880, 「各船来翰下 明治13年本社」 [Incoming Correspondence from Overseas to the Tokyo Office, 1880, Vol. 2], The Mitsubishi Archives, MA-00925-001.

70. 川田小一郎 (東京三菱本社) 宛 本田長十郎 (神戸廣業商会) 書翰 [Letter from Honda's younger brother, Honda Chōjūrō, an employee at Kōgyō Shōkai in Kobe, to Kawada Koichirō at Mitsubishi headquarters in Tokyo] dated November 9, 1880, 「他向来簡 完 明治13年分 本社」 [Miscellaneous Incoming Correspondence to the Tokyo Office, 1880], The Mitsubishi Archives, MA-00940-005.

71. *China Mail*, November 3, 1880, 2.

72. 石川七財・川田小一郎 (東京三菱本社) 宛 本田正造・本田宇兵衛書翰 [Letter from Honda Masazō (or possibly Shōzō) and Uemon to Mitsubishi's Ishikawa Shichizai and Kawada Koichirō] dated November 5, 1880, The Mitsubishi Archives, MA-00940-005.

73. 「香港支社支配人本田政二郎氏死去ノ節諸入費」 [Expenses in Connection with the Death of Hong Kong General Manager Honda Masajirō], dated January 10, 1881 「社内願伺写」 [Internal Expenses Claim], The Mitsubishi Archives, MA-00972.

74. The obelisk was erected at the initiative of the Japanese Seafarers Relief Association in the early 1910s. 日本海員掖済会 Japan Seafarers Relief Association, 『海之世界』 *Umino Sekai* 8, no. 5 (May 1914): 44–45.

75. Murakami's family name in Japanese also appears as 村上 in Mitsubishi archival records.

76. 'Hongkong fever' is given as the cause of death in the *China Mail*, June 9, 1881, 3.

77. 「邨上秀士死亡費明細書」 [Expenses in Connection with the Death of Murakami Hideshi], dated September 5, 1881, The Mitsubishi Archives, MA-00972.

78. *China Mail*, June 9, 1881, 3.

79. Stephen Davies, *Strong to Save: Maritime Mission in Hong Kong from Whampoa Reach to the Mariners' Club* (Hong Kong: City University of Hong Kong Press, 2017), 17, 46.

80. Davies, *Strong to Save*, 16–28, 109–19. There is no mention of seamen's boarding houses run by Japanese until an entry in the 1899 *Chronicle & Directory*. For more on crimping and predatory recruitment practices, see the case of INOUE Teijirō (井上貞治郎) in Chapter 3.

81. Davies, *Strong to Save*, 29–33.

82. Yokote's letter is reprinted on page 205 of OKUDA Otojirō's 1937 book. In a side note, Okuda expressed both his shock at the cost of the grave, which he considered very expensive, and his dismay that Yokote's obelisk should be half the size of that erected in memory of a prostitute. 奥田, 『明治初年に於ける香港日本人』, 205. For more on Kiya Saki, see Chapter 2.

83. *China Mail*, May 23, 1879, 4. For more on the Japan Seafarers Relief Association, which was established in Japan in 1880, see the *Shipping Gazette and Lloyd's List*, February 25, 1896, 11; and 日本海員掖済会 Japan Seafarers Relief Association, 「掖济会のあゆみ」 [History of the Seafarers Relief Association], https://www.ekisaikai.com/pages/31/.

84. 'Kaustioni Oto' does not sound like a Japanese name though his nationality is confirmed as Japanese in the Burial Registers 1853–1930 held by the Hong Kong Sheng Kung Hui Archives, PRO HKMS44–1. 'Kaustioni Oto' must be the name by which he was known aboard the S.S. *Brutus*.

85. 赤岩昭滋 Akaiwa Teruji, 「香港の日本人墓地——船員の墓碑を中心として」 [Japanese Graves in Hong Kong: Graves of Sailors and Others] 『海事史研究』 *Journal of the Japan Society for Nautical Research* 21 (1973): 66–81.

86. This section on the establishment of the NYK and OSK draws primarily on Wray, *Mitsubishi and the N.Y.K., 1870–1914*, 125–27, 146–52, 169–225.

Notes 157

87. 岩崎家傳記刊行會 編, 『岩崎彌之助傳』, 153.

88. Wilson penned the memoir shortly before his death in 1914. His wife, Dutch-born Charlotte Henriette (née Noordhoek Hegt; 1859–1937), survived him. She moved to Shanghai in 1920, where one of her daughters lived. She fled to Hong Kong in the summer of 1937 to escape the fighting between Japanese and Chinese forces but passed away a few weeks after her arrival, on September 26 or 27, 1937. Her grave still stands in the Hong Kong Cemetery. Burke-Gaffney, *Nagasaki: The British Experience*, 94 (Wilson Walker memoir quote); 125, 200–1, 218.

89. Businessman ASANO Sōichirō (浅野宗一郎; 1848–1930) established Toyo Kisen Kaisha in 1896. Wray, *Mitsubishi and the N.Y.K., 1870–1914*, 277–78; and *Chronicle & Directory*, 1902, 360. A list of all NYK, OSK, and Toyo Kisen services operating in 1909 appeared in the chapter on the mercantile marine written by Kondō Renpei, NYK president from 1895 to 1921, for the volume *Fifty Years of New Japan*, Vol. 1, compiled by Shigenobu Ōkuma, English editor Marcus B. Huish (London: Smith, Elder and Co., 1909), 447–64.

90. Sugiyama, *Japan's Industrialization*, 170–212; see also Catherine L. Phipps, *Empires on the Waterfront: Japan's Ports and Power, 1858–1899* (Cambridge, MA: Harvard University Asia Center, 2015), 147–48.

91. *Hong Kong Blue Book* for 1872, Shipping section 145–54.

92. *Hong Kong Blue Book* for 1880, Shipping section S 1–9.

93. *Hong Kong Blue Book* for 1901, Shipping section S 1–9.

94. *Hong Kong Blue Book* for 1904 (Shipping section S 1–9) and 1905 (Shipping section T 1–9). For more on the impact of the Russo-Japanese War, see Wray, *Mitsubishi and the N.Y.K., 1870–1914*, 373–84.

95. *Hong Kong Blue Book* for 1912, Shipping section T 1–14.

96. 井口丑二 Inokuchi Ushiji, 『世界一周実記』 [*Journal of a Trip around the World*] (Tokyo: Keizaizasshi-sha, 1904), 18–19. The NYK office was at 7 Praya Central in 1899. *China Mail*, April 6, 1899, 4.

97. *China Mail*, July 22, 1905, 3; and *China Mail*, October 13, 1905, 5.

98. *Who's Who in the Far East 1907–08* (London: Japan Press, 1907), 229; and *China Mail*, August 27, 1907, 4.

99. *South China Morning Post*, September 13, 1907, 2. The Mihara grave is badly damaged and the dates of birth and death of the two infants are impossible to make out, though from the numbers inscribed on the grave's pedestal (6142 and 7117), one may have been born on June 25, 1899, and died two days later, on June 27, 1899, and the other stillborn on August 25, 1906.

Chapter 5

1. Section in the memoirs of ATAKA Yakichi describing his thoughts as a twenty-two-year-old upon his arrival in Hong Kong on November 6, 1895, to work for the Japanese trading firm of Kusakabe & Co. Authors' own translation. 安宅彌吉 Ataka Yakichi, 『回顧録』 [*Memoirs*] (Osaka: Ataka Yakichi, 1922), 111.

2. William D. Wray, 'National Alliances and Global Webs: The Internationalization of Japanese Shipping', in *Global Markets: The Internationalization of the Sea Transport Industries since 1850*, ed. David J. Starkey and Gelina Hrlaftis (St John's, Newfoundland: International Maritime Economic History Association, 1998), 88–89.

3. 奥田乙治郎 Okuda Otojirō, 『明治初年に於ける香港日本人』 [*Japanese Residents in Hong Kong during the Early Meiji Era*] (Taipei: Taiwan Sōtokufu Nettai Sangyō Chōsa-kai, 1937), 313–16; and Joshua A. Fogel, *Articulating the Sinosphere: Sino-Japanese Relations in Space and Time* (Cambridge, MA: Harvard University Press, 2009), 80.

4. Chushichi Tsuzuki, *The Pursuit of Power in Modern Japan, 1825–1995* (Oxford: Oxford University Press, 2000), 121–30.

5. Benjamin Wai-ming Ng, 'Making of a Japanese Community in Prewar Period (1841–1941)', in *Foreign Communities in Hong Kong, 1840s–1950s*, ed. Cindy Yik-yi Chu (New York: Palgrave Macmillan, 2005), 114–15.

6. Andrew Gordon, *A Modern History of Japan: From Tokugawa Times to the Present*, 4th ed. (New York: Oxford University Press, 2020), 75.

7. Fogel, *Articulating the Sinosphere*, 79.

8. Kasano was born in either 1837 or 1838. 札幌市教育委員会 編 Sapporo City Education Board, ed., 『新札幌市史』第7巻 (史料編 2) [*A New History of Sapporo City*, Vol. 7, *Historical Documents 2*] (Sapporo: Hokkaidō Shimbun-sha, 1986), 628.

9. Fogel, *Articulating the Sinosphere*, 81.

10. 'Mr. Hennessy's Speech at Hakodate', *China Mail*, September 1, 1879, 3. Pope Hennessy's speech repeated figures from his June address to the Tokyo Chamber of Commerce, which was widely derided by the governor's detractors in the press. The *Japan Gazette*, in an article reprinted in the *China Mail* issue of July 3, lambasted Pope Hennessy for misrepresenting the situation in Hokkaido and glossing over the impact of the government's monopoly, exercised through the agency of Kōgyō Shōkai, on local suppliers. The latter were forced to accept prices that were well below market rates for their wares. 'Mr. Hennessy's Tokio Lecture', *China Mail*, July 3, 1879, 3.

11. 宮本又次・内田勝敏 Miyamoto Mataji and Uchida Katsutoshi, 『日本貿易人の系譜――総合商社への道のり』 [*Early International Traders in Japan: A Prehistory of Comprehensive Trading Companies*] (Tokyo: Yuhikaku, 1980), 97.

12. 奥田, 『明治初年に於ける香港日本人』, Appendix 5–6.

13. 日下部商店 広告 [Advertisement for Kusakabe & Co.], 『海商通報』 *Kaishō Tsūhō* 587, April 22, 1902, 11; and 奥田, 『明治初年に於ける香港日本人』, 110.

14. The northern China drought-induced famine of 1876–1879 is also known as the Ding-Wu Disaster. 『朝野新聞』 *Chōya Shimbun*, no. 1353, March 18, 1878, Tokyo Metropolitan Library, https://archive.library.metro.tokyo.lg.jp/da/detail?tilcod=0000000003-00007121.

15. 黄栄光 Huang Ronggwang, 『近代日中貿易成立史論』 [*Early Years of Modern Sino-Japanese Trade*] (Tokyo: Hikaku Bunka Keinkyū-jo, 2008). See also Fogel, *Articulating the Sinosphere*, 79. For more on Godai, see Donald Calman, *The Nature and Origins of Japanese Imperialism: A Reinterpretation of the Great Crisis of 1873* (London: Routledge, 1992), 292–311.

16. 安宅, 『回顧録』, 132. Ataka's name appears on the 'Jurors List for 1896' with his abode given as 4 Lower Mosque Terrace, just off Caine Road in Mid-Levels. Mrs Kusakabe is listed at the same address in the 1896 Hong Kong Ladies Directory. Kusakabe likely leased the flat to accommodate the company's employees and he and his wife may have stayed there during their visits to the city. *Hong Kong Government Gazette*, February 15, 1896; and *Chronicle & Directory*, 1896, 271.

17. 安宅産業株式会社社史編集室 編 Ataka & Co. Corporate History Project, ed., 『安宅産業六十年史』 [*Sixty-Year History of Ataka & Co.*] (Osaka: Ataka Sangyō, 1968), 24.

18. 安宅, 『回顧録』, 108–9.

19. *China Mail*, November 6, 1895, 2.

20. 安宅, 『回顧録』, 111. KAWAJI Kandō (川路寛堂, 1845–1927), for example, who passed through the city in late 1866 with a group of *bakufu* students bound for Britain, observed that 'it would be no mistake to think of Hong Kong as first and foremost part of Europe'. Quoted in Andrew Cobbing, *The Japanese Discovery of Victorian Britain: Early Travel Encounters in the Far West* (Richmond, Surrey: Japan Library, 1998), 39.

21. *Chronicle & Directory*, 1898, 281. The glass and lampshade factory was part-owned with a German businessman surnamed Becker, a partner in the firm of Sander & Co. and later Sander, Wieler and Co., and Becker's Chinese comprador. 安宅, 『回顧録』, 146–47.

Notes 159

22. 平井健介 Hirai Kensuke, 「1900–1920年代東アジアにおける砂糖貿易と台湾糖」 [The Sugar Trade and Taiwanese Sugar in East Asia: 1900–1920], 『社会経済史学』 *Shakai Keizai Shigaku* 73, no. 1 (2007): 38–49. For more on Ataka's partnership with Kian Gwan, see 安宅, 『回顧録』, 184–210.

23. 安宅, 『回顧録』, 122–23.

24. 安宅, 『回顧録』, 153–54. Authors' own translation.

25. *Chronicle & Directory*, 1901, 370.

26. 安宅, 『回顧録』, 107, 168–83, 210–24, 237. Before his death, Kusakabe sent KANEDA Rinzō (金田林蔵), an accounting specialist, to Hong Kong as a future replacement for Ataka. The plan was that Kaneda would marry Kusakabe's daughter Nobuko and become Kusakabe's adopted son. Following Kusakabe's death in 1899, Kaneda did indeed marry Nobuko and took over the business and Kusakabe's name. He and Ataka did not get along but the latter continued in his efforts to make Kusakabe & Co. profitable. Kaneda died of lung disease in 1904. Ataka operated his own company under the English name of Kusakabe Ataka & Co. for a couple of years, before dropping 'Kusakabe' altogether.

27. 「雑事 大阪安宅商店の開設」 [Miscellaneous: Opening of Ataka & Co. in Osaka], 『海商通報』 *Kaihō Tsūshō* 969, January 7, 1905, 3–4; 安宅, 『回顧録』, 224–32; *Chronicle & Directory*, 1904, 448; and *Chronicle & Directory*, 1908, 992.

28. Arnold Wright, ed., *Twentieth Century Impressions of Hong Kong, Shanghai, and other Treaty Ports of China: Their History, People, Commerce, Industries, and Resources* (London: Lloyd's Greater Britain Publishing Company, 1908), 232.

29. Sin-kiong Wong, 'The Tatsu Maru Incident and the Anti-Japanese Boycott of 1908: A Study of Conflicting Interpretations', *Chinese Culture* 34, no. 3 (September 1993): 77–92; and *China Mail*, February 18, 1908, 4. The Japan Shipowners' Association is also referred to as the Japan Shipowners' Union.

30. Terumine's letter was translated and summarised in the English-language press. 'The Tatsu Maru. Japanese Account of the Seizure', *South China Morning Post*, March 4, 1908, 7.

31. 吉澤誠一郎 Yoshizawa Seiichirō, 『愛国とボイコット——近代中国の地域的文脈と対日関係』 [*Patriotism and Boycotts: Modern China from a Regional Perspective and the Sino-Japanese Relationship*] (Nagoya: Nagoya University Press, 2021), 27–33.

32. In his memoirs, Ataka claimed that the guns were the type used at Japanese middle school sports days. 安宅, 『回顧録』, 264.

33. Wong, 'The Tatsu Maru Incident', 77–92. See also 'The Tatsu Maru', *South China Morning Post*, March 4, 1908, 7.

34. Editorial Comment, 'International Law Involved in the Seizure of the Tatsu Maru', *The American Journal of International Law* 2, no. 2 (April 1908): 391–97.

35. *The Times*, March 14, 1908, 7.

36. 「故辰丸船長性格」 [The Late Captain of the *Tatsu Maru*], 『東京朝日新聞』 *Tokyo Asahi Shimbun*, March 29, 1908, Morning Edition, 2; and 'Death of the "Tatsu Maru" Captain', *Japan Times*, March 31, 1908, 3.

37. 'The Tatsu Maru Incident: Death of the Captain', *China Mail*, April 1, 1908, 6.

38. 「故辰丸船長照峯廣吉氏」 [The Late Captain of the *Tatsu Maru* Terumine Hirokichi], 『東京朝日新聞』 *Tokyo Asahi Shimbun*, April 1, 1908, Morning Edition, 3.

39. Jung-fang Tsai, *Hong Kong in Chinese History: Community and Social Unrest in the British Colony, 1842–1913* (New York: Columbia University Press, 1993), 212–13.

40. Chinese merchants selling Japanese goods in Hong Kong also suffered material losses because of the boycott. Some were beaten up by groups supporting the boycott, with one losing an ear; others had their stores vandalised. Tsai, *Hong Kong in Chinese History*, 226; and 吉澤, 『愛国とボイコット』, 27.

41. The boycott flared up again briefly in April and October 1909 in response to Japan's expansionist moves in the South China Sea and northern China. Tsai, *Hong Kong in Chinese History*, 237.

42. Edward A. Irving, 'Report of the Registrar General' for the year 1908, dated April 7, 1909, Appendix C9.

43. 'Japanese "At Home". Reception on Board the Otowa: Japanese and Chinese Fraternizing', *Hongkong Telegraph*, July 19, 1909, 4.

44. 安宅, 『回顧録』, 312.

45. For more on Suzuki & Co., see Sojitz History Museum, https://www.sojitz.com/history/en/company/suzukishoten/. The sale was announced in the *South China Morning Post* on January 1, 1913, 4.

46. Losses incurred during the 1973 oil crisis would lead to Ataka & Co's eventual acquisition by Itochu Corporation in 1977. https://www.itochu.co.jp/en/about/history/index.html.

47. Satoshi Inotani, 'The Translation of Zen: A Tribute to D. T. Suzuki', *Nippon.com*, November 11, 2020. https://www.nippon.com/en/japan-topics/b07214/. See also Richard M. Jaffe, ed., *Selected Works of D. T. Suzuki*, Vol. 1, *Zen*, 1st ed. (Oakland: University of California Press, 2015), xi–lvi.

48. *China Mail*, August 20, 1878, 2. His name is romanised as 'Shugio Heromich' in both the *China Mail* announcement and the Mitsui Bussan Kaisha entry in the *Chronicle & Directory*, 1879, 215. Shugyō would depart for New York in 1880 and become a major art curator. Following his return to Japan, he worked as an agent for Frank Lloyd Wright, sourcing prints for his collection. Julia Meech, 'Shugio Hiromichi and the Grolier Club', *Gazette of the Grolier Club* 49 (New Series) (1998): 79–90.

49. Seiichiro Yonekura and Hiroshi Shimizu, 'Entrepreneurship in Pre–World War II Japan: The Role and Logic of the Zaibatsu', in *The Invention of Enterprise: Entrepreneurship from Ancient Mesopotamia to Modern Times*, ed. David S. Landes, Joel Mokyr, and William J. Baumol (Princeton: Princeton University Press, 2010), 507–8.

50. Yonekura and Shimizu, 'Entrepreneurship in Pre–World War II Japan', 508–12. The presidency was nominally assumed by a member of the Mitsui family.

51. *Chronicle & Directory*, 1883, 240, 269; and Nicholas Guoth, 'Advancing Trade with China: The Eastern and Australian Mail Steam Company and the 1873–1880 Mail Contract', *The International Journal of Maritime History* 31, no. 2 (2019): 276.

52. Shinya Sugiyama, *Japan's Industrialization in the World Economy, 1859–1899* (London: The Athlone Press, 1988), 198.

53. *Chronicle & Directory*, 1885, 403.

54. Yonekura and Shimizu, 'Entrepreneurship in Pre–World War II Japan', 510; and 奥田, 『明治初年に於ける香港日本人』, 255–56.

55. *China Mail*, February 16, 1886, 2. Fukuhara's initial is often given as 'Y' rather than 'E' in English-language publications of the time, such as the *Chronicle & Directory*, 1886.

56. Yonekura and Shimizu, 'Entrepreneurship in Pre–World War II Japan', 514.

57. 『人事興信録』データベース [Jinji Kōshinroku (Who's Who) Database], Nagoya University Graduate School of Law, originally published in January 1915.

58. Seiichiro Yonekura, 'The Emergence of the Prototype of Enterprise Group Capitalism: The Case of Mitsui', *Hitotsubashi Journal of Commerce and Management* 20 (1985): 95; and *Chronicle & Directory*, 1885, 417.

59. Fukuhara's manager in Shanghai was Wooyeda (Ueda) Yasusaburō. *Chronicle & Directory* 1886, 513; and *Chronicle & Directory*, 1888, 444.

60. Yonekura, 'The Emergence of the Prototype', 83–84; and 奥田, 『明治初年に於ける香港日本人』, 256.

61. Yonekura and Shimizu, 'Entrepreneurship in Pre–World War II Japan', 513.

Notes 161

62. Sugiyama, *Japan's Industrialization*, 196.

63. *China Mail*, May 10, 1892, 2.

64. The lot was later renumbered 39–41 MacDonnell Road. The British army requisitioned the site as 'enemy property' in 1945 and eventually sold it at auction in 1959. Hong Kong Public Records Office HKRS58-1-49-60 and HKRS251-3-35; and 'Government Notification No. 303', *Hong Kong Government Gazette*, August 1, 1896.

65. *HKGCC Report for the Year 1894*, 29; and *HKGCC Report for the Year 1896*, 30. Established in 1861, the Hong Kong General Chamber of Commerce (HKGCC) began admitting Chinese members in 1880. 'About Us', Hong Kong General Chamber of Commerce website, https://www.chamber.org.hk/en/about/hkgcc_history.aspx (accessed March 1, 2024); see also John M. Carroll, *Edge of Empires: Chinese Elites and British Colonials in Hong Kong* (Hong Kong: Hong Kong University Press, 2005), 85.

66. The opium trade was banned in Japan, with the exception of restricted amounts for medicinal purposes, but Japanese ships could transport it as cargo to other destinations. For Meiji-era attitudes to opium, see Bob Tadashi Wakabayashi, 'From Peril to Profit: Opium in Late-Edo to Meiji Eyes', in *Opium Regimes: China, Britain, and Japan, 1839–1952*, ed. Timothy Brook and Bob Tadashi Wakabayashi (Berkeley: University of California Press, 2000), 55–76.

67. *Chronicle & Directory*, 1908.

68. It is unclear whether the grouping of children's graves pre- or post-dates the construction of the Aberdeen tunnel in the 1970s, for which the government relocated thousands of graves. For more on Mihara, see Chapter 4.

69. Yonekura, 'The Emergence of the Prototype', 95.

70. 安宅彌吉, 『回顧録』, 108.

71. *China Mail*, September 22, 1896, 2.

72. Norio Tamaki, *Japanese Banking: A History, 1859–1959* (Cambridge: Cambridge University Press, 1995), 4, 13–14.

73. Tamaki, *Japanese Banking*, 22–23.

74. The coinage circulating in Hong Kong during the mid- to late nineteenth century included the Carolus or Spanish dollar, the Mexican dollar, the Indian rupee, the English sovereign, and Chinese coinage, with the Mexican dollar widely used for trade. Wilfrid Victor Pennell, *History of the Hong Kong General Chamber of Commerce, 1861–1961* (Hong Kong: Cathay Press, 1961), 46–47. The Hong Kong Mint was located in Causeway Bay, near present-day Great George Street. After its closure, the land was acquired by Jardine Matheson & Co. to build a sugar refinery. Ernest John Eitel, *Europe in China: The History of Hong Kong from the Beginning to the Year 1882* (London: Luzac & Company; Hong Kong: Kelly & Walsh, 1895), 442. See also P. Kevin MacKeown, 'The Hong Kong Mint, 1864–1868: The History of an Early Engineering Experiment', *Journal of the Royal Asiatic Society Hong Kong Branch* 47 (2007): 41–79.

75. Susumu Mizuta, 'Making a Mint: British Mercantile Influence and the Building of the Japanese Imperial Mint', *Architectural History* 62 (2019): 89–111. Godai stepped down from government in 1869 to concentrate on his business dealings and led Kōgyō Shōkai from 1879 until his death in 1885, as mentioned at the beginning of this chapter.

76. For a variety of reasons, not least a shortage of the metal, the adoption of the gold standard in Japan would remain nominal until 1897. Tamaki, *Japanese Banking*, 24.

77. Tamaki, *Japanese Banking*, 30–39.

78. *China Mail*, September 4, 1879, 2.

79. 'Recognition of the Japanese "Yen" as a legal tender.' The National Archives of the UK (TNA): CO129/182, 97–116. Though Europeans were involved with the construction and early operation of the Osaka Mint, only a few metallurgists remained after 1874. Mizuta, 'Making a Mint', 96.

80. P. Kevin MacKeown, *A Stormy Petrel: The Life and Times of John Pope Hennessy* (Hong Kong: City University of Hong Kong Press, 2020), 248–51.

81. Tamaki, *Japanese Banking*, 46–47.

82. The new central bank was largely modelled on the Bank of Belgium. Tamaki, *Japanese Banking*, 58–63.

83. Tamaki, *Japanese Banking*, 46, 58–61, 69–73. YSB opened overseas offices in New York in 1880, London in 1881, Lyons in 1882, San Francisco in 1886, Hawaii in 1892, Shanghai in 1893, and Mumbai [Bombay] in 1894. For more on Lyons's role in the Japanese silk market, see Sugiyama, *Japan's Industrialization*, 92–98.

84. Tamaki, *Japanese Banking*, 82–85. The amount in sterling was close to 38 million pounds. Keiko Itoh, 'The Yokohama Specie Bank in London', in *Britain & Japan: Biographical Portraits*, Vol. 5, ed. Hugh Cortazzi (Folkestone: Global Oriental, 2005), 235. See also Michael Schiltz, 'Money on the Road to Empire: Japan's Adoption of Gold Monometallism, 1873–97', *The Economic History Review* 65, no. 3 (2012): 1147–68.

85. *Chronicle & Directory*, 1901, 393. Prince's Building was built for Sir C. Paul Chater and Sir Hormusjee N. Mody on the Central Praya Land Reclamation, completed in 1904. 'Progress of Hongkong: Prince's Building', *South China Morning Post*, September 30, 1904, 5; and *Hongkong Land at 125*, published in Hong Kong in 2014, 31–45. https://hklandblob.blob. core.windows.net/assets/125_anniversary/mobile/index.html#p=1.

86. 「銀塊處分の結末」 [What Happened to Silver Bullion], 『東京朝日新聞』 *Tokyo Asahi Shimbun*, April 20, 1899, Morning Edition, 2.

87. 東京銀行 編 Bank of Tokyo, ed., 『横濱正金銀行全史 第 2 巻——創立から関東大震災ま で』 [*The History of the Yokohama Specie Bank*, Vol. 2, *From Its Establishment to the Great Kantō Earthquake*] (Tokyo: Bank of Tokyo, 1981), 110; and 小野一一郎 Ono Kazuichirō, 「日清 戦争賠償金の領収と貨幣制度——日本における金本位制の成立(3)」 [The Payment of the Indemnity after the Sino-Japanese War and the Monetary System: Introduction of the Gold Standard Part 3], 『經濟論叢』 *The Economic Review* 94, no. 3 (1964): 62–79.

88. *Chronicle & Directory*, 1896, 156; *Chronicle & Directory*, 1897, 285; and *Chronicle & Directory*, 1900, 359. Hirota's first manager in Hong Kong was Nabekura Nao.

89. *Hong Kong Government Gazette*, February 26, 1898 and February 28, 1900. Not being 'ignorant of the English language' was a prerequisite for inclusion on the jurors' list.

90. Nakasono is first listed as a YSB employee in the *Chronicle & Directory*, 1904, 474.

91. 『龍南同窓会々報』 [Ryūnan Alumni Association Bulletin] Vol. 2 (Tokyo: Ryūnan Dōsōkai, 1897), 4.; *South China Morning Post*, December 7, 1906, 6; and *Hongkong Telegraph*, December 8, 1906, 14.

92. Remains exhumed according to burial records kept by the Hong Kong Cemeteries and Crematoria Office in Happy Valley. 税田祖山 Saita Sozan, 『地方自治政の沿革と其の人 物——福岡県』 [*History of Local Government and Politicians in Fukuoka*] (Tokyo: Jichi Tsūshin-sha, 1931), Appendix: Jinbutsu-hen [People] 60.

93. Sakae Tsunoyama, 'Japanese Consular Reports', *Business History* 23, no. 3 (1981): 284–87. Japanese consul Noma Masaichi provided translations of Japanese government cables on the Russo-Japanese War to the *South China Morning Post*. See, for example, 'Peace Treaty: Ratifications Exchanged', *South China Morning Post*, October 18, 1905, 7.

94. 'Levée at Government House', *China Mail*, May 1, 1877, 2–3.

95. 'Japanese Consul "At Home": The Emperor's Birthday', *China Mail*, November 3, 1906, 5.

96. For more on the 1902 and 1905 Anglo-Japanese Alliances and the Russo-Japanese War, see Tsuzuki, *The Pursuit of Power*, 163–81. Japan eventually annexed Korea as a colony in 1910. Gordon, *A Modern History of Japan*, 74–75, 117–26.

97. 'Mikado's Birthday: Celebration in Hongkong. The Anglo-Japanese Alliance', *South China Morning Post*, November 4, 1905, 2.

Notes

98. 'Mikado's Birthday', *South China Morning Post*, November 4, 1905, 2.

99. Born in Kagoshima, Satsuma, in 1864, Noma Masaichi studied at the Columbian University in Washington, DC (now George Washington University), graduating with a Master of Laws (LLM) in 1890. Howard L. Hodgkins, *Historical Catalogue of the Officers and Graduates of The Columbian University, Washington, D. C., 1821–1891* (Washington, DC: Byron S. Adams, 1891), 162, 170; and *Who's Who in the Far East 1907–08* (London: Japan Press, 1907), 250.

100. For more on Majima Keinosuke and Era Hikotarō, see Chapter 6.

101. 'Mikado Day: Celebrating the Emperor's Birthday', *Hongkong Telegraph*, November 3, 1905, 5; and 'Mikado Day: The Japanese Ball', *Hongkong Telegraph*, November 4, 1905, 5.

102. Ayako Hotta-Lister, *The Japan-British Exhibition of 1910: Gateway to the Island Empire of the East* (Richmond, Surrey: Japan Library, 1999), 3, 61.

103. 'Mikado Day: The Japanese Ball', *Hongkong Telegraph*, November 4, 1905, 5.

104. Letter from Matthew Nathan to his mother dated November 4, 1905, Oxford, Bodleian Libraries, Archive of Sir Matthew Nathan, MS. Nathan 117.

105. 'Tiffin on Board the M. B. S. S. Co's Steamer "*Niigata Maru*"', *China Mail*, November 13, 1879, 3.

106. *Overland China Mail*, January 23, 1906, 13.

107. For more on the history of the Hongkong Club, see Vaudine England, *Kindred Spirits: A History of the Hong Kong Club* (Hong Kong: The Hong Kong Club, 2016).

108. Ricardo K. S. Mak, 'Nineteenth-Century German Community', in *Foreign Communities in Hong Kong, 1840s–1950s*, ed. Cindy Yik-yi Chu (New York: Palgrave Macmillan, 2005), 74.

109. The Nippon Club was originally developed from Yamato Kai (大和會), a Japanese association founded by two company executives in 1903. Ng, 'Making of a Japanese Community', 114–15.

110. Wright, *Twentieth Century Impressions*, 172; and 外務省通商局 編, 『香港事情』, 350.

111. Kusakabe and his wife listed their address as 4 Lower Mosque Terrace, just off Caine Road in Mid-Levels in 1892, whereas the Fukuharas were living at 3 Lower Mosque Terrace at the time of Kayo's birth in January 1892. *Chronicle & Directory*, 1892, 250. See Figure 1.3 in Chapter 1 for the location of Lower Mosque Terrace.

112. 安宅, 『回顧録』, 132–33. Authors' own translation.

113. 安宅, 『回顧録』, 108.

Chapter 6

1. Oral history interview with Mrs KUSANO Kakuma conducted by OKUDA Otojirō in 1935. 奥田乙治郎 Okuda Otojirō, 『明治初年に於ける香港日本人』 [*Japanese Residents in Hong Kong during the Early Meiji Era*] (Taipei: Taiwan Sōtokufu Nettai Sangyō Chōsa-kai, 1937), Appendix 12. Authors' own translation.

2. The store's operators were from Shizuoka. 奥田, 『明治初年に於ける香港日本人』, 20, 47–50.

3. For more on the co-location of brothels and sundry goods stores, see Chapter 2. This was a duplication of the situation in 1870s Shanghai. See Joshua A. Fogel, *Articulating the Sinosphere: Sino-Japanese Relations in Space and Time* (Cambridge, MA: Harvard University Press, 2009), 74–77.

4. MIYANO Yoshijirō (宮野芳治良／芳次郎) ran a 'café' in 1886 then opened a sundry goods store that handled kimonos. 奥田, 『明治初年に於ける香港日本人』, 258–59.

5. For more on Rikimatsu, see Chapter 1.

6. 奥田, 『明治初年に於ける香港日本人』, 204.

7. Andrew Cobbing, *The Satsuma Students in Britain: Japan's Early Search for the 'Essence of the West'* (Richmond, Surrey: Japan Library, 2000), 40–41.

8. Suzanne G. O'Brien, 'Splitting Hairs: History and the Politics of Daily Life in Nineteenth-Century Japan', *The Journal of Asian Studies* 67, no. 4 (2008): 1325, 1328.

9. P. Kevin MacKeown, *A Stormy Petrel: The Life and Times of John Pope Hennessy* (Hong Kong: City University of Hong Kong Press, 2020), 248–51.

10. Henry James Lethbridge, 'Condition of the European Working Class in Nineteenth Century Hong Kong', *Journal of the Hong Kong Branch of the Royal Asiatic Society* 15 (1975): 96.

11. Though there is no grave marker for Hirasawa, his date and place of death, as well as his profession, match those for 'Jorio Kitchey' in the Hong Kong Cemetery burial register, entry 4386. 'Jorio' must be an anglicisation of 'Rokujirō'. Jorio Kitchey's remains were removed to the Hong Kong Cemetery Ossuary in the 1960s or 1970s, niche 451. Burial Registers 1853–1930, Hong Kong Sheng Kung Hui Archives, PRO HKMS44–1.

12. *Hongkong Telegraph*, May 25, 1882, 3.

13. *Chronicle & Directory*, 1882, 245.

14. 奥田，『明治初年に於ける香港日本人』，189–90. Kojima Jisaburō's death certificate confirms that he was a barber and lists his address as 13 Aberdeen Street. Tōyōkan translates as 'Oriental House'. The boarding house was run by YOKOSE Yōkichi (横瀬要吉). See Chapter 3.

15. Moore and Campbell united to form Campbell, Moore & Co., Limited, hairdressers, perfumers, and wigmakers, on July 1, 1886. Campbell, Moore & Co. was still operating in 1910, with four Japanese staff among its employees. *Chronicle & Directory*, 1870, 160; 'Campbell, Moore & Co.', *China Mail*, October 30, 1886, 3; *Chronicle & Directory*, 1885, 274; and *Chronicle & Directory*, 1910, 1104.

16. 'A Barber Wanted', *China Mail*, August 19, 1885, 3; and 'Fatal Result of a Gambling Row', *China Mail*, May 13 and 14, 1889, 3.

17. Himi was not involved in the incident that resulted in the serious wounding of the unemployed seaman who was staying in the same house at the time. 'Stabbing Case amongst Japanese', *China Mail*, January 19, 1881, 3; and 'The Japanese Stabbing Case', *China Mail*, March 7, 1881, 3.

18. 安宅彌吉 Ataka Yakichi, 『回顧録』 [*Memoirs*] (Osaka: Ataka Yakichi, 1922), 133.

19. *Chronicle and Directory*, 1886; *Chronicle and Directory*, 1888; and 奥田，『明治初年に於ける香港日本人』，275.

20. 'The Paris Toilet Co. Ltd.', *China Mail*, December 17, 1906, 5; and *South China Morning Post*, October 30, 1909, 3. Yayoye was meant to be pronounced 'yayoi (彌生)', meaning the month of March.

21. 外務省通商局 編 International Trade Bureau, Foreign Ministry, ed., 『香港事情』 [*Hong Kong Current Affairs*] (Tokyo: Keisei-sha, 1917), 348–49. In addition to 1,399 Japanese residents, the 1916 Ministry of Foreign Affairs included thirty-eight Taiwanese and twenty-three Koreans in its count. The counts for each occupation included dependents, such as children, spouses, and servants, if applicable.

22. 'A New Craze in Hongkong: Tattooing Is Fashionable', *Hongkong Telegraph*, March 1, 1889, 2–3.

23. John Skutlin, 'Fashioning Tattooed Bodies: An Exploration of Japan's Tattoo Stigma', *Asia Pacific Perspectives* 16, no. 1 (2019): 9–12; and 山本芳美 Yamamoto Yoshimi, 『イレズミと日本人』 [*Tattooing and the Japanese*] (Tokyo: Heibonsha Shinsho, 2016), 39–41.

24. Noboru Koyama, 'Japanese Tattooists and the British Royal Family during the Meiji Period', in *Britain and Japan: Biographical Portraits*, Vol. 6, ed. Hugh Cortazzi (Folkestone: Global Oriental, 2007), 71–80.

25. 'A New Craze in Hongkong', *Hongkong Telegraph*, March 1, 1889, 2–3.

26. *Hong Kong Blue Book* for 1889 (Section I, page 60) reported the annual salary earned by the colonial surgeon, Philip Ayres, as 6,168 dollars.

Notes 165

27. Noboru Koyama argues that Hori Chiyo's real name was actually Miyazaki Tadashi and that he was likely too young to have tattooed Prince George in 1881. See 小山騰 Koyama Noboru, 『日本の刺青と英国王室——明治期から第一次世界大戦まで』 [*Japanese Tattoos and the British Royal Family: From the Meiji Era to World War I*] (Tokyo: Fujiwara Shoten, 2010), 209–45; and Koyama, 'Japanese Tattooists', 71–80. Tattoo artists running businesses under assumed names and making false claims was clearly an issue. Hong Kong–based tattoo artist Noma Denjirō added disclaimers to his advertisements disavowing any connection with the 'D. Nomas' in Singapore and Shanghai. *Who's Who in the Far East 1907–08* (London: Japan Press, 1907).

28. The historian David Sissons remarked on the prevalence of second and third sons in the Broome and Thursday Island pearling industries. David Sissons, 'The Japanese in the Australian Pearling Industry', *Queensland Heritage* 3, no. 10 (1979): 18. (Reprinted in *Bridging Australia and Japan*, Vol. 1, *The Writings of David Sissons, Historian and Political Scientist*, ed. Arthur Stockwin and Keiko Tamura (Canberra: Australian National University Press, 2016).) For more on the Japanese in the Australian pearling industry, see Chapter 3.

29. 'A Queer School of Art: A Hongkong Tatooer's Atelier', *Hongkong Telegraph*, March 14, 1898, 2.

30. *Hongkong Telegraph*, November 16, 1904, 2. Noma's premises were at 60 Queen's Road by this time.

31. Inokuchi spent a couple of days in Hong Kong in April 1899. 井口丑二 Inokuchi Ushiji, 『世界一周実記』 [*Journal of a Trip Around the World*] (Tokyo: Keizaizasshi-sha, 1904), 42.

32. 奥田, 『明治初年に於ける香港日本人』, Appendix 16.

33. For more on the Mikado Ball of 1905, see Chapter 5.

34. Gwenneth and John Stokes, *Queen's College: Its History 1862–1987* (Hong Kong: Queen's College Old Boys' Association, 1987), 4. See also Ernest John Eitel, *Europe in China: The History of Hong Kong from the Beginning to the Year 1882* (London: Luzac & Company; Hong Kong: Kelly & Walsh, 1895), 247.

35. Queen's College's was first called Government Central School at its founding in 1862. The school relocated to Aberdeen Street and was renamed Victoria College in 1889. It adopted the name Queen's College in 1894. Stokes, *Queen's College*, 4, 8, 14, 29, 40.

36. Inspector of Government Schools' Report published in the *Hong Kong Government Gazette* Vol. 27, no. 11, March 18, 1871.

37. 石附実 Ishizuki Minoru, 「海外留学生リスト——明治第一期（元一七年）の留学者」 [List of Students Sent Abroad: From 1868 to 1874], in 『近代日本の海外留学史』 [*A History of Study Abroad in Modern Japan*] (Chūkō Bunko, [1972] 1992), 443; and 「本官勘合帳外國官一號」 [Record of International Passport Issuance, Vol. 1], from the Diplomatic Archives of the Ministry of Foreign Affairs, Call Number: 3-8-5-5. The writer and journalist NARUSHIMA Ryūhoku (成島柳北; 1837–1884) encountered Igawa at a cheap boarding house on 12 Aberdeen Street when he passed through Hong Kong on his way to France in September 1872. 成島柳北, 「航西日乗」, 256–57; Maeda Ai, *Text and the City: Essays on Japanese Modernity*, ed. James A. Fujii (Durham, NC: Duke University Press, 2004), 276; and Ryūhoku Narushima, *'New Chronicles of Yanagibashi' and 'Diary of a Journey to the West': Narushima Ryūhoku Reports from Home and Abroad*, trans. Matthew Fraleigh (Ithaca, NY: Cornell University Press, 2010), 157. Japanese students also attended other schools run by religious or private organisations, such as the Diocesan School. *China Mail*, January 27, 1896, 3.

38. *China Mail*, January 18, 1888, 2–3; and *China Mail*, January 13, 1890, 3.

39. 'Actual Specimens of Composition, 1905–6: Class I.A., YAMASAKI M.', *The Yellow Dragon* 7, no. 7 (April 1906): 139.

40. *Overland Chinese Mail*, March 24, 1906, 5.

41. Y.S. 「批評紹介 英米を眺めて」 [Book Reviews: On the UK and the U.S.], 『英文学研究』 *Studies in English Literature* 10, no. 2 (1930): 309–11.

42. 'Girls' School' Sessional Paper 18/89, July 5, 1889. See also Stokes, *Queen's College*, 38.

43. *Belilios Public School 120 Years Memoir* (Hong Kong: Belilios Old Girls Foundation, 2010), 12–42.

44. 'Belilios Public School: Prize Distribution', *China Mail*, March 5, 1902, 5. Noma's daughters' names are anglicised in the prize list to 'Ida' and 'Esther'.

45. 奥田，『明治初年に於ける香港日本人』, Appendix 19; and 林金五郎 Hayashi Kingorō, 『南洋——前編』 [*The South Seas, Part 1*] (Tokyo: Kiryūya Shōkai Shuppan-bu, 1917), 86–88.

46. 外務省通商局 編，『香港事情』, 355. The school later moved to Kennedy Road. For more on the Japanese Benevolent Society, see Chapter 3.

47. 末永山彦 編 Suenaga Yamahiko, ed., 『父の記録』 [*Remembering Our Father*] (Osaka: Suenaga Yamahiko, 1941), 129. Asai Umeko went on to become a respected haiku poet, writing under the name YAMAGUCHI Hatsujyo (山口波津女).

48. Terry Bennett, *History of Photography in China: Chinese Photographers 1844–1879* (London: Quaritch, 2013), 66.

49. Ueno is romanised as 'Uyeno' in English-language advertisements and entries in the *Chronicle & Directory*. Ueno and the names of two younger Japanese photographers, probably his assistants, appear on the 1886 list of Japanese residents in Hong Kong. 奥田，『明治初年に於ける香港日本人』, 254–59.

50. Anne Wilkes Tucker et al., *The History of Japanese Photography*. Exhibition catalogue (London: Yale University Press in association with the Museum of Fine Arts, Houston, 2003), 6, 20. See also Terry Bennett, *Photography in Japan 1853–1912* (Tokyo: Tuttle Publishing, 2006), 16, 73–76.

51. Claude Estèbe, 'Ueno Hikoma, un Portraitiste à la Fin du Shôgunat', *Ebisu* 24 (2000): 121. Pierre Loti is the pen name of French naval lieutenant Julien Viaud (1850–1923).

52. Pierre Loti, *Madame Chrysanthème*, trans. Laura Ensor (London: George Routledge and Sons, 1897), 151, 250–51. Loti visited Ueno's with 'Okané-san', the future 'Madame Chrysanthème', and his shipmate Pierre Le Cor for a group portrait on July 29, 1885. Pierre Loti, *Journal*, Vol. 2, *1879–1886*, ed. Alain Quella-Villéger and Bruno Vercier (Paris: Les Indes Savantes, 2008), 635–36.

53. Era is rendered as 'Yera' in English-language advertisements and the *Chronicle & Directory*. H. Yera is listed as Ueno's employee in the 1889 *Chronicle & Directory*. Notice of the closure of Ueno's studio appeared in the *Hongkong Telegraph* on August 28, 1889, 3. Era's studio in Arsenal Street is first listed in the *Chronicle & Directory*, 1891, 242. The 14 Beaconsfield Arcade address appears in the *Chronicle & Directory*, 1900, 359. The Arcade was demolished in the 1930s and is now the location of the Cheung Kong Center. 'Old Hongkong (by "Colonial")', *South China Morning Post*, June 17, 1933, 13.

54. Unlike tattoo artist Noma, however, 'Mr. and Mrs. Yera' appeared on the ball's prestigious guest list. 'Mikado Day: Celebrating the Emperor's Birthday', *Hongkong Telegraph*, November 3, 1905, 5.

55. Nagamatsu's first name is given as 'Maromoto' on his death certificate but can also be read as 'Shōki'. An S. Nagamatsu is listed under Era's studio in the *Chronicle & Directory*, 1892, 245, along with two other Japanese employees.

56. Umeya is romanised as 'Mumeya' in advertisements in the English-language press and entries in the *Chronicle & Directory*.

57. 小坂文乃 Kosaka Ayano, 『革命をプロデュースした日本人——評伝　梅屋庄吉』 [*The Japanese Man Who Produced a Revolution: Biography of Umeya Shōkichi*] (Tokyo: Kodansha, 2009), 24–39; and Peter B. High, 'Shokichi Umeya: The Revolutionist as Impresario', in *Tagen Bunka to Mirai Shakai Kenkyu Project* (Nagoya: Nagoya University, 2005), 105–34.

Notes 167

58. 小坂『革命をプロデュースした日本人』, 54–70, 80–87, 130–37; and High, 'Shokichi Umeya', 105–34. For more on Sun Yat-sen's contacts with Japanese supporters of his cause in Hong Kong, see Marius B. Jansen, *The Japanese and Sun Yat-sen* (Cambridge, MA: Harvard University Press, 1954). Miyazaki Tōten is the pen name of Miyazaki Torazō (宮崎寅蔵).

59. 村岡伊平治,『村岡伊平治自伝』, 264–66. For more on the dispute between the Ōtaka and Suzuki crime families, see Chapter 3.

60. 奥田,『明治初年に於ける香港日本人』, Appendix 23.

61. 「紙幣偽造事件判決」 [Judgement in the Fake Bill Case],『法律日日』 *Hōritsu Hibi* 204, November 1913, 12–14.

62. 'The Bank Note Case: Proceedings at the Magistracy', *South China Morning Post*, December 31, 1912, 3.

63. Masujima spent two years at the Middle Temple in London and qualified as a barrister in 1883. He was recalled to Japan halfway through the trial and took no active part in the court proceedings from April 1, 1913, onwards. For more on Masujima, see Morikuni Sugawara, 'Chuo University and London', *Chuo Online*, 2012, https://yab.yomiuri.co.jp/adv/chuo/dy/research/20120816.html.

64. 'A Japanese Newspaper: The First to Be Published in Hongkong', *Hongkong Telegraph*, September 20, 1909, 4. For early editions of the newspaper, see 「新聞雑誌操縦関係雑纂／香港日報」 [Miscellaneous Matters Related to Newspapers and Magazines: *Honkon Nippō*], Japan Center for Asian Historical Records (JACAR), originally from the Diplomatic Archives of the Ministry of Foreign Affairs, https://www.jacar.archives.go.jp/das/image/B03040612400. For more on the newspaper's history, see Wilson Wai Shing Lee, 'Honkon Nippō and Hong Kong–Japan Relations: Re-examining the Geopolitical Position of Colonial Hong Kong in East Asia before the End of World War II', in *Asian Cities: Colonial to Global*, ed. Gregory Bracken (Amsterdam: Amsterdam University Press, 2015), 125–42; and 'Old Hongkong (by "Colonial") – Foreign Papers of the Colony', *South China Morning Post*, November 29, 1934, 17.

65. The magistrate ordered Matsushima to insert an apology in his own publication, as well as in two Chinese newspapers, and to refrain from printing similar articles in the future. 'The Bank Note Case: Proceedings at the Magistracy', *South China Morning Post*, December 31, 1912, 3; and 'Contempt of Court: Action against Japanese Editor', *South China Morning Post*, January 30, 1913, 3.

66. The trial concluded on April 8, 1903. The arrests, arraignments, trial, and sentencing were covered extensively in the *South China Morning Post*, notably the issues of December 25, 27, and 31, 1912; January 8, 9, 10, 14, 16, 24; March 18, 20, 21, 26; and April 1, 2, 4, 5, 8, 9, 1913. The governor, Sir Henry May, also sent a report on the case, dated May 2, 1913, to the secretary of state for the colonies. The National Archives of the UK (TNA): CO 129/401, 28–30.

67. 'The Bank Note Case: "Hardship on the Jury"', *South China Morning Post*, April 4, 1913, 3.

68. 奥田『明治初年に於ける香港日本人』, 314; and *Chronicle & Directory*, 1901, 380.

69. Examples include 'Destruction of Shipping and Dock Property at Hongkong', *The Far Eastern Review* 3, no. 5 (October 1906): 150–52; and 'The Zoroastrian Club: Annual Meeting', *South China Morning Post*, August 15, 1910, 6.

70. 夏目漱石 Natsume Sōseki,『漱石全集——第15巻日記及断片』 [*The Sōseki Collection*, Vol. 15, *Diaries and Fragments*] (Tokyo: Sōseki Zenshū Kankō-kai, 1936), 10; and 長島弘明 Nagashima Hiroaki, 「芳賀矢一 『留学日誌』——東京大学国文学研究室蔵本の影印と翻刻」 [Haga Yaichi's *Study Abroad Journal*: Reprint from Tokyo University's Library of the Institute of Japanese Literature]『東京大学国文学論集』 *Journal of Japanese Literature, Tokyo University* 14 (2019): 119.

71. See, for example, *China Mail*, August 25, 1904, 2.

72. *Chronicle & Directory*, 1903 (between pages 384 and 385).

73. MIZUMOTO Inosuke was also known as FUKUSHIMA Yūzaburō (福島祐三郎). 香港日本人倶楽部 Hongkong Japanese Club, 『写真集——香港日本人墓地』 [*Photo Album: Japanese Graves in Hong Kong*] (Hong Kong: Hongkong Japanese Club, 2006), 105, 162.

74. *South China Morning Post*, December 9, 1918, 3. Upon his return to Japan, Umeya established the film promotion and production company M. Pathé, which would eventually merge with three others to form Nihon Katsudō Shashin Kabushiki-gaisha (Nikkatsu). 小坂, 『革命をプロデュースした日本人』, 91–123, 147–51.

75. 坂田敏夫 Sakata Toshio, 「上海邦人歯科醫界の回顧」 [Reminiscences of Japanese Dentists in Shanghai], 『臨床歯科』 *Rinshō Shika* 12, no. 1 (1940): 147–50.

76. *Hongkong Daily Press*, June 8, 1894, 3. Lam Sam Shing's name is given as 'Sui Sang' in the advertisement. Sakata's name is transliterated as 'Ishinoseki' in the English-language press.

77. The Hongkong Hotel advertised board and lodging from 5 dollars per day in the *China Mail*, October 8, 1894, 1.

78. The young man, Albert Byron Wilson, arrived in Hong Kong on October 11, 1894, and left a trail of unpaid bills. The magistrate's court found Wilson guilty and sentenced him to six months' imprisonment. 'Another Sensational Arrest: How the "Reverend" Alfred Byron Wilson Got His Teeth Stopped', *Hongkong Telegraph*, October 24, 1894, 2; and *China Mail*, October 31, 1894, 2.

79. 歯科研究会 Dental Study Association, 「雑報」 [Miscellaneous News], 『歯科研究会月報』 *Shika Kenkyūkai Geppō* 11 (1891): 34.

80. 奥田, 『明治初年に於ける香港日本人』, 311–13. The medical register was established under Ordinance 6 of 1884, which was published in the *Hong Kong Government Gazette* of April 10, 1884.

81. Tai Ping Shan's overcrowded Chinese tenement houses and lack of sanitation were the focus of the colonial administration's post-epidemic disease prevention efforts. The land was resumed and several rows of tenement houses razed in late 1894. Cecilia L. Chu, *Building Colonial Hong Kong: Speculative Development and Segregation in the City* (London: Routledge, 2022), 73–84.

82. The *Hygeia* was built by the Hongkong and Whampoa Dock Company. 'The Launching of the "Hygeia"', *Hongkong Daily Press*, February 6, 1891, 2.

83. The Tung Wah Hospital, as well as the Alice Memorial Hospital and its extension, the Nethersole Hospital, were involved in the treatment of Chinese patients during the epidemic, initially using Chinese traditional medical practices. Arthur Starling et al., eds, *Plague, SARS and the Story of Medicine in Hong Kong* (Hong Kong: Hong Kong University Press, 2006), 28–34.

84. Jerome J. Platt, Maurice E. Jones, and Arleen Kay, *The Whitewash Brigade: The Hong Kong Plague of 1894* (London: Dix Noonan Webb, 1998), 34–37.

85. This number does not include dead bodies found in town and sent directly to designated plague burial grounds. James Lowson, 'The Epidemic of Bubonic Plague in Hongkong, 1894.' Lowson's report was published in the *Hong Kong Government Gazette* of April 13, 1895. See also Edward George Pryor, 'The Great Plague of Hong Kong', *Journal of the Hong Kong Branch of the Royal Asiatic Society* 15 (1975): 61–70.

86. 木下正中 Kinoshita Seichū, 「香港 『ペスト』 研究當時の追憶」 [Reminiscences of the Hong Kong 'Plague' Investigation], 『日本伝染病学会雑誌』 *Nihon Densenbyō Gakkai Zasshi* 2, no. 1 (1927): 62; reprinted edition with the correct spelling for Nakahara's name 「青山胤通先生」 [Dr Aoyama Tanemichi], 『日本医事新報』 *Nihon Iji Shinpō* (Special Issue, November 1937): 24; and 「岡田義行氏より加藤内務属へ宛てたる書」 [A Letter from Okada Yoshiyuki to Katō in the Home Ministry], 『醫海時報』 *Ikai Jihō* 18 (1894): 3.

Notes

87. For more on Lowson, see Gerald H. Choa, 'The Lowson Diary: A Record of the Early Phase of the Hong Kong Bubonic Plague 1894', *Journal of the Hong Kong Branch of the Royal Asiatic Society* 33 (1993): 129–45.

88. 「青山胤通先生」, 128; and 上山明博 Ueyama Akihiro, 『北里柴三郎——感染症と闘いつづけた男』 [*Kitasato Shibasaburō: A Man Who Fought with Infectious Diseases*] (Tokyo: Seidosha, 2021), 30.

89. 木下, 「香港『ペスト』研究當時の追憶」, 60; and 「青山胤通先生」, 21–22.

90. 上山, 『北里柴三郎』, 27.

91. 木下, 「香港『ペスト』研究當時の追憶」, 61.

92. 'Discovery of the Plague Bacillus: Interview with Professor Kitasato', *China Mail*, June 20, 1894, 3; 'Professor Kitasato on the Plague', *Hongkong Telegraph*, July 20, 1894, 2–3; and Shibasaburō Kitasato, 'The Bacillus of Bubonic Plague', *The Lancet* 144, no. 3704 (August 25, 1894): 428–30.

93. For more on the controversy, see Tom Solomon, 'Hong Kong, 1894: The Role of James A Lowson in the Controversial Discovery of the Plague Bacillus', *The Lancet* 350, no. 9070 (1997): 59–62; and 上山, 『北里柴三郎』, 51–62.

94. 木下, 「香港『ペスト』研究當時の追憶」, 62.

95. Entry for June 28, 1894, in Jack Lowson's diary, courtesy of the Hong Kong Museum of Medical Sciences.

96. A full description of the treatment given to Aoyama and Ishigami is included in Lowson's 1895 report on the plague, Cases 2 and 3.

97. In his July 7, 1894, report to the secretary of state for the colonies, the governor enclosed a list of nine Japanese stricken by the plague. Haruno Ino is listed as 'O Jugo'. Both her and Nakahara's names appeared alongside a small '+' symbol indicating that they were deceased. TNA: CO 129/263, 538–42.

98. While the government did cordon off a section of the Hong Kong Cemetery for plague victims, this arrangement was reserved for the small number of Europeans who died from the disease. TNA: CO 129/266, 470–75. Ino was probably buried in one of the other plague cemeteries and Takano erected the gravestone at a later date.

99. Moira M. W. Chan-Yeung, *A Medical History of Hong Kong: 1842–1941* (Hong Kong: The Chinese University of Hong Kong Press, 2018), 153.

100. *China Mail*, September 27, 1904, 8.

101. *Japan Times*, August 21, 1904, 3; and 民天時報社編輯局 編 Mintenjihō-sha Editorial Bureau, ed. 『海外邦人の事業及人物 第1輯』 [*Overseas Japanese: Their Occupations and Biographies*] (Tokyo: Mintenjihō-sha, 1917), 90.

102. Chieko Nakajima, 'Medicine, Philanthropy, and Imperialism: The Dōjinkai in China, 1902–1945', *Sino-Japanese Studies* 17, no. 6 (2010): 47–84. See also Ming-Cheng M. Lo, *Doctors Within Borders: Profession, Ethnicity, and Modernity in Colonial Taiwan* (Berkeley: University of California Press, 2002), 151–80. For more on the Tōa Dōbunkai, see Chapter 3.

103. Majima's entry in the 1906 *Chronicle & Directory* stated that he was the 'ex-principal of the Formosa Government Hospital, and Civil Med. Officer to the Home Dept.'. *Chronicle & Directory*, 1906, 939.

104. 'Register of Medical and Surgical Practitioners' for 1905, published in the *Hong Kong Government Gazette* of May 5, 1905. Majima was not the first Japanese doctor included. The registers for 1903 and 1904 list KOBAYASHI Sanzaburō (小林 参三郎; 1863–1926) as practising in Room 97 of the Hongkong Hotel. Majima's practice was at 177 Wanchai Road prior to 1907.

105. The property was owned by Irishman William Lysaught. Hong Kong Public Records Office HKRS 265 11A-1869-1 and HKRS 265 11A-1790-3. For more on William Lysaught, see Patricia O'Sullivan, *Policing Hong Kong: An Irish History* (Hong Kong: Blacksmith Books, 2017), 139–58.

170   Notes

106. *Hongkong Daily Press*, November 16, 1911, 2.
107. 'Sub-manager of the Specie Bank', *Hongkong Telegraph*, December 8, 1906, 14; and 'Description of the Scene', *South China Morning Post*, February 27, 1918, 7.
108. 赤岩昭滋 Akaiwa Teruji, 「香港の日本人墓地──船員の墓碑を中心として」 [Japanese Graves in Hong Kong: Graves of Sailors and Others], 『海事史研究』 *Journal of the Japan Society for Nautical Research* 21 (1973): 73.
109. 外務省通商局 編,『香港事情』, 353–55. For more on the Japanese Benevolent Society, see Chapter 3.
110. 'Lease of Inland Lot no. 1879', dated December 6, 1911. Hong Kong Public Records Office HKRS 265 11A-1973-1.
111. *South China Morning Post*, October 6, 1919, 10.
112. 死亡広告 [Death Notice], 『東京朝日新聞』 *Tokyo Asahi Shimbun*, November 9, 1919, Morning Edition, 3.
113. Majima's practice was taken over by Dr MUNEHIRO Jungo (宗廣純吾), a graduate of the University of Tokyo. 'Register of Medical and Surgical Practitioners' for 1920, published in the *Hong Kong Government Gazette* of May 7, 1920. See also the *Chronicle & Directory*, 1920, 998.
114. Funatsu departed Hong Kong on February 27, 1912. 'Mr. & Mrs. Funatsu', *South China Morning Post*, February 26, 1912, 3.
115. 奥田,『明治初年に於ける香港日本人』, Appendix 21–23.

Chapter 7

1.   朝倉明宣 Asakura Meisen, 『清国巡遊誌』 [*Journal of Travel around China*] (Kyoto: Asakura Meisen, 1900), 72–73.
2.   Census Office, *Report on the Census of the Colony for 1921*, December 15, 1921, 8. Hong Kong's Portuguese and Indian residents typically had their separate columns in the colonial government censuses. The reason for this can be found on pages 1 and 2 of the *Report on the Census of the Colony for 1897*. The census administrator explains that the 'Portuguese of Hongkong form a European community settled in the Tropics, thoroughly acclimatised and apparently not recruited to any extent from Europe'. As to why 'Indians' are counted separately, the administrator argues that they 'are a sufficiently numerous and important body to appear separately'.
3.   This number is based on our own calculation and a 2006 compilation of the graves by the Hongkong Japanese Club. 香港日本人倶楽部 Hongkong Japanese Club, 『写真集──香港日本人墓地』 [*Photo Album: Japanese Graves in Hong Kong*] (Hong Kong: Hongkong Japanese Club, 2006), 36–169.
4.   香港日本人倶楽部,『香港日本人墓地』, 159–69.
5.   執行弘道 編 Shugyō Hiromichi, ed. 『日本美術帖』 [*Japanese Art Folio*] Parts 1–3, ed. K. Ogawa (Tokyo: K. Ogawa, 1898); and 帝国美術院附属美術研究所 編 Fine Arts Institute, Imperial Fine Arts Academy, ed., 『三原繁吉氏蔵浮世絵版画展覧会目録』 [*Exhibition Catalogue for the Mihara Shigekichi Ukiyoe Collection*] (Tokyo: Iwanami Shoten, 1930).
6.   Census Office, Report on the Census of the Colony for 1921, December 15, 1921, Table XVIII.
7.   Letter from Charles Anderson, Commander of His Majesty's Forces in South China and Hong Kong, to Hong Kong Governor Frederick Lugard dated August 25, 1911. Governor Frederick Lugard was generally in favour of granting the lease under certain conditions to Mitsui Bussan Kaisha, which at the time was the largest coal dealing firm in Hong Kong. Ultimately, however, Mitsui was unwilling to take the site under the terms offered and

Notes 171

sought an alternative arrangement. The National Archives of the UK (TNA): CO129/370, 25–43, 243–46; and TNA: CO129/381, 168–74.

8. 『官報』 [(Japanese Government) *Gazette*], March 19, 1904, Appendix 15–20; and April 20, 1904, Appendix 10–12; 「日露戦役二際シ軍資金献納雑件／欧州其他ノ部」 [Various Donations in Connection with the Russo-Japanese War: Europe and Other Areas] (5-2-10-0-3-5), Japan Center for Asian Historical Records, originally from the Diplomatic Archives of the Ministry of Foreign Affairs.

9. Hong Kong Public Records Office HKRS156-1-1349, BDN; 'Japan's Unfinished War Memorial', *China Mail*, November 4, 1946, 4; 'Japanese Memorial Shattered', *South China Morning Post*, February 27, 1947, 1; and Ken Barrett, 'My Search for the Secret Samurai', *South China Morning Post*, August 30, 1993, 14.

10. 香港日本人倶楽部 史料編纂委員会 Hongkong Japanese Club's History Book Committee, 『香港日本人社会の歴史——江戸から平成まで——』 [*History of the Japanese Community in Hong Kong: From Edo to Heisei*] (Hong Kong: Hongkong Japanese Club, 2006), 66–69.

11. 香港日本人倶楽部,『香港日本人墓地』, 12–19.

12. 日本海員掖済会 Japan Seafarers Relief Association, 『海之世界』 *Umino Sekai* 8, no. 5 (May 1914): 43–45; 赤岩昭滋 Akaiwa Teruji, 「香港の日本人墓地——船員の墓碑を中心として」 [Japanese Graves in Hong Kong: Graves of Sailors and Others], 『海事史研究』 *Journal of the Japan Society for Nautical Research* 21 (1973): 66–81; and 香港日本人倶楽部,『香港日本人墓地』.

Bibliography

Archives

Government archives

Bibliothèque nationale de France. Fonds Victor Hugo

Hong Kong Births and Deaths General Register Office

Hong Kong Public Records Office (PRO)

The National Archives of the UK

Queensland State Archives

国立公文書館アジア歴史資料センター [Japan Center for Asian Historical Records (JACAR), National Archives]

外務省外交史料館 [The Diplomatic Archives of the Ministry of Foreign Affairs]

Private archives

Archival records of Lobnitz & Co. UCS 004/4/6, University of Glasgow

Bibliothèque centrale de l'École polytechnique

Bodleian Libraries

Carl T. Smith Papers (Hong Kong Public Records Office)

Hong Kong Museum of Medical Sciences

Hong Kong Sheng Kung Hui Archives

Imperial College Archives

Queen's College History Museum

三菱史料館 [The Mitsubishi Archives]

Government Publications

Hong Kong Blue Book

Hong Kong Government Gazette

Report of the Commissioners Appointed to Inquire into the Working of the Contagious Disease Ordinance, 1867, in Hong Kong (Hong Kong: Noronha & Sons, Government Printers, 1879)

『官報』 [(Japanese Government) *Gazette*]

Other English-Language Publications

Chronicle & Directory for China, Corea, Japan, The Philippines, Cochin-China, Annam, Tonquin, Siam, Borneo, Straits Settlements, Malay States, &c. (*Chronicle & Directory*)

Hong Kong General Chamber of Commerce Reports

Who's Who in the Far East 1906–07

Who's Who in the Far East 1907–08

The Yellow Dragon (Queen's College publication)

Newspapers

English-language newspapers

China Mail

Edinburgh Evening News

Friend of China

Hongkong Daily Press

Hongkong Telegraph

Japan Times

Japan Weekly Mail

London and China Telegraph

Overland China Mail

Paisley and Renfrewshire Gazette

Shipping and Mercantile Gazette

Shipping Gazette and Lloyd's List

South China Morning Post

The Times

Japanese-language newspapers

『海商通報』 [*Kaishō Tsūhō*]

『東京朝日新聞』 [*Tokyo Asahi Shimbun*]

『朝野新聞』 [*Chōya Shimbun*]

『法律日日』 [*Hōritsu Hibi*]

Websites

Hong Kong General Chamber of Commerce
https://www.chamber.org.hk/en/

Hongkong Land at 125 (Hong Kong: Hongkong Land Limited, 2014)
https://hklandblob.blob.core.windows.net/assets/125_anniversary/mobile/index.html#p=1.

Tung Wah Group of Hospitals, "The Race Course Fire Memorial"
https://www.tungwah.org.hk/en/heritage/historical-architecture/the-race-course-fire-memorial/

伊藤忠商事　歴史・沿革 [Itochu History]
https://www.itochu.co.jp/en/about/history/index.html

国立国会図書館デジタルコレクション [National Diet Library (NDL) Digital Collections]
https://dl.ndl.go.jp/

『人事興信録』データベース [Jinji Kōshinroku (Who's Who) Database, Nagoya University Graduate School of Law]
https://jahis.law.nagoya-u.ac.jp/who/

双日歴史館 [Sojitz History Museum]
https://www.sojitz.com/history/en/company/suzukishoten/

東京海洋大学 [Tokyo University of Marine Science and Technology]
https://www.kaiyodai.ac.jp/

ニッポンドットコム [nippon.com]
https://www.nippon.com/

日本海員掖済会 [Japan Seafarers Relief Association]
https://www.ekisaikai.com/

福沢諭吉 Fukuzawa Yukichi, デジタルで読む福澤諭吉 [Digital Library of Yukichi Fukuzawa's Work], Keio University Libraries
https://dcollections.lib.keio.ac.jp/en/fukuzawa

三菱グループ [Mitsubishi Group]
https://www.mitsubishi.com/

English- and French-Language References

Ai, Maeda. *Text and the City: Essays on Japanese Modernity.* Edited by James A. Fujii. Durham, NC: Duke University Press, 2004.

Belilios Public School 120 Years Memoir. Hong Kong: Belilios Old Girls Foundation, 2010.

Benesch, Oleg, and Ran Zwigenberg. *Japan's Castles: Citadels of Modernity in War and Peace.* Cambridge: Cambridge University Press, 2019.

Bennett, Terry. *History of Photography in China: Chinese Photographers 1844–1879.* London: Quaritch, 2013.

Bennett, Terry. *Photography in Japan 1853–1912.* Tokyo: Tuttle Publishing, 2006.

Bernstein, Andrew. 'Fire and Earth: The Forging of Modern Cremation in Meiji Japan.' *Japanese Journal of Religious Studies* 27, no. 3/4 (2000): 297–334.

Bernstein, Andrew. *Modern Passings: Death Rites, Politics, and Social Change in Imperial Japan.* Honolulu: University of Hawai'i Press, 2006.

Bird, Isabella L. *The Golden Chersonese and the Way Thither.* Kuala Lumpur: Oxford University Press, 1967. (First edition published by John Murray, Albemarle Street, London, in 1883.)

Bird, Isabella L. *Unbeaten Tracks in Japan: An Account of Travels in the Interior, Including Visits to the Aborigines of Yezo and the Shrines of Nikkô and Isé.* In *Collected Travel Writings of Isabella Bird*, Vol. 5. Bristol: Ganesha Publishing and Tokyo: Edition Synapse, 1997. (First edition published by John Murray, Albemarle Street, London, in 1880.)

'Blue Funnel's "Butterflies".' *Swire News* 25, no. 3 (1998): 28.

Borscheid, Peter, and Niels Viggo Haueter, eds. *World Insurance: The Evolution of a Global Risk Network.* Oxford: Oxford University Press, 2012.

Burke-Gaffney, Brian. *Nagasaki: The British Experience, 1854–1945.* Folkestone: Global Oriental, 2009.

Bibliography

Burke-Gaffney, Brian. 'The Tattoos of Michinaga Ei and Nicholas II.' *Crossroads: A Journal of Nagasaki History and Culture* 1 (1993), http://www.uwosh.edu/faculty_staff/earns/nick&ei.html.

Bush, Lewis. *The Life and Times of the Illustrious Captain Brown: A Chronicle of the Sea and of Japan's Emergence as a World Power.* Tokyo: The Voyagers' Press and Rutland: The Charles E. Tuttle Company, 1969.

Calman, Donald. *The Nature and Origins of Japanese Imperialism: A Reinterpretation of the Great Crisis of 1873.* London: Routledge, 1992.

Carroll, John M. *A Concise History of Hong Kong.* Hong Kong: Hong Kong University Press, 2007.

Carroll, John M. *Edge of Empires: Chinese Elites and British Colonials in Hong Kong.* Hong Kong: Hong Kong University Press, 2005.

Carroll, John M. 'A National Custom: Debating Female Servitude in Late Nineteenth-Century Hong Kong.' *Modern Asian Studies* 43, no. 6 (2009): 1463–93.

Chadwick, Osbert. *Mr. Chadwick's Reports on the Sanitary Condition of Hong Kong; with Appendices and Plans.* Hong Kong, 1882.

Chan-Yeung, Moira M. W. *A Medical History of Hong Kong: 1842–1941.* Hong Kong: The Chinese University of Hong Kong Press, 2018.

Checkland, Olive. *Japan and Britain after 1859: Creating Cultural Bridges.* New York: Routledge, 2003.

Cheng, Po Hung. *Early Hong Kong Eateries.* Hong Kong: University Museum and Art Gallery, University of Hong Kong, 2003.

Ching, Henry. *Pow Mah: A Historical Sketch of Horse and Pony Racing in Hong Kong and of the Royal Hong Kong Jockey Club.* Hong Kong: South China Morning Post, 1965.

Chiu, Patricia Pok-kwan. 'A Position of Usefulness: Gendering History of Girls' Education in Colonial Hong Kong (1850s–1890s).' *History of Education* 37, no. 6 (2008): 789–805.

Choa, Gerald H. 'The Lowson Diary: A Record of the Early Phase of the Hong Kong Bubonic Plague 1894.' *Journal of the Hong Kong Branch of the Royal Asiatic Society* 33 (1993): 129–45.

Chu, Cecilia L. *Building Colonial Hong Kong: Speculative Development and Segregation in the City.* London: Routledge, 2022.

Chubbuck, Kay, ed. *Letters to Henrietta.* London: John Murray, 2002.

Cobbing, Andrew. *The Japanese Discovery of Victorian Britain: Early Travel Encounters in the Far West.* Richmond, Surrey: Japan Library, 1998.

Cobbing, Andrew. *Kyushu: Gateway to Japan: A Concise History.* Leiden: Brill, 2008.

Cobbing, Andrew. *The Satsuma Students in Britain: Japan's Early Search for the 'Essence of the West'.* Richmond, Surrey: Japan Library, 2000.

Cobbing, Andrew. 'Ueno Kagenori, 1845–1888: A Most Influential Diplomat [London, 1874–1879].' In *Japanese Envoys in Britain, 1862–1964*, edited by Ian Nish, 35–45. Boston: Brill, 2007.

Daniels, Roger. 'The Japanese Diaspora in the New World.' In *Japanese Diasporas: Unsung Pasts, Conflicting Presents, and Uncertain Futures*, edited by Nobuko Adachi, 25–34. Abingdon: Routledge, 2006.

Davies, Stephen. *Strong to Save: Maritime Mission in Hong Kong from Whampoa Reach to the Mariners' Club.* Hong Kong: City University of Hong Kong Press, 2017.

'Destruction of Shipping and Dock Property at Hongkong.' *The Far Eastern Review* 3, no. 5 (October 1906): 150–52.

Drixler, Fabian. *Mabiki: Infanticide and Population Growth in Eastern Japan, 1660–1950.* Berkeley: University of California Press, 2013.

Dusinberre, Martin. 'Japan, Global History, and the Great Silence.' *History Workshop Journal* 83, no. 1 (Spring 2017): 130–50.

Ealing-Godbold, Christina. 'Pearling Luggers of the Torres Strait.' *State Library of Queensland*, posted November 19, 2014. https://www.slq.qld.gov.au/blog/pearling-luggers-torres-strait.

Eitel, Ernest John. *Europe in China: The History of Hong Kong from the Beginning to the Year 1882.* London: Luzac & Company; Hong Kong: Kelly & Walsh, 1895.

Empson, Hal. *Mapping Hong Kong: A Historical Atlas.* Hong Kong: Government Information Services, 1992.

England, Vaudine. *Kindred Spirits: A History of the Hong Kong Club.* Hong Kong: The Hong Kong Club, 2016.

Estèbe, Claude. 'Ueno Hikoma, un Portraitiste à la Fin du Shôgunat.' *Ebisu* 24 (2000): 107–30.

Fogel, Joshua A. *Articulating the Sinosphere: Sino-Japanese Relations in Space and Time.* Cambridge, MA: Harvard University Press, 2009.

Fogel, Joshua A. *The Literature of Travel in the Japanese Rediscovery of China, 1862–1945.* Stanford: Stanford University Press, 1996.

Fraleigh, Matthew. *'New Chronicles of Yanagibashi' and 'Diary of a Journey to the West': Narushima Ryuhoku Reports from Home and Abroad.* Ithaca, NY: Cornell University Press, 2010.

Gluck, Carol. *Japan's Modern Myths: Ideology in the Late Meiji Period.* Princeton: Princeton University Press, 1985.

Gordon, Andrew. *A Modern History of Japan: From Tokugawa Times to the Present*, 4th ed. New York: Oxford University Press, 2020.

Guoth, Nicholas. 'Advancing Trade with China: The Eastern and Australian Mail Steam Company and the 1873–1880 Mail Contract.' *The International Journal of Maritime History* 31, no. 2 (2019): 263–84.

Hamilton, Sheila E. *Watching Over Hong: Private Policing 1841–1941.* Hong Kong: Hong Kong University Press, 2008.

Hane, Mikiso. *Peasants, Rebels, and Outcastes: The Underside of Modern Japan.* New York: Pantheon, 1982.

Hartman, Elwood. 'Japonisme and Nineteenth-Century French Literature.' *Comparative Literature Studies* 18, no. 2 (June 1981): 141–66.

High, Peter B. 'Shokichi Umeya: The Revolutionist as Impresario.' In *Tagen Bunka to Mirai Shakai Kenkyu Project*, 105–34. Nagoya: Nagoya University, 2005.

Hoare, James, ed. *Culture, Power & Politics in Treaty Port Japan, 1854–1899: Key Papers, Press and Contemporary Writings*, Vol. 1, *Historical Perspectives*. Amsterdam: Amsterdam University Press, 2018.

Hodgkins, Howard L. *Historical Catalogue of the Officers and Graduates of the Columbian University, Washington, D. C., 1821–1891.* Washington, DC: Byron S. Adams, 1891.

Hoe, Susanna. *The Private Life of Old Hong Kong: Western Women in the British Colony, 1841–1941.* Hong Kong: Oxford University Press, 1991.

Hotta-Lister, Ayako. *The Japan-British Exhibition of 1910: Gateway to the Island Empire of the East.* Richmond, Surrey: Japan Library, 1999.

Howell, Philip. 'Race, Space and the Regulation of Prostitution in Colonial Hong Kong.' *Urban History* 31, no. 2 (2004): 229–48.

'Incidents in the Life of a Missionary Candidate.' *Female Missionary Intelligencer* 4, New Series (1884): 42–47.

Inotani, Satoshi. 'The Translation of Zen: A Tribute to D. T. Suzuki.' *Nippon.com*, November 11, 2020, https://www.nippon.com/en/japan-topics/b07214/.

'International Law Involved in the Seizure of the Tatsu Maru.' *The American Journal of International Law* 2, no. 2 (April 1908): 391–97.

Itoh, Keiko. 'The Yokohama Specie Bank in London.' In *Britain & Japan: Biographical Portraits*, Vol. 5, edited by Hugh Cortazzi, 233–46. Folkestone: Global Oriental, 2005.

Jaffe, Richard M. 'Buddhist Material Culture, "Indianism," and the Construction of Pan-Asian Buddhism in Prewar Japan.' *Material Religion* 2, no. 3 (2006): 266–92.

Jaffe, Richard M., ed. *Selected Works of D.T. Suzuki*, Vol. 1, *Zen*, 1st ed. Oakland: University of California Press, 2015.

Jansen, Marius B. *The Japanese and Sun Yat-sen.* Cambridge, MA: Harvard University Press, 1954.

Japan Business History Institute, eds. *The Tokio Marine & Fire Insurance: The First Century, 1879–1979.* Tokyo: The Tokio Marine and Fire Insurance Co., 1980.

Jorge Cotton, Doreen. 'A Man on Fire.' January 31, 2011, https://doreenjorgecotton.com/?cat=4.

Kawata, T., ed. *Glimpses of the East: Official Shipper's Guide and Commercial Year-book of the World, 9th Annual Issue, 1925–1927.* Tokyo: Nippon Yusen Kaisha,1926. NDL Digital Collections, https://dl.ndl.go.jp/pid/1700326.

Keene, Donald. *Modern Japanese Diaries: The Japanese at Home and Abroad as Revealed through Their Diaries.* New York: Henry Holt and Company, 1995.

Kitasato, Shibasaburō. 'The Bacillus of Bubonic Plague.' *The Lancet* 144, no. 3704 (August 25, 1894): 428–30.

Ko, Tim-Keung. 'A Review of Development of Cemeteries in Hong Kong: 1841–1950.' *Journal of the Royal Asiatic Society Hong Kong Branch* 41 (2001): 241–80.

Kohl, Stephen W. 'Strangers in a Strange Land: Japanese Castaways and the Opening of Japan.' *Pacific Northwest Quarterly* 73, no. 1 (1982): 20–28.

Koyama, Noboru. 'Japanese Tattooists and the British Royal Family During the Meiji Period.' In *Britain and Japan: Biographical Portraits*, Vol. 6, edited by Hugh Cortazzi, 71–80. Folkestone: Global Oriental, 2007.

Koyama, Noboru. 'Three Meiji Marriages between Japanese Men and English Women.' In *Britain and Japan: Biographical Portraits*, Vol. 4, edited by Hugh Cortazzi, 383–96. Leiden: Brill, 2002.

Kume, Kunitake. *The Iwakura Embassy, 1871–1873: A True Account of the Ambassador Extraordinary and Plenipotentiary's Journal of Observation Through the United States of America and Europe*, Vol. 5, edited by Graham Healey and Chushichi Tsuzuki, translated by Graham Healey, Eugene Soviak, and Chushichi Tsuzuki. Chiba: The Japan Documents, 2002.

Lee, Wilson Wai Shing. 'Honkon Nippō and Hong Kong-Japan Relations: Re-examining the Geopolitical Position of Colonial Hong Kong in East Asia before the End of World War II.' In *Asian Cities: Colonial to Global*, edited by Gregory Bracken, 125–42. Amsterdam: Amsterdam University Press, 2015.

Lengerer, Hans. 'Pre-history of the Sino-Japanese War 1894–1895: The Taiwan Expedition: Impulse to the IJN's First Expansion and Basis for the Formation of a Merchant Marine.' *Warship International* 56, no. 2 (2019): 115–36.

Lethbridge, Henry James. 'Condition of the European Working Class in Nineteenth Century Hong Kong.' *Journal of the Hong Kong Branch of the Royal Asiatic Society* 15 (1975): 88–112.

Lethbridge, Henry James. *Hong Kong: Stability and Change: A Collection of Essays.* Hong Kong: Oxford University Press, 1978.

Levine, Philippa. *Prostitution, Race, and Politics: Policing Venereal Disease in the British Empire.* New York: Routledge, 2003.

Lim, Patricia. *Forgotten Souls: A Social History of the Hong Kong Cemetery.* Hong Kong: Hong Kong University Press, 2011.

Liu-Farrer, Gracia. 'Creating a Transnational Community: Chinese Newcomers in Japan.' In *Japan's Minorities: The Illusion of Homogeneity*, 2nd ed., edited by Michael Weiner, 116–38. London: Routledge, 2009.

Lo, Ming-Cheng M. *Doctors Within Borders: Profession, Ethnicity, and Modernity in Colonial Taiwan*. Berkeley: University of California Press, 2002.

Loti, Pierre. *Journal*, Vol. 2, *1879–1886*, edited by Alain Quella-Villéger and Bruno Vercier. Paris: Les Indes Savantes, 2008.

Loti, Pierre. *Madame Chrysanthème*, translated by Laura Ensor. London: George Routledge and Sons, 1897.

Lowe, Kate, and Eugene McLaughlin. 'Sir John Pope Hennessy and the "Native Race Craze": Colonial Government in Hong Kong, 1877–1882.' *The Journal of Imperial and Commonwealth History* 20, no. 1 (January 1992): 223–47.

MacKeown, P. Kevin. 'The Hong Kong Mint, 1864–1868: The History of an Early Engineering Experiment.' *Journal of the Royal Asiatic Society Hong Kong Branch* 47 (2007): 41–79.

MacKeown, P. Kevin. *A Stormy Petrel: The Life and Times of John Pope Hennessy*. Hong Kong: City University of Hong Kong Press, 2020.

Maejima, Michiko. 'Édifier et Équiper les Bases de l'Armée Japonaise: Transferts de Technologie, France-Japon 1868–1930.' Doctoral thesis, Conservatoire National des Arts et Métiers, 2014.

Mak, Ricardo K. S. 'Nineteenth-Century German Community.' In *Foreign Communities in Hong Kong, 1840s–1950s*, edited by Cindy Yik-yi Chu, 61–83. New York: Palgrave Macmillan, 2005.

McMaster, John. 'The Takashima Mine: British Capital and Japanese Industrialization.' *The Business History Review* 37, no. 3 (1963): 217–39.

Meech, Julia. 'Shugio Hiromichi and the Grolier Club.' *Gazette of the Grolier Club* 49 (New Series) (1998): 79–90.

Mihalopoulos, Bill. 'The Making of Prostitutes: The Karayuki-san.' *Bulletin of Concerned Asian Scholars* 25, no. 1 (1993): 41–56.

Mihalopoulos, Bill. 'Women, Overseas Sex Work and Globalization in Meiji Japan.' *The Asia-Pacific Journal* 10.35, no. 1 (August 2012): 1–24.

Miners, R.J. 'State Regulation of Prostitution in Hong Kong, 1857 to 1941.' *Journal of the Hong Kong Branch of the Royal Asiatic Society* 24 (1984): 143–61.

Mizuta, Susumu. 'Making a Mint: British Mercantile Influence and the Building of the Japanese Imperial Mint.' *Architectural History* 62 (2019): 89–111.

Munn, Christopher. 'The Hong Kong Opium Revenue, 1845–1885.' In *Opium Regimes: China, Britain, and Japan, 1839–1952*, edited by Timothy Brook and Bob Tadashi Wakabayashi, 105–26. Berkeley: University of California Press, 2000.

Nakajima, Chieko. 'Medicine, Philanthropy, and Imperialism: The Dōjinkai in China, 1902–1945.' *Sino-Japanese Studies* 17, no. 6 (2010): 47–84.

Nakatsu, Masaya. 'Les Missions Militaires Françaises au Japon entre 1867 et 1889.' Doctoral thesis, Université Sorbonne Paris Cité, 2018.

Narushima, Ryūhoku. *'New Chronicles of Yanagibashi' and 'Diary of a Journey to the West': Narushima Ryūhoku Reports from Home and Abroad*, translated by Matthew Fraleigh. Ithaca, NY: Cornell University Press, 2010.

Ng, Benjamin Wai-ming. 'Making of a Japanese Community in Prewar Period (1841–1941).' In *Foreign Communities in Hong Kong, 1840s–1950s*, edited by Cindy Yik-yi Chu, 111–32. New York: Palgrave Macmillan, 2005.

Nicolson, Ken. *The Happy Valley: A History and Tour of the Hong Kong Cemetery*. Hong Kong: Hong Kong University Press, 2010.

Nish, Ian, ed. *The Iwakura Mission in America and Europe: A New Assessment*. Richmond, Surrey: Japan Library, 1998.

O'Brien, Suzanne G. 'Splitting Hairs: History and the Politics of Daily Life in Nineteenth-Century Japan.' *The Journal of Asian Studies* 67, no. 4 (2008): 1309–39.

Oharazeki, Kazuhiro. *Japanese Prostitutes in the North American West, 1887–1920*. Seattle: University of Washington Press, 2016.

Ōkuma, Shigenobu, compiler. *Fifty Years of New Japan*, Vol. 1, English editor Marcus B. Huish. London: Smith, Elder and Co., 1909.

O'Sullivan, Patricia. *Policing Hong Kong: An Irish History*. Hong Kong: Blacksmith Books, 2017.

Ōtani, Kosui. 'The Japanese Pilgrimage to the Buddhist Holy Land: A Personal Narrative of the Hongwanji Expedition of 1902–03.' *The Century Illustrated Monthly Magazine* 72 (October 1906): 866–78.

Pennell, Wilfrid Victor. *History of the Hong Kong General Chamber of Commerce, 1861–1961*. Hong Kong: Cathay Press, 1961.

Perry, John Curtis. 'Great Britain and the Emergence of Japan as a Naval Power.' *Monumenta Nipponica* 21, no. 3/4 (1966): 305–21.

Phipps, Catherine L. *Empires on the Waterfront: Japan's Ports and Power, 1858–1899*. Cambridge, MA: Harvard University Asia Center, 2015.

Platt, Jerome J., Maurice E. Jones, and Arleen Kay. *The Whitewash Brigade: The Hong Kong Plague of 1894*. London: Dix Noonan Webb, 1998.

Plummer, Katherine. *The Shogun's Reluctant Ambassadors: Japanese Sea Drifters in the North Pacific*, 3rd ed. Portland: Oregon Historical Society Press, 1991.

Pope-Hennessy, James. *Verandah: Some Episodes in the Crown Colonies, 1867–1889*. London: George Allen and Unwin, 1964.

Pryor, Edward George. 'The Great Plague of Hong Kong.' *Journal of the Hong Kong Branch of the Royal Asiatic Society* 15 (1975): 61–70.

Ramage, James A. *Gray Ghost: The Life of Col. John Singleton Mosby*. Lexington: University Press of Kentucky, 1999.

Reynolds, Douglas R. 'Training Young China Hands: Tōa Dōbun Shoin and Its Precursors, 1886–1945.' In *The Japanese Informal Empire in China, 1895–1937*, edited by Peter Duus, Ramon H. Myers, and Mark R. Peattie, 210–71. Princeton: Princeton University Press, 2014.

Samuels, Richard J. *Special Duty: A History of the Japanese Intelligence Community*. Ithaca, NY: Cornell University Press, 2019.

Schiltz, Michael. 'Money on the Road to Empire: Japan's Adoption of Gold Monometallism, 1873–97.' *The Economic History Review* 65, no. 3 (2012): 1147–68.

Shimizu, Hiroshi. 'Rise and Fall of the Karayuki-san in the Netherlands Indies from the Late Nineteenth Century to the 1930s.' *Review of Indonesian and Malaysian Affairs* 26, no. 2 (Summer 1992): 17–43.

Sinn, Elizabeth. *Pacific Crossing: California Gold, Chinese Migration, and the Making of Hong Kong*. Hong Kong: Hong Kong University Press, 2012.

Sinn, Elizabeth. *Power and Charity: The Early History of the Tung Wah Hospital, Hong Kong*. Hong Kong: Oxford University Press, 1989. (Republished in 2003 as *Power and Charity: A Chinese Merchant Elite in Colonial Hong Kong* by Hong Kong University Press.)

Sinn, Elizabeth. 'Women at Work: Chinese Brothel Keepers in Nineteenth-Century Hong Kong.' *Journal of Women's History* 19, no. 3 (2007): 87–111.

Sissons, David. 'The Japanese in the Australian Pearling Industry.' *Queensland Heritage* 3, no. 10 (1979): 9–27. (Reprinted in *Bridging Australia and Japan*, Vol. 1, *The Writings of David Sissons*,

Historian and Political Scientist, edited by Arthur Stockwin and Keiko Tamura, Canberra: Australian National University Press, 2016.)

Sissons, David. 'Karayuki-san: Japanese Prostitutes in Australia, 1887–1916 (1).' *Historical Studies* 17, no. 68 (1977): 323–41. (Reprinted in *Bridging Australia and Japan*, Vol. 1, *The Writings of David Sissons, Historian and Political Scientist*, edited by Arthur Stockwin and Keiko Tamura, Canberra: Australian National University Press, 2016.)

Sissons, David. 'Karayuki-san: Japanese Prostitutes in Australia, 1887–1916 (2).' *Historical Studies* 17, no. 69 (1977): 474–88. (Reprinted in *Bridging Australia and Japan*, Vol. 1, *The Writings of David Sissons, Historian and Political Scientist*, edited by Arthur Stockwin and Keiko Tamura, Canberra: Australian National University Press, 2016.)

Skutlin, John. 'Fashioning Tattooed Bodies: An Exploration of Japan's Tattoo Stigma.' *Asia Pacific Perspectives* 16, no. 1 (2019): 4–33.

Smith, Carl T. 'Wanchai: In Search of an Identity.' In *Hong Kong: A Reader in Social History*, edited by David Faure, 157–207. Hong Kong: Oxford University Press, 2003.

Solomon, Tom. 'Hong Kong, 1894: The Role of James A Lowson in the Controversial Discovery of the Plague Bacillus.' *The Lancet* 350, no. 9070 (1997): 59–62.

Sone, Sachiko. 'The Karayuki-san of Asia 1868–1938: The Role of Prostitutes Overseas in Japanese Economic and Social Development.' *Review of Indonesian and Malaysian Affairs* 26, no. 2 (Summer 1992): 44–62.

Starling, Arthur, Faith C.S. Ho, Lilian Luke, Tso Shiu-chiu, and Edwin C.L. Yu, eds. *Plague, SARS and the Story of Medicine in Hong Kong*. Hong Kong: Hong Kong University Press, 2006.

Stokes, Gwenneth and John. *Queen's College: Its History 1862–1987*. Hong Kong: Queen's College Old Boys' Association, 1987.

Stoler, Ann Laura. *Carnal Knowledge and Imperial Power*. Berkeley: University of California Press, 2002.

Stratton, D. 'History of Nursing in Government Hospitals.' *The Hong Kong Nursing Journal* 14 (May 1973): 34–37.

Sugawara, Morikuni. 'Chuo University and London.' *Chuo Online*, 2012, https://yab.yomiuri.co.jp/adv/chuo/dy/research/20120816.html.

Sugiyama, Shinya. *Japan's Industrialization in the World Economy, 1859–1899*. London: The Athlone Press, 1988.

Tamaki, Norio. *Japanese Banking: A History, 1859–1959*. Cambridge: Cambridge University Press, 1995.

Tankha, Brij. 'Exploring Asia, Reforming Japan: Ōtani Kōzui and Itō Chūta.' In *Japan on the Silk Road: Encounters and Perspectives of Politics and Culture in Eurasia*, edited by Selçuk Esenbel, 155–80. Leiden: Brill, 2018.

Terami-Wada, Motoe. 'Karayuki-san of Manila: 1890–1920.' *Philippine Studies* 34 (1986): 287–316.

Tsai, Jung-fang. *Hong Kong in Chinese History: Community and Social Unrest in the British Colony, 1842–1913*. New York: Columbia University Press, 1993.

Tsu, Yun Hui, ed. *Japan and Singapore: A Multidisciplinary Approach*. Singapore: McGraw-Hill Education [Asia], 2006.

Tsu, Yun Hui. 'Post-Mortem Identity and Burial Obligation: On Blood Relations, Place Relations, and Associational Relations in the Japanese Community in Singapore.' In *The Culture of Association and Associations in Contemporary Japanese Society*, edited by Hirochika Nakamaki, 93–114. Osaka: National Museum of Ethnology, 2002.

Tsunoyama, Sakae. 'Japanese Consular Reports.' *Business History* 23, no. 3 (1981): 284–87.

Tsuzuki, Chushichi. *The Pursuit of Power in Modern Japan, 1825–1995*. Oxford: Oxford University Press, 2000.

Bibliography   181

Tucker, Anne Wilkes, Dana Friis-Hansen, Kaneko Ryūichi, and Takeba Joe. *The History of Japanese Photography*. Exhibition catalogue. New Haven, CT: Yale University Press in association with the Museum of Fine Arts, Houston, 2003.

United States. *Compilation of Treaties in Force: Prepared under Act of July 7, 1898*. Washington, DC: Government Printing Office, https://heinonline-org.eproxy.lib.hku.hk/HOL/P?h=hein.ustreaties/ctforpu0001&i=1.

Wakabayashi, Bob Tadashi. 'From Peril to Profit: Opium in Late-Edo to Meiji Eyes.' In *Opium Regimes: China, Britain, and Japan, 1839–1952*, edited by Timothy Brook and Bob Tadashi Wakabayashi, 55–76. Berkeley: University of California Press, 2000.

Warren, James Francis. Ah Ku *and* Karayuki-san*: Prostitution in Singapore 1870–1940*. Singapore: Oxford University Press, 1993.

Wong, Sin-kiong. 'The Tatsu Maru Incident and the Anti-Japanese Boycott of 1908: A Study of Conflicting Interpretations.' *Chinese Culture* 34, no. 3 (September 1993): 77–92.

Wray, William D. *Mitsubishi and the N.Y.K., 1870–1914: Business Strategy in the Japanese Shipping Industry*. Cambridge, MA: Harvard University Press, 1984.

Wray, William D. 'National Alliances and Global Webs: The Internationalization of Japanese Shipping.' In *Global Markets: the Internationalization of the Sea Transport Industries since 1850*, edited by David J. Starkey and Gelina Hrlaftis, 81–101. St. John's, Newfoundland: International Maritime Economic History Association, 1998.

Wright, Arnold, ed. *Twentieth Century Impressions of Hong Kong, Shanghai, and Other Treaty Ports of China: Their History, People, Commerce, Industries, and Resources*. London: Lloyd's Greater Britain Publishing Company, 1908.

Xavier, Roy Eric. 'Death at the Races: The Portuguese Presence during the Happy Valley Fire of 1918.' *Journal of the Royal Asiatic Society Hong Kong Branch* 53 (2013): 89–107.

Yamazaki, Tomoko. *Sandakan Brothel No. 8: An Episode in the History of Lower-Class Japanese Women*, translated by Karen Colligan-Taylor. Armonk: M.E. Sharpe, 1999. (Original in Japanese published in Tokyo by Chikuma Shobō in 1972.)

Yonekura, Seiichiro. 'The Emergence of the Prototype of Enterprise Group Capitalism: The Case of Mitsui.' *Hitotsubashi Journal of Commerce and Management* 20 (1985): 63–104.

Yonekura, Seiichiro, and Hiroshi Shimizu. 'Entrepreneurship in Pre–World War II Japan: The Role and Logic of the Zaibatsu.' In *The Invention of Enterprise: Entrepreneurship from Ancient Mesopotamia to Modern Times*, edited by David S. Landes, Joel Mokyr, and William J. Baumol, 501–26. Princeton: Princeton University Press, 2012.

Japanese-Language References

「青山胤通先生」 [Dr Aoyama Tanemichi]. 『日本医事新報』 *Nihon Iji Shinpō*, Special Issue (November 1937): 7–46.

赤岩昭滋 Akaiwa Teruji. 「香港の日本人墓地──船員の墓碑を中心として」 [Japanese Graves in Hong Kong: Graves of Sailors and Others]. 『海事史研究』 *Journal of the Japan Society for Nautical Research* 21 (1973): 66–81, NDL Digital Collections. https://dl.ndl.go.jp/pid/2642097.

朝倉明宣 Asakura Meisen. 『清国巡遊誌』 [*Journal of Travel around China*]. Kyoto: 朝倉明宣 Asakura Meisen, 1900.

安宅産業株式会社社史編集室 編 Ataka & Co. Corporate History Project, ed. 『安宅産業六十年史』 [*Sixty-Year History of Ataka & Co.*]. Osaka: 安宅産業 Ataka Sangyō, 1968, NDL Digital Collections. https://dl.ndl.go.jp/pid/3442354.

安宅彌吉 Ataka Yakichi. 『回顧録』 [*Memoirs*]. Osaka: 安宅彌吉 Ataka Yakichi, 1922, NDL Digital Collections. https://dl.ndl.go.jp/pid/971920.

安藤太郎 Andō Tarō. 「美家古廼波奈誌」 [Stories from the Battle in Miyako]. In 『舊幕府』 [*The Former Government*] 3, 1–11. Tokyo: 旧幕府雑誌社 Kyūbakufu-zasshi-sha, 1897, NDL Digital Collections. https://dl.ndl.go.jp/pid/1559394.

石附実 Ishizuki Minoru. 『近代日本の海外留学史』 [*A History of Study Abroad in Modern Japan*]. Tokyo: 中公文庫 Chūkō Bunko, [1972] 1992.

井上貞次郎 Inoue Teijirō. 「私の履歴書」 [*My Personal Story*]. 『日本経済新聞』 *The Nikkei*. June 28 to July 17, 1959, republished at https://www.rengo.co.jp/history/inoue/index.html.

井口丑二 Inokuchi Ushiji. 『世界一周実記』 [*Journal of a Trip around the World*]. Tokyo: 経済雑誌社 Keizai-zasshi-sha, 1904, NDL Digital Collections. https://dl.ndl.go.jp/pid/761271.

岩崎家傳記刊行會 編 Iwasaki Family Biography Project Team, ed. 『岩崎彌太郎傳』 上・下 [*Biography of Iwasaki Yatarō*, Vols. 1 and 2]. Tokyo: 東京大学出版会 Tokyo University Press, 1980.

岩崎家傳記刊行會 編 Iwasaki Family Biography Project Team, ed. 『岩崎彌之助傳』 [*Biography of Iwasaki Yanosuke*]. Tokyo: 東京大学出版会 Tokyo University Press, 1980.

上山明博 Ueyama Akihiro. 『北里柴三郎――感染症と闘いつづけた男』 [*Kitasato Shibasaburō: A Man Who Fought with Infectious Diseases*]. Tokyo: 青土社 Seidosha, 2021.

『英文学研究』 [*Studies in English Literature*] 10, no. 2 (1930).

江森泰吉 編 Emori Taikichi, ed. 『大隈伯百話』 [*One Hundred Tales of Earl Okuma*]. Tokyo: 実業之日本社 Jitsugyō no Nihon Sha, 1909.

黄栄光 Huang Ronggwang. 『近代日中貿易成立史論』 [*Early Years of Modern Sino-Japanese Trade*]. Tokyo: 比較文化研究所 Hikaku Bunka Kenkyū-jo, 2008.

大橋乙羽 Ōhashi Otowa. 『歐山米水』 [*European Mountains, American Waters*]. Tokyo: 博文館 Hakubun-kan, 1900.

大原関 一浩 Ōharazeki Kazuhiro. 「20世紀転換期オーストラリアにおける日本人売買春――合衆国の事例との比較から」 [Japanese Prostitution in Turn-of-the-Century Australia: In Comparison with the Cases in the United States]. 『西南学院大学 国際文化論集』 *Seinan Journal of Cultures* 36, no. 1 (2021): 105–68.

「岡田義行氏より加藤内務属へ宛てたる書」 [A Letter from Okada Yoshiyuki to Katō in the Home Ministry]. 『醫海時報』 *Ikai Jihō* 18 (1894): 3, NDL Digital Collections. https://dl.ndl.go.jp/pid/11182865.

奥田乙治郎 Okuda Otojirō. 『明治初年に於ける香港日本人』熱帯産業調査會叢書 第5號 [*Japanese Residents in Hong Kong during the Early Meiji Era*, Association for Commercial Research in the Tropics Series, vol. 5]. Taipei: 臺灣總督府熱帶産業調査會 Taiwan Sōtokufu Nettai Sangyō Chōsa-kai, 1937.

奥村功 Okumura Isao. 「明治初期のあるフランス留学生――湯川温作」 [A Student in France during the Early Meiji Period]. In 『幕末・明治期の国民国家形成と文化変容』 [*The Formation of the Nation-State and Transformation of Culture in the Late Tokugawa and Meiji Periods*], edited by 西川長夫・松宮秀治 Nishikawa Nagao and Matsumiya Hideharu, 581–603. Tokyo: 新曜社 Shinyō-sha, 1995.

小野一一郎 Ono Kazuichirō. 「日清戦争賠償金の領収と貨幣制度――日本における金本位制の成立(3)」 [The Payment of the Indemnity after the Sino-Japanese War and the Monetary System: Introduction of the Gold Standard Part 3]. 『經濟論叢』 *The Economic Review* 94, no. 3 (1964): 62–79.

外務省通商局 編 International Trade Bureau, Foreign Ministry, ed. 『香港事情』 [*Hong Kong Current Affairs*]. Tokyo: 啓成社 Keisei-sha, 1917, NDL Digital Collections. https://dl.ndl.go.jp/pid/1878063.

Bibliography

外務省通商局第二課 Section 2 of the International Trade Bureau, Foreign Ministry. 『濠州探検報告書』 [*Report of the Australian Expedition*]. Tokyo: 外務省通商局第二課 Gaimushō Tsūshō Dai-ni-ka, 1894, NDL Digital Collections. https://dl.ndl.go.jp/pid/767453.

河東碧梧桐 Kawahigashi Hekigotō. 『支那に遊びて』 [*Touring China*]. Tokyo: 大阪屋号書店 Ōsakayagō Shoten, 1919.

木下正中 Kinoshita Seichū. 「香港『ペスト』研究當時の追憶」 [Reminiscences of the Hong Kong 'Plague' Investigation]. 『日本伝染病学会雑誌』 *Nihon Densenbyō Gakkai Zasshi* 2, no.1 (1927): 60–63, NDL Digital Collections. https://dl.ndl.go.jp/pid/1726410.

小坂文乃 Kosaka Ayano. 『革命をプロデュースした日本人——評伝　梅屋庄吉』 [*The Japanese Man Who Produced a Revolution: Biography of Umeya Shōkichi*]. Tokyo: 講談社 Kodansha, 2009.

小山健三 Koyama Kenzō. 『作州からみた明治百年』上巻 [*Sakushū City in the One Hundred Years since the Meiji Restoration*, Vol. 1]. Tsuyama: 津山朝日新聞社 Tsuyama Asahi Shimbun-sha, 1970, NDL Digital Collections. https://dl.ndl.go.jp/pid/9573265.

小山騰　Koyama　Noboru.　『日本の刺青と英国王室——明治期から第一次世界大戦まで』 [*Japanese Tattoos and the British Royal Family: From the Meiji Era to World War I*]. Tokyo: 藤原書店 Fujiwara Shoten, 2010.

税田祖山 Saita Sozan. 『地方自治政の沿革と其の人物——福岡県』 [*History of Local Government and Politicians in Fukuoka*]. Tokyo: 自治通信社 Jichi Tsūshin-sha, 1931, NDL Digital Collections. https://dl.ndl.go.jp/pid/1456886.

左右田昌幸 Sauda Masayuki. 「花山火葬場について」 [On the Kazan Crematorium]. 『本願寺史料研究所報』 *Hongwanji Shiryō Kenkyūjo Hō* 29 (July 2006): 1–12.

坂田敏夫 Sakata Toshio. 「上海邦人歯科醫界の回顧」 [Reminiscences of Japanese Dentists in Shanghai]. 『臨床歯科』 *Rinshō Shika* 12, no. 1 (1940): 147–50, NDL Digital Collections. https://dl.ndl.go.jp/pid/1780606.

札幌市教育委員会 編 Sapporo City Education Board, ed. 『新札幌市史』第7巻 (史料編 2) [*A New History of Sapporo City*, Vol. 7, *Historical Documents 2*]. Sapporo: 北海道新聞社 Hokkaidō Shimbun-sha, 1986, NDL Digital Collections. https://dl.ndl.go.jp/pid/9501866.

塩山正純 Shioyama Masazumi. 「『大旅行誌』の思い出に記された香港——昭和期の記述より」 [Hong Kong in the *Journal of the Grand Tour* during the Shōwa Period]. 『愛知大学国際コミュニケーション学会 文明21』 *Civilization 21*, Association for International Communication, Aichi University 40 (March 2018): 37–64.

歯科研究会 Dental Study Association. 「雑報」 [Miscellaneous News]. 『歯科研究会月報』 *Shika Kenkyūkai Geppō* 11 (1891), NDL Digital Collections. https://dl.ndl.go.jp/pid/1507200.

執行弘道 編 Shugyō Hiromichi, ed. 『日本美術帖』 [*Japanese Art Folio*] Parts 1–3, edited by K. Ogawa. Tokyo: K. Ogawa, 1898, NDL Digital Collections. https://dl.ndl.go.jp/pid/1700882.

末永山彦 編 Suenaga Yamahiko, ed. 『父の記録』 [*Remembering Our Father*]. Osaka: 末永山彦 Suenaga Yamahiko, 1941, NDL Digital Collections. https://dl.ndl.go.jp/pid/1907048.

曽根俊虎 Sone Toshitora. 『東亜各港日本人職業姓名録——世界各国日本人職業一覧』 [*Directory of Japanese Nationals in East Asian Ports (with the Occupations of Japanese Overseas Residents around the World)*]. Tokyo: 曽根俊虎 Sone Toshitora, 1907, NDL Digital Collections. https://dl.ndl.go.jp/pid/994851.

武田尚子 Takeda Naoko. 『ミルクと日本人——近代社会の「元気の源」』 [*Milk and the Japanese: A 'Source of Energy' in Modern Society*]. Tokyo: 中央公論新社 Chūō Kōron Shinsha, 2017.

帝国美術院附属美術研究所 編 Fine Arts Institute, Imperial Fine Arts Academy, ed. 『三原繁吉氏蔵浮世絵版画展覧会目録』 [*Exhibition Catalogue for the Mihara Shigekichi Ukiyoe Collection*]. Tokyo: 岩波書店 Iwanami Shoten, 1930, NDL Digital Collections. https://dl.ndl.go.jp/pid/1192795.

東京銀行 編 Bank of Tokyo, ed. 『横濱正金銀行全史 第2巻──創立から関東大震災まで』 [*The History of the Yokohama Specie Bank*, Vol. 2: *From Its Establishment to the Great Kantō Earthquake*]. Tokyo: 東京銀行 Bank of Tokyo, 1981.

東京大学史料編纂所 編 Historiographical Institute, University of Tokyo, ed. 「三月十二日より十六日に至る英船箱館沖碇泊中日記」 [Diary of the British Ship's Stay in Hakodate, March 12 to 16]. In 『大日本古文書──幕末外国関係文書之10』 [*Historical Documents of Great Japan: International Relations in Late Tokugawa*, Vol. 10], 49–79. Tokyo: 東京大学出版会 Tokyo University Press, 1918, NDL Digital Collections. https://dl.ndl.go.jp/pid/12212200.

「長崎入墨見本帳」 [Nagasaki Tattoo Template]. 長崎歴史文化博物館 [Nagasaki Museum of History and Culture], n.d.

長崎県南高来郡役所 Minami-Takaki County Office, Nagasaki Prefecture. 『長崎県南高来郡町村要覧 上・下』 [*Annals of the Minami-Takaki Counties, Towns and Villages, Nagasaki Prefecture*, Vols. 1 and 2]. 1893, NDL Digital Collections. https://dl.ndl.go.jp/info:ndljp/pid/766696.

長島弘明 Nagashima Hiroaki. 「芳賀矢一『留学日誌』──東京大学国文学研究室蔵本の影印と翻刻」 [Haga Yaichi's *Study Abroad Journal*: Reprint from Tokyo University's Library of the Institute of Japanese Literature]. 『東京大学国文学論集』 *Journal of Japanese Literature, Tokyo University* 14 (2019): 107–69.

夏目漱石 Natsume Sōseki. 『漱石全集──第15巻日記及断片』 [*The Sōseki Collection*, Vol. 15, *Diaries and Fragments*]. Tokyo: 漱石全集刊行会 Sōseki Zenshū Kankō-kai, 1936.

成島柳北 Narushima Ryūhoku. 「航西日乗」 [Journal of a Voyage to the West]. 『新日本古典文学大系 明治編 5 海外見聞集』 [*New Collection of Japanese Classics: Meiji*, Vol. 5, *International Travels*], edited by 中野三敏,十川信介, 延広真治, 日野龍夫 Nakano Mitsutoshi, Togawa Shinsuke, Nobuhiro Shinji, and Hino Tatsuo, 249–356. Tokyo: 岩波書店 Iwanami Shoten, 2009.

日本海員掖済会 Japan Seafarers Relief Association. 『海之世界』 *Umino Sekai* 8: 5 (May 1914), NDL Digital Collections. https://dl.ndl.go.jp/pid/1499468.

日本青年會 Japan Youth Association (in Hong Kong). 「香港青年」 [*Hong Kong Youth*] 7, July 10, 1911. In 『香港都市案内集成』 [*Collection of Writings on the City of Hong Kong*], Vol. 7, edited by 濱下武志 and 李培德 Hamashita Takeshi and Lee Pui-tak, 383–413. Tokyo: ゆまに書房 Yumani Shobō, 2013.

濱下武志・李培德 監修 Hamashita Takeshi and Lee Pui-tak, eds. 『香港都市案内集成』 [*Collection of Writings on the City of Hong Kong*]. Tokyo: ゆまに書房 Yumani Shobō, 2013.

春名徹 Haruna Akira. 『世界を見てしまった男たち』 [*Men Who Travelled the World*]. Tokyo: 文芸春秋 Bungei Shunju, 1981, NDL Digital Collections. https://dl.ndl.go.jp/pid/12281967.

林金五郎 Hayashi Kingorō. 『南洋──前編』 [*The South Seas*, Part 1]. Tokyo: 桐生屋商会出版部 Kiryūya Shōkai Shuppan-bu, 1917.

林陸朗 Hayashi Rokurō. 『長崎唐通事──大通事林道栄とその周辺 増補版』 [*Chinese-Language Interpreters in Nagasaki: Head Interpreter Hayashi Dōei and His Associates*, Revised edition]. Nagasaki: 長崎文献社 Nagasaki Bunken-sha, 2010.

平井健介 Hirai Kensuke. 「1900–1920年代東アジアにおける砂糖貿易と台湾糖」 [The Sugar Trade and Taiwanese Sugar in East Asia: 1900–1920]. 『社会経済史学』 *Shakai Keizai Shigaku* 73, no. 1 (2007): 27–49.

『婦人雑誌』 *Fujin Zasshi* 15, no. 6 (1900), NDL Digital Collections. https://dl.ndl.go.jp/pid/1580201.

本願寺史料研究所 編 Hongwanji Historical Institute, ed. 『本願寺史 第三巻』 [*The History of Hongwanji*, Vol. 3]. Kyoto: 本願寺出版社 Hongwanji Shuppan-sha, 2019.

Bibliography

香港日本人倶楽部 Hongkong Japanese Club. 『写真集──香港日本人墓地』 [*Photo Album: Japanese Graves in Hong Kong*]. Hong Kong: 香港日本人倶楽部 Hongkong Japanese Club, 2006.

香港日本人倶楽部 史料編纂委員会 Hongkong Japanese Club's History Book Committee. 『香港日本人社会の歴史──江戸から平成まで──』 [*History of the Japanese Community in Hong Kong: From Edo to Heisei*]. Hong Kong: 香港日本人倶楽部 Hongkong Japanese Club, 2006.

本多静六 Honda Seiroku. 『明治二十三年 洋行日誌』巻一 [*Travel Diary, 1890*], Vol. 1. Shōbu-machi, Saitama: 本多静六博士を記念する会 Honda Seiroku Hakase o Kinensuru-kai, 1998.

前田寶治郎 Maeda Hōjirō. 『香港概観』 [*Hong Kong Overview*]. Tokyo: 前田寶治郎 Maeda Hōjirō, 1915.

横山榮次 Makiyama Eiji. 『百年前の留学記』 [*Study Abroad Diary from a Century Ago*]. Tokyo: 新風舎 Shinpū-sha, 2005.

民天時報社編輯局 編 Mintenjihō-sha Editorial Bureau, ed. 『海外邦人の事業及人物 第1輯』 [*Overseas Japanese: Their Occupations and Biographies*]. Tokyo: 民天時報社 Mintenjihō-sha, 1917, NDL Digital Collections. https://dl.ndl.go.jp/pid/950506.

三菱社誌刊行会 編 Mitsubishi Corporate History Project, ed. 『三菱社誌』 [*Mitsubishi Corporate History*]. Tokyo: 東京大学出版会 Tokyo University Press, 1979.

三宅克己 Miyake Kokki. 『欧洲絵行脚』 [*Art Journey around Europe*]. Tokyo: 画報社 Gahō-sha, 1910, NDL Digital Collections. https://dl.ndl.go.jp/pid/767282.

宮本又次・内田勝敏 Miyamoto Mataji and Uchida Katsutoshi. 『日本貿易人の系譜──総合商社への道のり』 [*Early International Traders in Japan: A Prehistory of Comprehensive Trading Companies*]. Tokyo: 有斐閣 Yuhikaku, 1980.

村岡伊平治 Muraoka Iheiji. 『村岡伊平治自伝』 [*Autobiography of Muraoka Iheiji*]. Tokyo: 講談社 Kodansha, 1987.

目賀多信順 編 Megata Nobuyori, ed. 「陸軍埋葬地ニ葬ルノ法則」 [Burial Rules at Army Burial Grounds]. In 『官省布告類纂』明治8年巻1 [*Government Rules and Announcements: 1875*] Vol. 1, 82–83. Tokyo: 目賀多信順 Megata Nobuyori, 1875, NDL Digital Collections. https://dl.ndl.go.jp/pid/787151.

森鴎外 Mori Ōgai. 「航西日記」 [Diary of a Voyage to the West]. In 『新日本古典文学大系──明治編5海外見聞集』 [*New Collection of Japanese Classics: Meiji*, Vol. 5, *International Travels*], edited by 中野三敏, 十川信介, 延広真治, 日野龍夫 Nakano Mitsutoshi, Togawa Shinsuke, Nobuhiro Shinji, and Hino Tatsuo, 407–54. Tokyo: 岩波書店 Iwanami Shoten, 2009.

森崎和江 Morisaki Kazue. 『からゆきさん』 [*Karayuki-san*]. Tokyo: 朝日新聞社 Asahi Shimbun-sha, [1976] 2022.

師岡国 編 Morooka Kuni, ed. 『板垣君欧米漫遊日記』 [*Itagaki's Diary of a Journey to Europe and the U.S.*]. Tokyo: 松井忠兵衛 Matsui Chūbei, 1883.

『龍南同窓会々報』 [Ryūnan Alumni Association Bulletin] 2. Tokyo: 龍南同窓会 Ryūnan Dōsōkai, 1897, NDL Digital Collections. https://dl.ndl.go.jp/pid/1602261.

山崎朋子 Yamazaki Tomoko. 『サンダカン八番娼館──底辺女性史序章』 [*Sandakan Brothel No. 8: Journey into the History of Lower-Class Japanese Women*]. Tokyo: 筑摩書房 Chikuma Shobō, 1972.

山田迪生 Yamada Michio. 「漱石の欧州航路体験」 [Soseki's Experiences on His Way to Europe]. 『海事史研究』 [*Journal of the Japan Society for Nautical Research*] 74 (2017): 33–51.

山本芳美 Yamamoto Yoshimi. 『イレズミと日本人』 [*Tattooing and the Japanese*]. Tokyo: 平凡社新書 Heibonsha Shinsho, 2016.

横山篤夫 Yokoyama Atsuo. 「戦没者の遺骨と陸軍墓地──夫が戦没した妻たちの六〇年後の意識から」 [The Remains of the War Dead and Military Cemeteries: From the Viewpoint of War

Widows 60 Years On]. 『国立歴史民俗博物館研究報告』 *Bulletin of the National Museum of Japanese History* 147 (December 2008): 93–130.

吉澤誠一郎 Yoshizawa Seiichirō. 『愛国とボイコット——近代中国の地域的文脈と対日関係』 [*Patriotism and Boycotts: Modern China from a Regional Perspective and the Sino-Japanese Relationship*]. Nagoya: 名古屋大学出版会 Nagoya University Press, 2021.

Chinese-Language References

陳湛頤 Chan Cham-yi. 〈香港早年的日本娼妓〉 [Japanese Prostitutes in the Early Years of Hong Kong]. In 《日本與亞洲華人社會　歷史文化篇》 [*Chinese Societies in Japan and East Asia: History and Culture*], edited by 原武道, 陳湛頤 and 王向華 Hara Takemichi, Chan Cham-yi, and Wong Heung-wah, 133–52. Hong Kong: 商務印書館 Commercial Press, 1999.

陳湛頤 Chan Cham-yi. 《日本人訪港見聞錄: 1898–1941》 [*Japanese Visitors to Hong Kong: 1898–1941*]. Hong Kong: 三聯書店 Joint Publishing, 2005.

Index

Amakusa, 1, 23–24

America, 64, 73, 84, 85, 119; and dentistry, 111; and international commerce, 4, 8, 61, 75, 78, 90, 117; and the *karayuki-san*, 39. *See also* United States (US)

Americans in Hong Kong, 1, 6, 8, 36, 47, 64, 99, 102, 106, 111, 119; and the Hong Kong Cemetery, 17, 19, 121; and shipping, 70, 73, 76 table 4.2; and social stratification, 8, 85, 95, 120

Andō Tarō, 4, 5, 16, 93; 1879 trip to Japan, 16, 63, 64, 90, 99; and the Mitsubishi Mail Steamship Company, 63–64, 70–72; and the traffic of *karayuki-san*, 28

Anglo-Japanese Alliance, 93, 95, 120, 139n39

Aoyama Tanemichi, 112–13

army, Japanese, 11, 14, 16, 17, 40, 46, 56, 61, 66, 120, 121, 122. *See also* navy, Japanese

Asai Umeko (Yamaguchi Hatsujyo), 106, 166n47

Ataka Yakichi, 78, 79, 81–85, 90, 97. *See also* Kusakabe Heijirō

Australia, 6, 74, 86, 136n5; and coal, 70, 75; and pearl-diving, 13, 44–45; and the traffic of *karayuki-san*, 39, 49, 118

Bank of Japan, 91

Bank of Tokyo, 124

barbers. *See* hairdressers

Belilios, Emanuel Raphael, 105

Bird, Isabella, 68, 70

boarding houses, 10, 12 fig. 1.3, 13 table 1.4, 40–48, 58–59, 73, 77, 103, 109 fig. 6.6, 116, 118, 122; and the traffic of *karayuki-san*, 11, 20, 33, 39, 49–50, 108, 116, 118. *See also* Matsubara Jisaburō; Ōtaka Saichi;

Tokyo Hotel; Tōyōkan; Uetsuki Kakuzō; Yokose Yōkichi

Boshin War (1868–1869), 137n18

Botanic Gardens, 42, 68

Britain, 1, 10, 29, 49, 84, 91, 102, 118; and the cession of Hong Kong, 1, 6, 122; and coal, 70, 75; and imperialism, 3, 7, 28, 60, 93, 120, 121; Japanese in, 3, 4, 99, 147n82; and shipping, 6, 26, 61. *See also* Anglo-Japanese Alliance

British in Hong Kong, 85, 104, 112, 118, 119, 121, 137n4; and the Hong Kong Cemetery, 15, 18; and recognition of the yen, 90–91; and shipping, 25, 26, 45, 60, 62, 75, 76 table 4.2; and social stratification, 13, 16, 48, 93, 95, 99, 120

brothels, 4, 11, 13 table 1.4, 24, 29, 30, 32 fig. 2.2, 41, 114; and boarding house owners, 49–50, 118; Chinese, 30–31; Japanese, 22, 31–39, 105, 119; and other small businesses, 11, 12 fig. 1.3, 39, 98, 100, 118; and social stratification, 11, 29, 97, 98, 116, 118, 120. *See also* 'cafés'; Graham Street; *karayuki-san*; *kashizashiki*

Buddhism and Buddhists, 18, 19, 20, 43, 52, 53, 54, 58, 85, 121. *See also* Nishi Hongwanji

Butterfield & Swire, 26

'cafés', 9, 10 table 1.3, 23, 31, 33, 34 table 2.1, 50, 100, 116. *See also* brothels; *karayuki-san*; *kashizashiki*

Chater, Paul, 94, 162n85

cherry blossom trees, 125

China, 46, 52, 93, 104, 107, 112, 115, 120; and Japanese travellers perceptions of,

7, 68, 120; and migration, 6, 10, 13, 45; and opium, 6, 7, 68, 120; and trade, 3, 6, 25, 66, 75, 76 table 4.2, 78, 79, 80; treaty ports, 3, 60, 75, 85. *See also* Sino-Japanese War (1894–1895) and *Tatsu Maru* affair

Chinese in Hong Kong, 6, 85, 91, 94, 104, 106, 112; and burials, 15–16, 19; and prostitution, 25, 29–31, 36, 99, 119; and social stratification, 8, 9, 13–14, 16, 30, 39, 47, 52, 115, 120–21

Chinese language training, 46, 104, 138n30

Chōshū, 4, 14

'Chōshū Five', 137n20

Christianity, 1, 28; and burials in the Hong Kong Cemetery, 2, 15, 18–20, 33, 99, 120, 121, 122, 125; in Japan, 24, 52, 53

coal, 24, 70, 75, 83, 84, 86–87, 89, 119, 121; and the traffic of *karayuki-san*, 25–27, 118. See also *Fushiki Maru* tragedy; Miike mines; Takashima mine

Colonial Cemetery. *See* Hong Kong Cemetery

concubinage, 9, 10 table 1.3, 11, 13 table 1.4, 23, 34 table 2.1, 35–36, 38, 114, 119, 125

crimping, 45, 73. *See also* Inoue Teijirō; pearl-diving industry

currency, 90, 91, 92, 108. *See also* gold standard; silver yen

Dejima, 3

dentists, 111

diaspora, Japanese, 13, 98, 121, 122

discrimination, 7, 11, 13, 16, 20, 24, 47, 121

disease, 6, 79, 82, 112–13, 114; venereal, 29, 30, 73. *See also* plague

doctors, 20, 29, 30, 40, 71, 94, 98, 111, 112–16. *See also* Majima Keinosuke; Nakahara Tomisaburō

Dōjinkai (Association for Universal Benevolence), 114–15

Douglas, Archibald Lucius, 64

education, 78, 93, 104–6, 119. *See also* Japanese primary school; Queen's College

Era Hikotarō, 55 fig. 3.6, 94, 106, 108

First National Bank (Daiichi Kokuritsu Ginkō), 80, 86, 90

First Opium War (1839–1842), 3, 6

Fukuhara Eitarō, 10, 86–87, 89, 90, 97, 119

Fukuzawa Yukichi, 138n34

Funatsu Tatsuichirō, 20, 85, 108, 115, 116

Fushiki Maru tragedy, 27

geisha, 13 table 1.4, 48, 56

Glover, Thomas Blake, 25, 62, 70, 90

Godai Tomoatsu, 81, 90

gold standard, 90, 91

Gotō Shōjirō, 70

Government Central School. *See* Queen's College

Government Civil Hospital, 22, 31, 43, 73, 92, 99, 106, 110, 112

Graham Street, 22, 31–33

graves, Japanese: afterlife names, 18, 37, 43; bilingual inscriptions, 18, 22, 38, 103, 125; design, 17, 18, 22, 44, 114; location within the cemetery, 18, 120, 124; as markers of social status, 3, 20, 33, 37, 41, 44, 57, 59, 73, 119, 122

Guangzhou [Canton], 42, 60, 71, 84, 107, 111, 112, 120

Gutzlaff, Karl, 1

hairdressers, 2, 10 table 1.3, 11, 23, 57, 98, 99–100, 118, 119

Hakodate, 1, 3, 16, 25, 60, 79

Happy Valley, 15, 118, 123 fig. 7.1; horse races, 50, 116, 118. *See also* Hong Kong Cemetery

Happy Valley Racecourse Fire, 54–58, 116, 125. *See also* Memorial to Ten Thousand Souls

Hawaii, 13

Hayashi Michisaburō, 6–7

Hayashizaki (Hayasaki) Kiku, 36, 37

Heng Fa Lou Chinese restaurant, 42–43

Hirose Matsujirō, 82. *See also* Ataka Yakichi; Kusakabe & Co.

Hirota Kōkichi, 82, 90, 92, 97

Ho Kai, 94, 146n71

Honda Masajirō, 60, 75, 77; death, 70–71; grave, 2 table 1.1, 71–72; impressions of Hong Kong, 68–70; launch of Yokohama to Hong Kong service, 60, 64, 67–68. *See also* Iwasaki Yatarō; Mitsubishi Mail Steamship Company

Honda Seiroku, 27, 42–43, 118

Hong Kong: cession of to Britain, 1, 6, 22; as a free port, 6, 25, 68, 75; plague of 1894,

Index 189

111, 112–14; and social stratification, 13–14, 20, 29, 30, 47, 85, 93, 95, 97, 120, 121; as a transit hub, 6, 7, 26, 40, 49, 60, 66, 70, 74–76, 85, 117, 118

Hong Kong Cemetery (Protestant Graveyard/ Colonial Cemetery): division and consecration of, 20; history of, 1–2, 15; Sanitary Board bye-laws, 18–19, 121–22

Hong Kong General Chamber of Commerce, 89

Hongkong and Shanghai Banking Corporation, 92

Hongkong Club, 13, 95, 120

Hongkong Hotel, 57, 68, 99, 100, 113, 169n104

Hongkong Japanese Club, 124–25

Honkon Nippō (*Hong Kong Daily News*), 108

Hori Chiyo, 101–2

Hugo, Victor, 14

identity, national, 39, 117, 122

India, 6, 49, 54, 66, 74, 90

Indians, 31, 73, 119; in Hong Kong, 6, 75, 104, 118

Inokuchi Ushiji, 75, 103

Inoue Kaoru, 86. *See also* 'Chōshū Five'

Inoue Teijirō, 45–46, 118

intelligence gathering, 6, 46, 93, 121

international marriages, 36, 147n82

Itagaki Taisuke, 25

Itō Chūta, 54

Itō Hirobumi, 4. *See also* 'Chōshū Five'

Iwakura Embassy, 4–5, 14, 16, 120

Iwasaki Yanosuke, 70, 74

Iwasaki Yatarō, 25, 60–61, 67 fig. 4.4, 74, 75, 80; and the Takashima mine, 70; and the Yokohama to Hong Kong service, 62–64, 70, 71. *See also* Mitsubishi Mail Steamship Company; Nippon Yusen Kaisha (NYK)

Japan Shipowners' Association/Union, 83

Japan–British Exhibition (1910), 95, 139n39

Japanese Benevolent Society, 50–52, 53, 116, 122; and education, 116, 122; and graves, 52, 118; and the Happy Valley Racecourse Fire, 54, 56–58, 125; and the Japanese crematorium, 53–54, 121. *See also* Nishi Hongwanji

Japanese Consulate in Hong Kong, 10, 11, 40, 42, 45, 63, 64, 73, 85, 104, 124; and

the Emperor's Birthday, 93, 97; and the Hong Kong Cemetery, 2 table 1.1, 3, 14, 16, 17, 73, 125; and the Japanese Crematorium, 20, 53–54, 121; and the *karayuki-san*, 27, 28, 37, 38, 48, 120; opening of (1873), 5, 6–7, 13, 39, 93, 119; and social stratification, 77, 79, 95, 98, 105, 116, 120, 122; surveys of residents, 9, 23, 25, 48. *See also* Andō Tarō; Funatsu Tatsuichirō; Hayashi Michisaburō; Mikado Ball; Noma Masaichi

Japanese crematorium, 53–54, 57, 58, 116, 121, 122, 124 fig. 7.2, 125; impact on cemetery burials, 54, 59, 122. *See also* Japanese Benevolent Society; Nishi Hongwanji

Japanese Imperial Mint, 90, 91

Japanese in Hong Kong: ambiguous position, 2, 13, 14, 30, 39, 95, 120–21, 122; community of two halves, 2, 8, 20, 59, 98, 118; discussion group, 105–6, 116, 122. *See also* diaspora, Japanese

Japanese primary school, 52–53, 105–6. *See also* education; Japanese Benevolent Society; Nishi Hongwanji

Japanese Seafarers Relief Association, 72 fig. 4.6, 73

Japanese War Memorial, 124

Japonisme, 14, 140n65

Jardine Matheson & Co., 26, 66, 70, 90, 137n20, 161n74

karayuki-san, 9, 22–39, 97, 98, 99, 119, 122; future prospects, 35–38; and the Japanese Benevolent Society, 50, 56; origins of the term, 24–25, 144n14; regions of origin, 24, 118; regulation of, 28, 29; solidarity between, 33–35, 39; traffic of, 11, 26, 45, 49–50. *See also* brothels; 'cafés'; Graham Street; *kashizashiki*; Kiya Saki

Kasano Kumakichi, 79, 80. *See also* Kōgyō Shōkai

kashizashiki, 9, 10 table 1.3, 23, 31, 33, 34 table 2.1, 37. *See also* brothels; 'cafés'; *karayuki-san*

Kawahigashi Hekigotō, 31, 32, 35

Kian Gwan trading company, 82

Kitasato Shibasaburō, 112–13, 114

Kiya Saki, 22–23, 26, 31–35, 38, 39, 73, 118.
    See also Graham Street
Kobe [Hyōgo], 34 table 2.1, 45, 84, 85, 119;
    treaty port, 3, 25, 28, 60; and the traffic
    of *karayuki-san*, 28, 37; and the Yokohama
    to Hong Kong service, 18, 61, 71
Kōgyō Shōkai, 68, 79–81, 90, 119, 139n42,
    156n70, 158n10. *See also* Kusakabe
    Heijirō
Kowloon City, 100
Kowloon Peninsula, 22, 45, 58; cession of to
    Britain, 6
Kusakabe & Co., 78, 79, 80, 81, 82, 97, 119.
    See also Ataka Yakichi; Kōgyō Shōkai;
    Kusakabe Heijirō
Kusakabe Heijirō, 79, 81, 82, 86, 97. *See also*
    Ataka Yakichi; Kōgyō Shōkai; Kusakabe
    & Co.
Kyōdo Un'yu Kaisha (KUK), 74. *See also*
    Nippon Yusen Kaisha

language issues, 6, 7, 60, 92, 93, 95, 111, 119
liquor licences, 47–48, 58–59, 120. *See also* Sei
    Foo Row; Tokyo Hotel; Uetsuki Kakuzō
Lock Hospital, 29
Loti, Pierre, 36, 106
Lowson, James, 112, 113

Macau, 1, 6, 75, 83–84, 136n4. See also *Tatsu
    Maru* affair
Majima Keinosuke, 53, 55 fig. 3.6, 57, 94, 109
    fig. 6.6, 114–16, 151n74
Mallory, Lawrence, 36, 37
Masuda Takashi, 80, 86
Masujima Rokuichirō, 108
Matsubara Jisaburō, 41, 44–46, 49, 50, 55 fig.
    3.6, 59; and the Happy Valley Racecourse
    Fire, 54, 56–57, 116; and the Japanese
    Benevolent Society, 50, 52, 53
Meiji emperor (Mutsuhito), 16, 39, 63, 64, 99,
    117; accession, 4; birthday, 93, 97, 103,
    116, 119. *See also* Mikado Ball
Meiji government: coming to power, 4; inter-
    national marriages, 36; and the Miike
    coal mines, 26, 70, 87; and the Mitsubishi
    Mail Steamship Company, 26, 61, 63,
    74; modernisation initiatives, 3, 4–5, 11,
    24, 26, 40, 52, 64, 66, 90, 99; national
    identity, 39, 117; overseas students, 6,
    14, 40, 46, 104; subsidies, 74, 78, 79,

115, 158n10. *See also* Iwakura Embassy;
    Japanese Consulate in Hong Kong; *Tatsu
    Maru* affair
Memorial to Ten Thousand Souls, 58, 124 fig.
    7.2, 125. *See also* Happy Valley Racecourse
    Fire
merchant shipping, Japanese, 10 table 1.3,
    11, 13 table 1.4, 26, 60–61, 73, 74–75,
    79, 84–85, 119. *See also* Mitsubishi Mail
    Steamship Company; navy, Japanese;
    seamen; Tokio Marine Insurance
    Company
Messageries Maritimes, 3, 5, 6, 15, 40, 66, 68,
    70, 87
Michinaga Ei, 36
Mid-Levels, 11, 87, 89, 106
Mihara, Andrew Shigekichi, 75, 77, 89, 95,
    119
Miike coal mines, 25–26, 70, 75, 86, 87, 119
Mikado Ball, 93–95, 97, 103, 106, 120
Minami Takaki district, 24, 38
Minami Teisuke, 10, 147n82. *See also* interna-
    tional marriages
Mitsubishi Mail Steamship Company, 2,
    60–61, 73, 74, 78, 80, 87; Yokohama to
    Hong Kong service, 26, 60, 62–68, 70,
    71–72, 74–75, 85, 95, 110, 119, 120;
    Yokohama to Shanghai service, 26, 61,
    68; Takashima mine, 25, 70, 74, 75, 83,
    87, 119. *See also* Honda Masajirō; Iwasaki
    Yatarō; Nippon Yusen Kaisha (NYK)
Mitsui Bussan Kaisha (Sam Ching), 10, 11, 57,
    68, 77, 78, 80, 89, 97, 110, 121; history of,
    86; MacDonnell Road mansion, 89; Miike
    mines, 26, 70, 75, 87, 119; opening of the
    Hong Kong office, 86–87, 119; shipping,
    28, 74. *See also* Fukuhara Eitarō; Shugyō
    Hiromichi
Miura Seiichi, 124 fig. 7.2
Miyake Kokki, 47
Mody, Hormusjee Naorojee, 95, 162n85
Moji, 75
Mori Ōgai, 40
Morisaki Kazue, 24, 39
Mosby, John Singleton, 64
mui-tsai, 29–30
Muraoka Iheiji, 41–42, 49, 50, 108

Nagasaki, 36, 62, 64, 70, 74, 106; as a place of
    origin, 22, 32, 33–34, 41, 60, 73, 107, 119;

as a training location, 61, 67, 78; and the traffic of *karayuki-san*, 9, 24, 25–28, 49–50, 118; treaty port, 3, 25, 60, 118
Nakahara Tomisaburō, 98, 112–14
Narushima Ryūhoku, 7, 165n37
Nathan, Matthew, 93, 95
Natsume Sōseki, 40, 59, 110, 118
navy, Japanese, 64, 73, 84, 85, 94, 116, 120, 122. *See also* army, Japanese; merchant shipping, Japanese; seamen
Niigata, 45, 46; treaty port, 3, 25, 60
Niigata Maru, 62–67, 73. *See also* Mitsubishi Mail Steamship Company; Walker, Wilson
1908 Anti-Japanese boycott. See *Tatsu Maru* affair
Nippon Club, 53, 79, 97, 105, 108, 116
Nippon Yusen Kaisha (NYK), 55 fig. 3.6, 74–75, 77, 78, 79, 89, 97, 119, 121. *See also* Mihara, Andrew Shigekichi
Nishi Hongwanji, 19, 52–53, 54, 55 fig. 3.6, 105, 117, 121. *See also* Ōtani Kōzui
Noma Denjirō, 102–4, 105, 106, 116, 165n27
Noma Masaichi, 94, 95, 122, 162n93

Ōhashi Otowa, 35
Ōkuma Shigenobu, 16 fig. 1.6, 86
opium, 3, 4, 6, 7, 68, 75, 89, 120
Osaka, 3, 14, 16, 66, 67, 89, 98; and Ataka & Co., 84, 85; Japanese Imperial Mint in, 90; and Kusakabe & Co., 78–82, 119
Osaka Shosen Kaisha (OSK), 74–75, 106, 109 fig. 6.6
Ōtaka Saichi, 41–44, 50, 59
Ōtani Kōzui, 52–53, 54, 55 fig. 3.6, 58, 117. *See also* Nishi Hongwanji; Japanese Benevolent Society
overseas travel ban, 1, 3–4, 6, 73, 117

Pacific Mail Steamship Company, 61, 66, 70
Parkes, Harry, 6
Peak, The, 42, 68, 82, 89, 92
pearl-diving industry, 13, 44, 45, 165n28. *See also* crimping; Thursday Island
Peninsular and Oriental Steam Navigation Company (P&O), 6, 61, 62, 63, 64, 66
photographers, 10 table 1.3, 106–11, 55 fig. 3.6, 94, 118, 119
plague, 81, 82, 92, 116; of 1894, 111–14
Po Leung Kuk, 30. See also *mui-tsai*

Pope Hennessy, Catherine 'Kitty' (née Low), 16, 93
Pope Hennessy, John, 16, 64; advocacy for the yen as legal tender, 91; attitude to the Chinese, 16, 17; 1879 trip to Japan, 16, 63, 64, 79, 90, 99
prostitutes and prostitution. *See* brothels; 'cafés'; *karayuki-san*; *kashizashiki*
Protestant Graveyard. *See* Hong Kong Cemetery

Queen's College (formerly Government Central School), 10, 104–5

Rikimatsu (Rickomartz, Adonia), 1–2, 3, 15, 99
Russo-Japanese War (1904–1905), 11, 39, 75, 84, 95, 103, 104, 105; donations to the war effort, 122; Japan's enhanced standing, 93, 120

sailors. *See* seamen
samurai, 11, 22, 67, 78, 86, 99, 101
Satsuma, 4, 14, 79, 81, 99, 137n18
seamen, 1, 2, 3, 4, 9, 15, 49, 73–74, 102; and boarding houses, 41, 42, 45, 73; as brothel customers, 25, 29, 30, 31; and pearl-diving, 45; and the Yokohama to Hong Kong service, 62, 66, 67
Second Opium War (1856–1860), 6
Second World War, 85, 124
Sei Foo Row, 41, 46–48. *See also* liquor licences; Tokyo Hotel; Uetsuki Kakuzō; Uetsuki Yoneko
Shanghai, 46, 80, 92, 107, 111, 122, 163n3; and coal, 70; Japanese consulate in, 6, 28; Japanese company executives in, 60, 68, 78, 79, 81, 86, 90, 97, 119; *karayuki-san* in, 41, 49, 50; Mitsubishi Mail Steamship Company service to, 26, 61, 68; treaty port, 7, 60
Shimabara Peninsula, 23–28, 35. *See also* Minami Takaki district
Shimonoseki, Treaty of, 78, 84. *See also* Sino-Japanese War (1894–1895)
Shintō, 19, 52, 139n40
Shugyō Hiromichi, 86, 119
silk, 66, 85, 91
silver yen: as legal tender in Hong Kong, 91

Singapore, 98, 107; Japanese community in, 13, 17, 122; and the traffic of *karayuki-san*, 24, 26, 39, 41, 49, 118
Sino-Japanese War (1894–1895), 11, 39, 91, 93, 107, 122; tensions resulting from, 78–79, 120. *See also* Shimonoseki, Treaty of; *Tatsu Maru* affair
spying. *See* intelligence gathering
students, 11, 62, 85, 104–5; and overseas travel, 2, 3, 4, 7, 14, 17–18, 40, 42, 46, 99, 104. *See also* Japanese primary school; Queen's College; Tōa Dōbun Shoin
Suez Canal, 6, 70
sugar, 66, 70, 75, 82, 83, 84, 161n74
Sun Yat-sen, 107
sundry goods stores, 9, 13 table 1.4, 98, 116, 118
Suzuki Teitarō Daisetsu (D. T. Suzuki), 85

Taiwan Expedition (1874), 61, 62
Takada Seigan, 52
Takasago Maru, 62, 64–66, 72. *See also* Mitsubishi Mail Steamship Company
Takashima mine, 25, 26, 70, 74, 75, 83, 87, 119
Tatsu Maru affair, 79, 83–85, 120. *See also* Sino-Japanese War; Terumine Hirokichi
tattoo artists, 98, 100–104, 105, 116, 118, 119; government ban on, 102
Terada Ichirō, 2 table 1.1, 3
Terumine Hirokichi, 84
Thursday Island, 74; pearl-diving industry, 13, 44, 45, 165n28; and the traffic of *karayuki-san*, 49
Tianjin [Tientsin], 60, 73
Tōa Dōbun Shoin (East Asia Common Culture Academy), 46
Tokio Marine Insurance Company, 66, 74, 89
Tokugawa government (*bakufu*, shogunate), 2, 4, 14, 25, 90, 117; and Christianity, 24; fall of, 4; and the *karayuki-san*, 25; and mining, 25–26; and the Mitsubishi Mail Steamship Company, 60–61; overseas travel ban, 1, 3, 4; unequal treaties, 3, 5, 25, 60
Tokyo Hotel, 41, 46–48, 55 fig. 3.6, 58, 59 table 3.1, 108. *See also* liquor licences; Sei Foo Row; Uetsuki Kakuzō; Uetsuki Yoneko
Tosa, 4, 61, 62, 67

Tōyōkan, 41–42, 55 fig. 3.6, 99, 164n14. *See also* Yokose Yōkichi
Toyo Kisen Kaisha, 75
treaties, unequal, 3–4, 5, 25, 60
treaty ports, 3–4, 7, 25, 26, 36, 60, 78, 83, 85, 90, 118
Tripp, Henry John Howard, 64, 66, 70, 71, 72
Tsukumo Shōkai, 61, 67. *See also* Iwasaki Yatarō; Mitsubishi Mail Steamship Company
Tung Wah Hospital, 16, 53, 152n92, 168n83

Ueno Hikoma, 106
Ueno Kagenori, 3, 6
Uetsuki Kakuzō, 41, 46–48, 55 fig. 3.6, 57, 59; and the Happy Valley Racecourse Fire, 54, 56–57; and the Japanese Benevolent Society, 50, 52. *See also* liquor licences; Sei Foo Row; Tokyo Hotel
Uetsuki Yoneko, 48, 59 table 3.1. *See also* Sei Foo Row; Tokyo Hotel
ukiyo-e woodblock prints, 14, 101, 119
Umeya (Mumeya) Shōkichi, 107–8, 110–11; friendship with Sun Yat-sen, 107
United States (US), 10 table 1.3, 28, 64; Iwakura Embassy to, 4, 16; Japanese studying/working in, 3, 4, 75, 78, 85, 80, 104; labour migration to, 6, 13; shipping routes to, 6, 74; unequal treaties with Japan, 3–4, 5, 25, 60. *See also* America; Americans in Hong Kong

Walker, Wilson, 62–63, 66, 67, 74. See also *Niigata Maru*
Wan Chai, 9, 36, 52, 54, 58, 59 table 3.1, 105, 118; Japanese brothels in, 30, 31, 32, 35, 98, 120; Japanese clinic in, 54, 57, 115–16
Wei Yuk, 94

Xiamen [Amoy], 60, 73

Yamamoto Hisa, 36–37
Yamazaki Tomoko, 39
Yersin, Alexandre, 113
Yokohama, 66, 78, 98, 102, 111, 119; service to Hong Kong, 26, 60, 61, 62–67, 75, 95, 119; service to Shanghai, 26, 61, 65 fig. 4.2, 68; treaty port, 3, 25, 60

Yokohama Specie Bank (YSB), 78, 81, 124;
Hong Kong office, 79, 89, 90–92, 97, 108,
109 fig. 6.6, 110 fig. 6.7, 114, 116, 119
Yokose Yōkichi, 41, 55 fig. 3.6, 164n14. *See also*
Tōyōkan
Yoshioka copper mine, 61, 74
Yukawa Onsaku, 2–3, 14–18, 99